Hello! Python

Hello! Python

Anthony Briggs

MANNING

SHELTER ISLAND

For online information and ordering of this and other Manning books, please visit
www.manning.com. The publisher offers discounts on this book when ordered in
quantity. For more information, please contact:

Special Sales Department
Manning Publications Co.
20 Baldwin Road
PO Box 261
Shelter Island, NY 11964
Email: orders@manning.com

Manning Publications Co.
20 Baldwin Road
PO Box 261
Shelter Island, NY 11964

Development editor: Sebastian Stirling
Technical proofreader: Marion Newlevant
Copyeditors: June Eding, Tiffany Taylor
Typesetter: Marija Tudor
Cover designer: Leslie Haimes

ISBN: 9781935182085

Printed in the United States of America
1 2 3 4 5 6 7 8 9 10 – MAL – 17 16 15 14 13 12

Brief contents

Contents

Foreword

When Anthony asked me if I would write a foreword to this book, I thought, "Oh, no! Another job! I'll just refuse." But something urged me to at least take a look at the text, which I soon saw was sprinkled with frames from the *User Friendly* cartoon series (a firm favorite, I am sure, with those few surviving individuals who like me have been working with computers since the days of punched cards and tape). So I thought I would take a look at the manuscript, and found that in 12 short chapters you can learn enough about Python and some of its most popular applications to either get started programming or decide that the programmer's life is not for you.

Even the latter conclusion would make the money invested in buying *Hello! Python* worthwhile—if you don't enjoy programming in Python, you are unlikely to enjoy programming at all, in which case you might save yourself the trouble of years spent in a mismatched career.

The book is full of sound practical advice, and nowhere does it try to make pretentious and unbelievable claims. It is a solid work that will, I am sure, introduce many more people who might not currently think of themselves as programmers to the Python language.

I hope that *Hello! Python* will give a broad audience new insights into programming and the fascinating world of information technology. In the absence of sensible computer science education in secondary schooling (which many U.S. states appear unable to afford at present), this book is appealing enough to draw students to the subject. By the time they discern the educational purpose they will be so engaged with the text that they will digest the whole volume.

STEVE HOLDEN
PRESIDENT, THE OPEN BASTION

Preface

When I was first asked to write *Hello! Python*, I didn't want to write just another introductory book — I wanted to write something different. The programming books that I've read in the past have often been just a laundry list of features: a list can have things in it, and you can call `len(mylist)` to find out exactly how many things, `.pop()` to chop an element from the end, `.append()` to add ... There you go, that's all you need to know about lists, now on to the next feature. If you're shown a program, it's usually either a trivial few lines or a couple of chapters tacked on to the end of the book as an afterthought.

Then I thought back to how I first learned to program. I didn't read an entire programming book from cover to cover and then write a program after I knew everything there was to know. Instead I started with a goal, something that I wanted to do, and worked toward it, figuring things out as I went. I read programming books from time to time, but really only to figure out the bits I was stuck on. When I was done, my programs weren't particularly elegant or fast, but they were *mine* — I knew how they worked, and they solved a real problem that I was having.

Fast-forward to today, and my programs *are* elegant and fast, for the most part. And most of the really good programmers I know have learned to program the same way. In *Hello! Python*, I've tried to re-create that process, but speeded up, with all the things I've learned about programming and the pitfalls I've encountered. Every chapter (except the first and last) includes a practical program at its core to illustrate either a particular Python feature or a library — often several. Some of them are fun, some of them are useful, but there are no boring beginning chapters where you learn, in excruciating detail, every feature of a list or dictionary—or, worse, learn how Python adds numbers together.

Instead, you'll watch a program being written and learn about Python features as you need them, not before. Several of the chapters build on previous ones, so you'll learn how to extend existing programs to add new features and keep their design under control—essential if you're going to be writing programs of any scope. The book also explores several different styles of program, from simple scripts, to object-oriented programs, to event-based games.

The idea is to provide a book that's different—that lets you begin writing programs from the first chapter and learn how to use Python's features by seeing them used in action. I hope this is the sort of book that will help people really understand how to use Python.

Acknowledgments

First I'd like to thank Lyndall, my beautiful wife, for being supportive and giving me the time I needed to write this book. It took much longer than we originally thought, but her enthusiasm was unwavering, despite the many weekends that I spent cloistered in the study.

Second, I'd like to thank the team at Manning: my editor, Sebastian Stirling, for his suggestions and experience; June Eding and Tiffany Taylor for the final editing, proofreading, and push across the line; Karen Tegtmeyer for organizing the whole thing; and Michael Stephens for helping me develop the initial concept of the book.

Third, I'd like to acknowledge J.D. "Illiad" Fraser of *User Friendly* for letting Manning use the *User Friendly* cartoons in the *Hello!* Series and allowing me to put my own words in the characters' mouths in this book.

Next, I'd like to thank all of my beta testers who helped find errors—Daniel Hadson, Eldar Marcussen, William Taylor, David Hepworth, and Tony Haig—as well as everyone in the MEAP program who offered advice and criticism or discovered errors.

Finally, I would like to thank the following peer reviewers who provided invaluable feedback on the manuscript at various stages of its development: Tray Skates, Curtis Miller, Joe Hoover, Michael R. Bain, Francesco Goggi, Mike Stok, Michael R. Head, Cheryl M. Davis, Daniel Bretoi, Amos Bannister, Rob Allen, Dr. John Grayson, William Z. Taylor, Munch Paulson, David Hepworth, Eldar Marcussen, Daniel Hadson, Tony Niemann, Paolo Corti, Edmon Begoli, Lester Lobo, Robby

O'Connor, and Sopan Shewale. And special thanks to Marion Newlevant for her careful technical review of the final manuscript during production and to Steve Holden for agreeing to write the foreword to my book.

About this book

Hello! Python is written for people who'd like to learn more about Python and how to program. You might be completely new to programming, or you might have some prior experience; either way, *Hello! Python* will take you from your first steps through writing networked games and web applications.

The style of this book is different from most programming books. Rather than present a laundry list of every possible feature, I've chosen to show you a more real-world picture. Starting with chapter 2, you'll be following along as we write real, useful programs—warts and all. All programming language features have a purpose, and it's hard to recognize that purpose if you don't see all the bugs, broken code, and badly written programs that the feature is supposed to help with.

Some of the programs in *Hello! Python* are improved and expanded as the book progresses, so you'll see how Python features such as functions, classes, and modules can help keep your code under control as it expands. They will also reduce the amount of work you have to do when you need to add new parts.

I think of *Hello! Python* as being split into three rough sections, although that's not explicitly mentioned in the book. The first chapters cover the basic syntax of Python, how to use libraries, some common concepts, and all the other pieces you'll need to know to understand how things work. The middle section covers more advanced features and introduces libraries that will help you get more done without having to reinvent the wheel.

In the final section, we write complete programs using frameworks, which will help you even more.

The fun doesn't stop when you've finished the book. All the programs in *Hello! Python* are intended to be extended and reused when you write your own programs. Most experienced programmers have a library of code that they've previously written, and the code in this book will give you a head start on your own projects.

Roadmap

Chapter 1 gives you an introduction to Python and programming, as well as an idea of what it's all about—why we program, and what you can do with your programs. I also step through how to install Python on Windows, Mac, or Linux, and some common issues you might run into when doing so.

Chapter 2 jumps straight into the basic building blocks of programs, and you write your first program based on Hunt the Wumpus. Over the course of the chapter, you see firsthand some of the issues that programmers face, such as how to manage complex programs and make them clear and easy to understand.

Chapter 3 teaches you about Python's famed standard library, as well as how to import its code along with code that other programmers have written to perform common tasks. You learn how to use this code in your own programs, saving you tons of time and making your programs easier to read.

Chapter 4 shows you how to test your programs, and covers both unit testing and system testing as well as some common testing issues and solutions. As you follow along, you'll write a simple and easily extendable todo-list application.

Chapter 5 covers how you might use Python for business-style programming by downloading web pages, parsing the information inside them, and using that to generate emails and CSV files. It also looks at how to make your programs more robust and harder to break in the face of bad information and other errors.

In chapter 6, we write an adventure game, complete with locations, monsters, and treasure. In the process, you learn how classes work and how to design object-oriented programs.

Chapter 7 extends what you've learned about classes with some more advanced features, like mixins, __getattribute__, and properties. We also look briefly at some of Python's other advanced features, such as iterators and generators, as well as regular expressions and functional programming.

Chapter 8 introduces Django and helps you get a personal todo list site up and running. You learn about Django's templates, database handling, forms, and admin functions. The chapter also covers some common web development patterns, including RESTful design and using the right HTTP methods.

Chapter 9 teaches you how to write an arcade game, loosely based on Asteroids and Lunar Lander, using a library called Pyglet. You'll learn about geometry, event-based programming, and timers.

Chapter 10 extends the adventure program you wrote in chapter 6 so that you and your friends can play it over a network using Telnet. You use a Python networking library called Twisted to handle all the connection handling, protocol definition, and logging needed to make the game work.

Chapter 11 takes the todo list application that we wrote in chapter 8 and updates it so that everyone can have their own todo list. You'll learn how to handle logins, create users in Django, use Django's generic views, secure your web applications, and deploy behind a server such as Apache or Nginx.

Finally, chapter 12 gives you some extra resources you can use as you continue learning about Python — mailing lists and user groups, as well as programs to read and explore, and other libraries you might want to investigate.

Code downloads and conventions

The source code for this book is released under the 3-clause BSD license. More information about the license is available within the source code, available from manning.com/HelloPython/.

Throughout the book, I've used the convention of formatting code in a `monospaced font`, as well as variable, class, and method names. Because this book is primarily about reading and writing code, there's a fair bit of it—Manning uses a numbering scheme with code annotations to more thoroughly explain what particular pieces of code do.

Author Online

Purchase of *Hello! Python* includes free access to a private web forum run by Manning Publications where you can make comments about the book, ask technical questions, and receive help from the author and from other users. To access the forum and subscribe to it, point your web browser to www.manning.com/HelloPython. This page provides information on how to get on the forum once you're registered, what kind of help is available, and the rules of conduct on the forum.

Manning's commitment to our readers is to provide a venue where a meaningful dialogue between individual readers and between readers and the author can take place. It's not a commitment to any specific amount of participation on the part of the author, whose contribution to the book's forum remains voluntary (and unpaid). We suggest you try asking the author some challenging questions, lest his interest stray!

The Author Online forum and the archives of previous discussions will be accessible from the publisher's website as long as the book is in print.

About the author

Anthony Briggs has been a Python programmer since early 2000. He's currently writing a web publishing system for Ramble Communications in Melbourne. Previously he worked on a core booking system for a travel firm in Australia and Canada, eventually becoming lead developer overseeing the entire project.

About *Hello!* books

At Manning, we think it should be just as much fun to learn new tools as it is to use them. And we know that fun learning gets better results. Our *Hello!* series demonstrates how to learn a new technology without getting bogged down in too many details. In each book, *User Friendly* cartoon characters offer commentary and humorous asides, as the book moves quickly from Hello World into practical techniques. Along the way, readers build a unique hands-on application that leverages the skills learned in the book.

Our *Hello!* books offer short, lighthearted introductions to new topics, with the author and cartoon characters acting as your guides.

1

Why Python?

If you've picked up this book, you're probably trying to learn how to program. Congratulations! Not many people set out to learn programming, but it's one of the most interesting and rewarding subjects that you can teach yourself. Programming is the new literacy; if you're not sure how to write a simple program, whether as a batch file, mail filter, or formula in a spreadsheet, you're at a disadvantage compared to those who do. Programming is also a lever. With programming, you can turn your ideas into reality.

HI. MY NAME IS GREG, AND I'LL BE YOUR CHARACTER FOR THIS BOOK.

I first started to program when I was around 10, using the Commodore 64. Back then, there wasn't much available in the way of preprogrammed software, unless you counted games or simple word processing. Computers like the Commodore came with BASIC built in, and programming was a lot more accessible—you didn't need to learn a great deal to be able to get results quickly.

Since then, computers have departed from that early ideal. Now you have to go out of your way to install something so that your computer can be programmed. But once you know how, you can create all sorts of wondrous programs which will do boring work for you, inform you, and entertain you. Especially that last part—programming is fun, and everybody should try it.

You'll notice the cartoons sprinkled throughout the book. I've used these to give you some background information about what's going on in the chapter, or to cover some common problems, all while having a bit of fun. Although the characters are from *User Friendly*, the text and jokes are all mine—so if you don't like them, you know who to blame.

Let's start by learning the basics of programming.

Learning to program

Because this book is about programming, it makes sense to give you some sort of overview before we jump in and start learning the details in chapter 2. What is programming? How does it work? The definition of programming is simple.

PROGRAMMING IS ART, MAN. THAT'S ALL YOU NEED TO KNOW.

DEFINITION   Programming is telling a computer what to do.

But, like most definitions, this is a drastic oversimplification. Like chess, learning the initial rules of programming is easy; but putting them together in a useful way and mastering them is much harder. Programming touches on most areas of human endeavor these days—if you want to create something meaningful with a computer, it's really hard to do so without having to program in some sense—and it's just as much about design and ideas and personal expression as it is about numbers and calculation.

Telling a computer what to do

Let's break down the different parts of our definition and look at them individually. In order to understand our definition, we need to know what a computer is; what we mean by "telling" it what to do; and what, exactly, "what to do" consists of.

A COMPUTER

A computer is a fast calculator that can make simple decisions based on your instructions. Computer instructions are simple and usually consist of tasks like adding numbers and making comparisons. But sets of instructions can be combined to create large programs that can do complex things like write documents, play games, balance your accounts, and control nuclear reactors.

Computers *seem* smart, but they're actually stupid and single-minded, and they lack common sense. After all, they're only machines; they will do exactly what you (or the developers of Python) tell them to do—no matter the consequences. Consider a command to delete an entire hard drive. Most people would find that to be a bit drastic, and they'd probably check to make sure that's what you wanted before proceeding. But a computer will go right ahead and destroy all your data, no questions asked.

NOTE   The great thing about computers is that they do exactly what you tell them. The terrible thing about computers is that they do exactly what you tell them.

If a program that you're using (or that you've written) is doing something odd or crashes for no reason, it's nothing personal—it's just following the instructions it was given.

TELLING

When working with Python, you'll typically instruct it by typing program code into a text file and then telling the Python program to run it; you'll find out how to do this later in the chapter. The instructions that you type can be complex or simple, and they cover a wide range of tasks—adding numbers, opening other files, placing things on screen, and so on. A simple Python program looks like this:

```
number = "42"
print "Guess my number..."
guess = raw_input(">")
if guess == number:
    print "Yes! that's it!"
else:
    print "No - it's", number

raw_input("hit enter to continue")
```

Don't worry too much about trying to understand this program yet; this example is just meant to provide you with some background.

WHAT TO DO

This is where the fun starts. Most modern computers are "Turing complete," which means they can do anything; anything you can think of, a computer can do. At least in theory—it might take longer or be more complicated than you first expected, or need special hardware if you want to interact in a certain way, but if the computer has access to enough data and you've programmed it properly, the sky's the limit. Here are some of the tasks that computers have been used for:

- Controlling manned and unmanned spacecraft and probes and guiding robots on other planets, including the Mars exploration rovers Spirit and Opportunity.

- Transmitting data around the world via a network of computers—the internet and World Wide Web! Online, you can transmit or receive information from around the world in a fraction of a second.

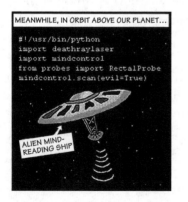

- Building robots, from industrial robot arms to Roomba vacuum cleaners to lifelike human robots that can climb stairs or mimic human emotions.

- Modeling real world processes such as gravity, light, and weather. This includes scientific models, but also most games.

You might not have the hardware that's needed to send a robot probe to another planet, but, in principle at least, you can still run the same programs. Incredibly, the computers used to drive Spirit and Opportunity, for example, are much less powerful than the computer sitting on your desk, in your lap, or even in your pocket (your mobile phone).

Programming is made of ideas

It's easy to focus on the concrete aspects of computer programming—instructions, adding numbers, networks, hardware, and so on—but the core of programming is about ideas: specifically, successfully capturing those ideas in a program so that other people can use them. Helping other people by discovering new, cool things has been hap-

pening since early man started using pointy sticks, and programming is no exception. Computers have helped to develop many new ideas since their invention, including the internet, spreadsheets, interactive games, and desktop publishing.

Unfortunately, I can't help you come up with new ideas, but I can show you some of the ideas that other people have come up with as inspiration to develop some of your own.

Programming is design

Most of the aspects of programming that we'll cover in this book deal with design. *Design* is typically described as a common solution to a particular problem. For example, architecture is the design of buildings and the space that they occupy. It addresses some of the problems common to buildings, such as how people get in and out and move around inside a building, how they occupy it, how to make people happy about being in a building, using materials sensibly, and so forth.

What makes a design good—and what makes one design better than another—is whether it solves your problems effectively. This means a design is never complete; there are always other, potentially better ways to solve a problem. Always question what you've designed. Is the solution accurate? Or does it only solve part of your problem? How easy is your design to build? If it's 10% better in some way but twice as hard to put into practice, then you might go with the simpler design.

If programming is the design of ideas, what are some of the problems that it solves? Some of the problems that you're likely to run into include the following:

- Your idea isn't fully formed—there are details that need to be worked out.
- Most ideas are complicated, and have a lot of details involved once you start writing them down.
- Your ideas need to be clear and easy to follow, so that other people can use them, understand them, and build on them.

The key thing that programs need to do is to express your ideas as clearly and simply as possible. One of the common themes in the development of computer languages is the management of complexity. Even when working on straightforward programs, it's easy to get bogged down in details and lose sight of what you're trying to do. When it comes time to make changes to a program, you can misunderstand the original purpose of the program and introduce errors or inconsistencies. A good programming language will have features to help you work at different levels of detail, allowing you to move to more (or less) detailed levels as necessary.

Another important factor is how flexible your programs are when written in a particular language. Exploratory programming is a useful tool when developing ideas, and we'll be doing a lot of it in this book—but if your programming language doesn't have strong facilities for managing complexity or hiding detail, then they become hard to change, and a lot of the benefit is lost.

Now that you have a basic understanding of programming, it's time to check out this book's chosen language, Python.

What makes Python so great?

In this book, you'll be learning Python, which, not so coincidentally, happens to be my favorite programming language. For a number of reasons, It's ideal for a beginner who's just started programming.

Python is easy

If you compare Python to other programming languages, the first thing you'll notice is that it's easy to read. Python's syntax is intended to be as clear as possible. Some features that make Python especially user-friendly include the following:

- It avoids the use of punctuation characters like { } $ / and \.
- Python uses whitespace to indent lines for program control, instead of using brackets.
- Programmers are encouraged to make their programs clear and easy to read.
- Python supports a number of different ways to structure your programs, so you can pick the best one for the job.

Python's developers try to do things "right," by making programming as straightforward as possible. There have been several cases where features have been delayed (or even cancelled outright) while the core developers figured out the best way to present a particular feature. Python even has its own philosophy on how programs should look and behave. Try typing "import this" once you have Python installed (later in the chapter).

Python is a real language

Although Python is an easy-to-use language, it's also a "real" language. Typically, languages come in two flavors: easy ones with training wheels, to teach people how to program; and harder ones with more features to let you get real work done. When you're learning how to program, you have two choices:

- Jump head first into a real language, but be prepared to be confused until you figure out the hard language.
- Start with a beginner's language, but be ready to throw away all of the work that you've done when you need a feature that it doesn't have.

Python skips the drawbacks and manages to combine the best aspects of these approaches. It's easy to use and learn, but as your programming skills grow, you'll be able to continue using Python, because it's fast and has lots of useful features. Best of all, jumping in and learning how to do things the real way is often easier than following all of the steps that you need to learn how to program "properly."

Python has "batteries included"

A large number of libraries are included with Python, and there are many more which you can download and install. *Libraries* are program code that other programmers have written that you can easily reuse. They let you read files, process data, connect to other computers via the internet, serve web pages, generate random numbers, and do pretty much any other sort of basic activity. Python is a good choice for the following:

- Web development
- Networking
- Graphical interfaces
- Scripting operating system tasks
- Games
- Data processing
- Business applications

MMM, GAMES ...

Often, when it comes time to write a program, most of the hard bits are already done for you, and all you have to do is join together a few libraries to be able to do what you need. You'll read more about Python's libraries and how to use them in chapter 3.

Python has a large community

Python is a popular language and has a large, friendly community that is happy to help out new Python developers. Questions are always welcome on the main mailing list, and there's also a specialized mailing list set up specifically to help new developers. There are also a lot of introductions and tutorials, and a great deal of example code, available on the internet.

TIP   "Good artists borrow, great artists steal." Because of the size of the Python developer community, there are a lot of programs to beg, borrow and steal, regardless of what type of program you're writing. Once you have some Python experience, reading other people's programs is an excellent way to learn more.

One of the other advantages of having a large community is that Python gets a lot of active development, so bugs are fixed rapidly and new features are added regularly. Python is constantly improving.

Now that you know about programming and why Python is a good choice, let's install Python on your computer so that you can run your own programs. If you're running Linux, skip ahead a section. If you're running Mac, skip ahead two sections.

Setting up Python for Windows

Over the next couple of sections, we'll go through the installation process step by step, create a simple program to make sure that Python is working on your system, and teach you the basic steps involved in running a program. Making sure that Python is working properly now will save you a lot of frustration later on.

Installing Python

We'll be using the latest version of Python 2, because most of the libraries that we'll use in this book don't yet support Python 3. At the time of writing, Python 2.6 is the standard version, but Python 2.7 should be available by the time you read this. To install Python, we need to download a program from the Python website and run it. That program includes Python, its libraries, and everything you need to run Python programs.

The first step is to go to http://python.org/ and click Download. That should take you to a page that lists all of the operating systems that Python can be installed on. Click the Windows version, and save it to your desktop.

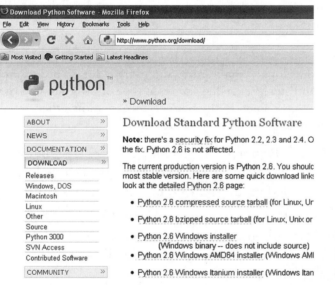

Figure 1.1
Python.org's
download page

Once it's finished download-ing, double-click the pro-gram's icon to open and run it. You'll probably be shown a screen similar to figure 1.2. Click Run to run the Python installer.

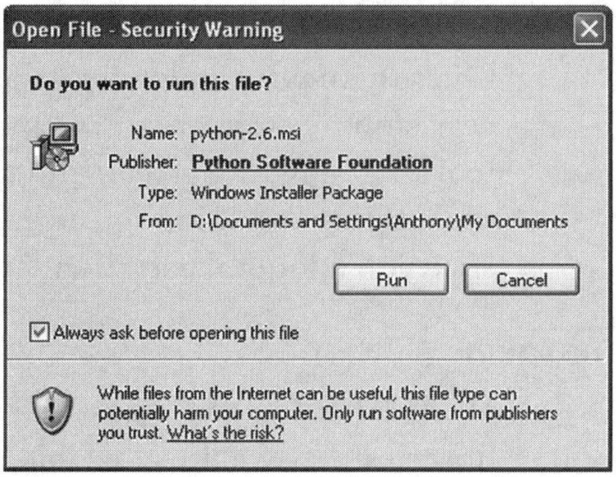

Figure 1.2 Are you sure you want to run this strange program from the internet? Yes!

You'll now be given a series of options for installing Python. Typically, the defaults (the options that have already been chosen for you) are good enough, unless your computer is low on disk space and needs to install to a different partition. If you're happy with the options at each step, click Next to go to the next screen.

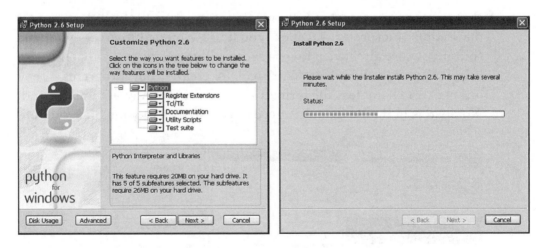

Figure 1.3 Install Python for all users. 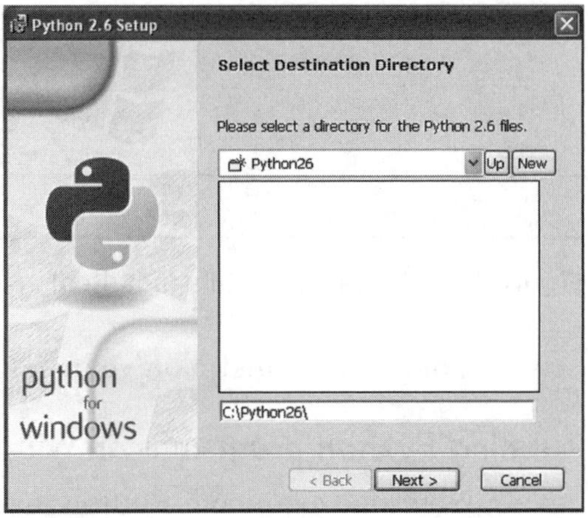   **Figure 1.4** Choose Python's location.

Figure 1.5 Choose which bits of Python you want.   **Figure 1.6** Installing Python

Figure 1.7   Hooray! Python's installed!

The final stage might take a little while depending on the speed of your computer, but once you see figure 1.7, you're done.

Congratulations! You've installed Python!

Running Python programs on Windows

Now that you have Python installed on your system, let's create a simple program. This will let you know that Python is installed correctly and also show you how to create a program and run it.

Python programs are normally written into a text file and then run by the Python interpreter. To start, you'll use Notepad to create your file (but if you already have a favorite text editor, you can use that). Avoid using Microsoft Word or Wordpad to create your programs—they insert extra characters for formatting which Python won't understand. Notepad is in the Programs > Accessories section of your Start menu.

Figure 1.8   Here's where Notepad lives.

In the Notepad window that opens, type the following code. Don't worry too much about what it does yet—for now you want to test out Python and make sure that you can run a program. Type the following:

```
print "Hello World!"
raw_input("hit enter to continue")
```

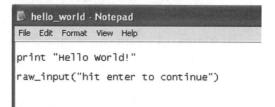

Figure 1.9
The test program for Python

When you're done, save it to your desktop as hello_world.py. The .py on the end is important—that's how Windows knows that it's a Python program.

AH, I REMEMBER MY FIRST HELLO WORLD PROGRAM LIKE IT WAS YESTERDAY ...

Figure 1.10 Save your test program to the desktop.

If you have a look on your desktop, you should be able to see your program, with the blue and yellow Python icon on it. Double-click the document icon, and your program should run.

IT WAS GREEN, AND IT SAID: "HELLO WORLD!"

Figure 1.11 Run your script by double-clicking it.

Congratulations! Python is installed and working properly on your computer! Read on to find out how to run Python from the command line—it can be an important troubleshooting tool when things go wrong. If you don't see the output, don't worry—the "Troubleshooting" section has some common problems and their solutions.

Running Python programs from the command line

It's also possible to run Python programs from the command line. This is often easier when you have a program that deals mainly with text input and output, or runs as an operating system script, or needs lots of input—using command-line options can be easier to program than a custom settings window.

NOTE   There are many different ways to access and run programs. Double-clicking through the GUI is one way; the command line is another. You'll learn several during the course of the book.

Running from the command line is also easier when you have a program that has a bug, because you'll see an error message, rather than seeing no window or having your window close immediately.

The Windows command-line program is available from Program Files > Accessories under the Windows Start menu.

If you run that program, you should see a black window with some white text. Type cd Desktop to change to the desktop directory, and

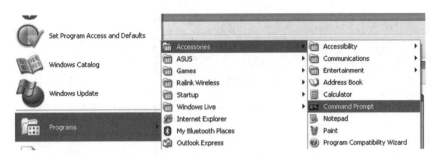

Figure 1.12 Where the Windows command line lives

then `python hello_world.py` to open Python and tell it to run the script file that you created earlier.

When you do this, one of two things will happen: either your program will run, in which case you're done; or you'll see an error message saying that the Python program couldn't be found. If that happens, don't panic—you just need to tell Windows where to find Python.

Figure 1.13 Windows doesn't know where Python is!

You need to make some changes to the path settings of Windows. The *path* is a list of places where Windows looks to find programs that you've asked it to run. To start, right-click your My Computer icon, and click Properties.

Figure 1.14
Looking in your computer's properties

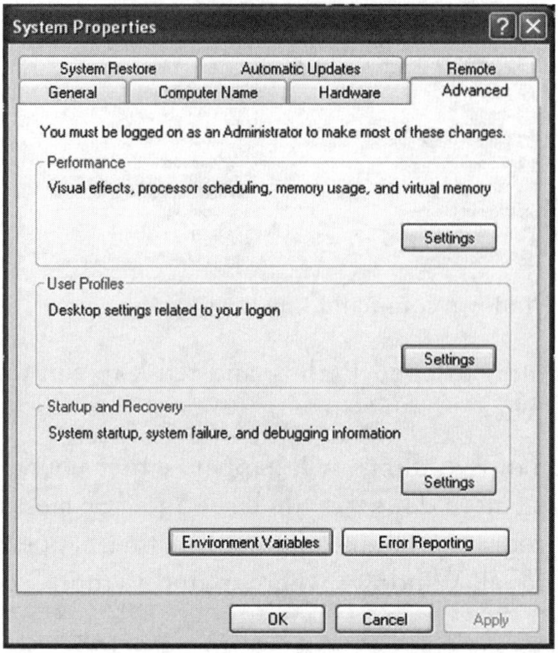

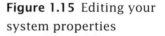

Figure 1.15 Editing your system properties

Then select the Advanced tab, and click the Environment Variables button at the bottom. You should see a list of environment variables like those in the figure at right.

In the bottom half, look for the line named Path and double-click it. In the edit box that appears, you need to add ;c:\python26 at the end of the line and click OK.

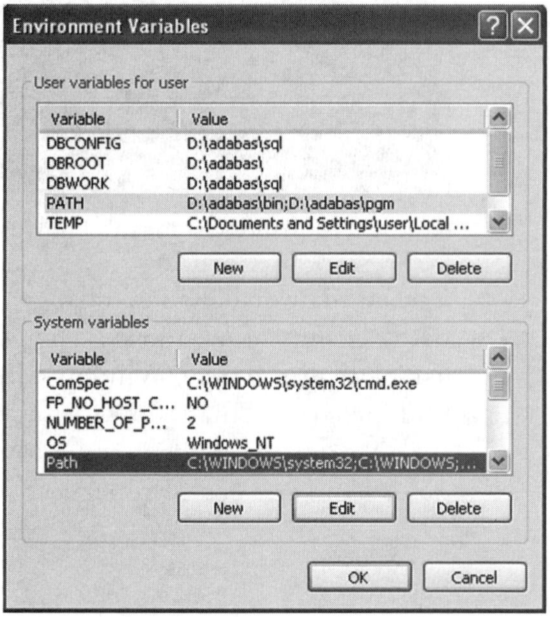

Figure 1.16 Opening the PATH variable

NOTE   Paths are what Windows uses to find files. Each individual file on your computer has a path. You'll learn more about paths and how to use them in chapter 3.

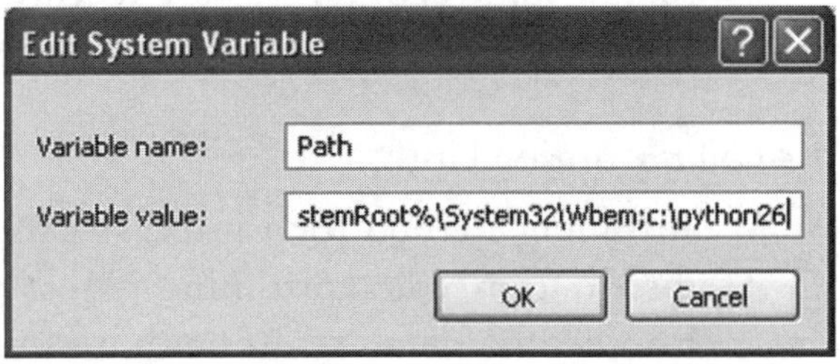

Figure 1.17
Adding Python to your
PATH variable

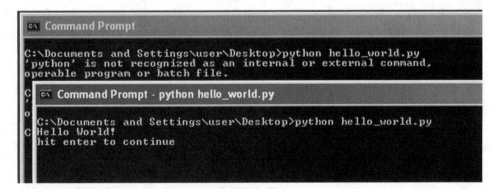

Once you've done that, click OK in all of the windows that you've opened until you're back at your desktop. Open another command prompt window (the old one will still have the old path settings), and type python hello_world.py again. You should see the output from your program.

Figure 1.18 Success! Now Windows knows where Python is.

Congratulations! You're now ready to start programming. You might want to read the "Troubleshooting" section first, though, to find a better program to edit your Python programs.

Next, we'll review how to install Python on Linux machines.

Linux

Using Python with Linux is harder to describe exactly, because there are a large number of Linux distributions available and they all do things in a slightly different way. I've chosen to use Gnome and Ubuntu as an example; other Linux distributions will be similar.

Installing under Linux

Installing Python for Linux isn't often necessary, depending on which distribution you're running. Most will have some version of Python installed by default, although it's often a few revisions out of date. You can use `python -V` to find out which one you have.

There are two main methods of installation under Linux: you can use a package or compile from source.

GREG? I'M JUST HEADING DOWN TO THE CORNER. DID YOU WANT ANYTHING? GREG?

... LIKE TO GAMBLE, BABY ...

TAPPITY
TAPPITY
TAPP
TAPP
TAPP

Package managers are straightforward to use and handle most of the dependency and compilation issues for you. Under Debian's apt-get system, you can type something like `sudo apt-get install python` and have the most up-to-date version of Python installed automatically. You can also use `apt-cache search python` to find out what else is available, because there are usually a number of other packages (python-dev or python-docs) that you'll probably want to install as well.

Compiling from source is also an option, but it's somewhat outside the scope of this book. It can be a complicated process, and you'll need several other libraries (like gnu-readlines and OpenSSL) installed if you want all of Python's features. It's usually easier to install via package, but you can find more information on compiling Python at www.python.org/download/source/ if you want to go down this route.

Linux GUI

In general, Linux users will be more comfortable with the command line, which we'll cover next, but you can also run Python programs from a GUI such as Gnome—although it's a little more involved than the Windows version. Type the following program into a text editor and save it:

```
#!/usr/bin/python
print "hello world!"
ignored = raw_input("Hit enter to continue")
```

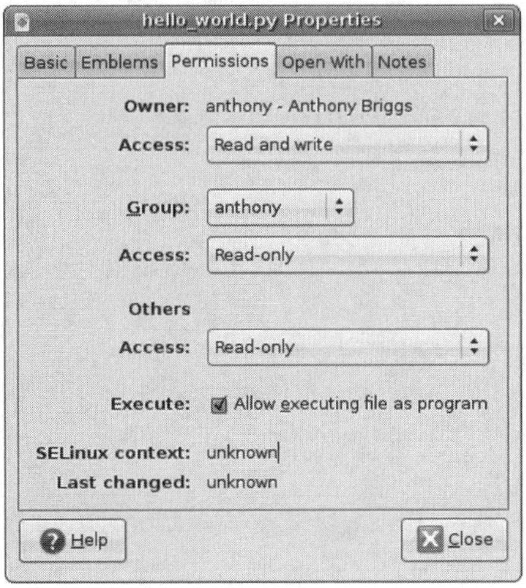

You'll also need to edit the permissions for the file to set it executable, so that you can run it directly, as shown in figure 1.19.

Figure 1.19
The permissions window for hello_world.py

Once you've done that, you can double-click the program file and click Run in Terminal to run your program.

When you see the window in figure 1.21, you're done. Although this is the easiest

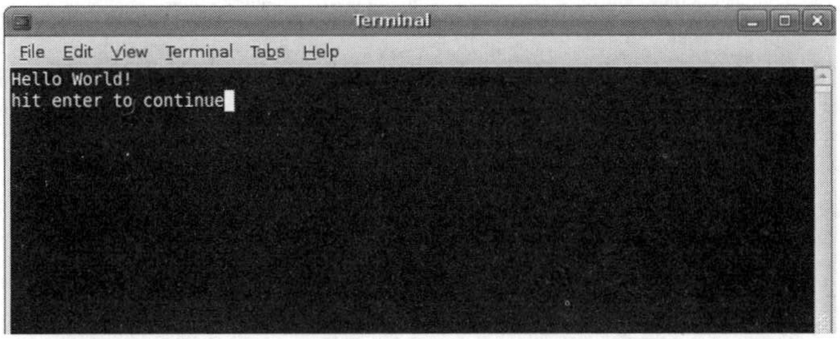

Figure 1.20 Choosing what to do with your program

Figure 1.21
Your test program running in a terminal window under Ubuntu Linux

method of running Python programs from the GUI, there are other options for running scripts that don't involve choosing whether to run or display your program. Under Gnome, you can set up a program launcher. The permissions window is displayed, as in the following figure.

Figure 1.22
Setting the command in a launcher

Bear in mind that for a terminal-based program such as your test script, you'll need to run it within a terminal window, by issuing something like the following command:

```
gnome-terminal -e '/usr/bin/python /home/anthony/Desktop/hello_world.py'
```

Although these examples are Gnome-specific, there are similar options for other distributions and window managers.

Linux command line

A lot of Linux programs are run from the command line, and Python is no exception. You'll need to be able to open a terminal window. If you're using Gnome, then this is available under the Applications > Accessories menu.

Once you've opened the terminal window, you'll see a command prompt. To execute your script, type

```
python path/to/your/script
```

If you've saved your script to the desktop, this can be shortened to

```
python ~/Desktop/hello_world.py
```

If you want to make your script look more like a system command, you can omit the .py on the end of the file, save it somewhere on your path (most systems support a ~/bin folder), and make it executable with a command like `chmod 755 path/to/script.py`. As long as you've kept the `#!/usr/bin/python` line as the first line of your file, you should be able to type your script's name from anywhere and have it run.

Now that Windows and Linux users have been covered, let's see how to install Python on the Mac.

Macintosh

Using Python on the Mac is pretty much like running under Linux, with the obvious exception of the graphical parts. Mac OS 10.5 comes with Python 2.5 preinstalled, and Snow Leopard (Mac OS 10.6) comes with Python 2.6. Either version should work with the code that you'll be using in Hello Python.

If you need to install a later version of Python, you can also download it from the Python website and install it via a standard .dmg image file—but there are a few details to take care of to get things running properly.

Updating the shell profile

The first thing you'll need to do is tell Mac OS X to use the new version of Python if you're running things from the Terminal. Otherwise, it will continue to use the built-in version. Fortunately, Python includes a script to set this for you. If you navigate to the Python folder within Applications and run the application called Update Shell Profile, future shell windows should use the right version.

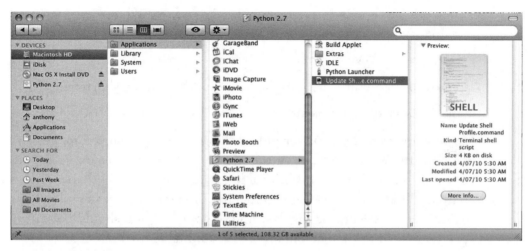

Figure 1.23 Setting the new Python path properly

Setting the default application

The second step is to set what Python programs do when you double-click them. By default, they will open in IDLE, the editor that comes with Python; but I prefer to have them run the Python program instead, so they behave more like a real application. If you right-click (or control-click) a .py Python file, you should see this pop-up menu.

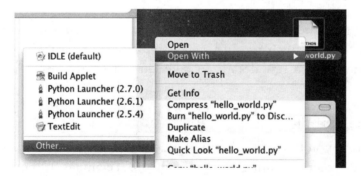

Figure 1.24 Setting the default action for Python files

This lets you choose which program to run your Python script this time; but if you select Other, you can pick which program will run each time.

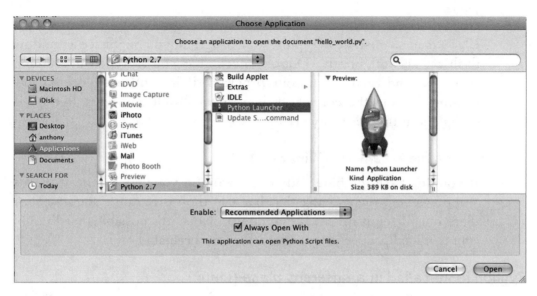

Figure 1.25 Setting the Python Launcher as the default app

Select the Python Launcher within the Python folder in the Applications directory, select the Always Open With check box, and click Open. Now, each time you double-click a .py script, it will run it instead of opening in IDLE. If you want to test that the command line is working properly, you can open the Terminal application and try out all of the previous commands in the Linux section.

Now that you have Python installed on your chosen operating system, it's time to figure out any hiccups.

Troubleshooting

If you don't see a window when you run your Python program, there could be a few things wrong. You'll potentially face a lot of errors like this as you learn to program. A good source of information is to do a web search for the exact error message or symptoms that you're getting when you try to run a program. Also, don't be afraid to ask for help (for example, on one of the Python mailing lists) if you get stuck. Here are some of the more common problems.

A syntax error

If you made a mistake in typing your program, you might see a window flash on and off briefly. Double-check that you've typed everything correctly, and then rerun your program. If it's still not working, try running it from the command line; that will tell you what Python is doing and if there are any errors.

An incorrect file extension (Windows)

If you don't see the blue and yellow icon on your document, it means Windows isn't recognizing that it's a Python program. Double-check that your file ends in .py. If that doesn't work, it's possible that Python isn't installed properly; try uninstalling and reinstalling it.

Python is installed in a different place (Linux)

Under Linux, the #! line you put at the start of your program tells the shell which program to use to run your script. If that program doesn't exist, then your command-line program will fail with something like the following error:

```
bash: ./hello_world.py: /usr/local/bin/python: bad interpreter:
   No such file or directory
```

To fix this, you need to find out where Python is installed and update the line. The easiest way is to type which python at the command line, which should respond with the current location of Python. Another option is to use #!/usr/bin/env python, which will use the env program to look for Python instead of referring to it directly.

Finally, let's see how text editors and IDEs can make programming easier.

Text editors and IDEs

To create your programs, you'll need to use a text editor to edit the files that Python reads. Programs like Microsoft Word and Wordpad are a bad choice, because they use a more complicated format that won't work with Python (or other programming languages). Instead, you'll want to use a program that edits text directly and doesn't support formatting like bold text or pages.

If you're using a Windows PC, you can always use Notepad, and similar applications are available under Linux and Mac OS X; but it's extremely basic and won't help you to catch many common programming errors, such as indenting your code properly or not closing quotes in strings.

A better option is to use the IDLE editor that comes with Python, or else download one of the editors listed in a moment, which are specifically designed for programming. Programming editors often have extra features that make programming much easier:

- They automatically indent your code.
- They can color in different instructions to make your program easier to read.
- They can run your program and send you back to the exact line where an error occurred, making it faster to write your programs.

A long list of editors that are usable for Python editing is available on Python's website at http://wiki.python.org/moin/PythonEditors. Some of the more commonly used ones include the following:

- IDLE, which is installed with Python.
- Emacs and Vim are used by a great many developers and are powerful, but they have a fairly steep learning curve. Cream is a variant of Vim that has more normal keybindings.
- Notepad++ is a Windows-specific editor with lots of features.

Some editors are also integrated development environments (IDEs). IDEs provide extra services above and beyond text editing, to save you time when programming. Typically, they will give you access to a Python interpreter, some sort of auto-completion, and more advanced code navigation (for example, jumping directly to the source of an error in your program), as well as interactive debugging tools so that you can run your code step by step and look at variables while your program is running. There's also a list of Python IDEs on the Python wiki at http://

wiki.python.org/moin/IntegratedDevelopmentEnvironments. Some IDEs that you might want to consider include the following:

- IDLE is a simple IDE—it has a Python interpreter included, as well as pop-up completion, and it takes you directly to errors.

- Wing IDE is a commercial IDE with integrated unit testing, source browsing, and auto-completion. Wingware offer a free license to developers working on open source projects.

- PyDev is an open source plugin for Eclipse.

- SPE is also open source and offers a wide range of features, including a code checker that tests for common programming mistakes and rates the quality of your code.

- Komodo is available in a number of forms, including an open source editor called OpenKomodo.

Ultimately, whether you use an IDE or an editor, and which one you use, tend to be decisions based on personal preference and the scope of

I.D.E.s? I.D.E.s?
IN MY DAY, WE TOGGLED
PROGRAMS IN THROUGH
THE FRONT PANEL ...
AND WE *LIKED* IT!

your project. As you start building larger programming projects, the investment in learning a more featured editor or an IDE will pay off. The best advice is to try a number of editors and see which ones you prefer.

Summary

In this chapter, we covered the basics that you'll need to know in order to get started programming in Python. You learned some high-level details: what programming is, the philosophy of programming, and the sorts of problems that programmers tend to face; and also some low-level details, such as how to install and run Python, how to create programs, and how to run them from both a graphical user interface and the command line.

One of the most important long-term skills to learn when you're programming is how to deal with errors that might occur. When this happens, tracing them back to their source and fixing the root cause of the problem can require some persistence and detective work, so being aware of the resources that are available to you is important. You'll learn how to deal with errors in your programs in later chapters.

Everything you've learned in this chapter—particularly how to run a Python program—will help you in the chapters to come, when we'll take a look at Python's basic statements and use them to write a game called Hunt the Wumpus.

2

Hunt the Wumpus

This chapter covers

- *Writing your first real program*
- *How programs work*
- *Some easy ways to organize programs*

Now that you have Python set up and installed and know how to enter and run a test program, let's get started with writing a real one. I'll begin by explaining a few of Python's basic features, and then you'll create a simple text-based adventure game called Hunt the Wumpus.

As you progress through the chapter, you'll add features to your game, building on the initial version. This is how most programmers (including the author) learned to program: learn just enough about the language to be able to write a simple program, and then build up from there. In order to do that, you need more knowledge—but you only need to learn a little bit more to be able to make small additions to your program. Repeat the process of adding small features a few more times, and you'll have a program that you couldn't have created in one sitting. Along the way, you'll have learned a lot about the programming language.

In this chapter, you'll experience the early days of programming first hand, as you write your own version of Hunt the Wumpus. The text-based interface is ideal for your first program because you only need to know two simple statements to handle all of your input and output. Because all of your input will be strings, the logic of your program is straightforward and you won't need to learn a lot to start being productive.

A brief history of Hunt the Wumpus

Hunt the Wumpus was a popular early computer game written by Gregory Yob in 1976. It puts you in the shoes of an intrepid explorer, delving into a network of caves in search of the hairy, smelly, mysterious beast known only as the wumpus. Many hazards faced the player, including bats, bottomless pits, and, of course, the wumpus. Because the original game was released with source code, it allowed users to create their own versions of Hunt the Wumpus with different caves and hazards. Ultimately, reinterpretations of Wumpus led to the development of an entire genre of first-person adventure games, such as Adventure and Zork.

By the end of this chapter, you'll know how to add features to your fully functioning version of Hunt the Wumpus, and you'll even be able to tweak it to create your own version.

HAIRY, SMELLY BEAST? SOUNDS LIKE PITR!

Before we get to the cave adventures, let's figure out the basics.

What's a program?

As you learned in chapter 1, a program consists of statements that tell the computer how to do something. Programs can execute simple tasks, such as printing a string to the screen, and can be combined to execute complex tasks, like balancing accounts or editing a document.

PROGRAM   A series of instructions, usually called *statements*, that tell your computer how to do certain things.

The basic mechanics of a program are straightforward: Python starts at the first line and does what it says, then moves to the next and does what that says, and so on. For example, enter this simple Python program:

```
print "Hello world!"
print "This is the next line of my program"
```

The code outputs output the following text to the screen:

```
Hello world!
This is the next line of my program
```

WHAT'S UP, GREG? HOW'S THE PYTHON COMING ALONG?

I HEARD ABOUT THIS "HUNT THE WUMPUS" GAME, SO I THOUGHT I'D WRITE MY OWN VERSION.

Python can do many different types of things. So that you can get started on your program as soon as possible, this chapter will give you a brief idea of the statements you can use to tell Python what to do. We won't go into extensive detail, but you'll learn everything you need so that you can follow what's going on.

There's a lot to take in, so don't worry too much if you don't understand it all at once. You can think of programming like this as painting a picture; you'll begin with a light pencil sketch before you get started properly. Some parts will be hazy at first, but it's important to get a sense of the whole before you try to make sense of the details.

You might also want to read this chapter at your computer, so that you can experiment with different statements to see what works and try out your own ideas.

We'll start by investigating that print statement you just tried out.

Writing to the screen

The print statement is used to tell the player what's happening in your game, such as which cave the player is in or whether there's a wumpus nearby. You've already seen the print statement in the Hello World program, but there are some extra things that it can do, too. You're not limited to printing out words; pretty much anything in Python can be printed:

```
print "Hello world!"
print 42
print 3.141592
```

You can print out lots of things at once by putting a comma between them, like this:

```
print "Hello", "world!"
print "The answer to life, the universe and everything is", 42
print 3.141592, "is pi!"
```

But printing statements wouldn't make for an interactive game. Let's see how you can add options.

Remembering things with variables

Python also needs some way to know what's happening. In the Hunt the Wumpus game, for example, Python needs to be able to tell which cave the wumpus is hiding in, so it will know when the player has found the wumpus. In programming, we call this memory *data*, and it's stored using a type of object called a *variable*. Variables have names so they can be referred to later in the program.

To tell Python to set a variable, you choose a name for the variable and then use the equals sign to tell Python what the variable should be. Variables can be letters, numbers, words, or sentences, as well as some other things that we'll cover later. Here's how to set a variable:

```
variable = 42
x = 123.2
abc_123 = "A string!"
```

In practice, your program can get quite complex, so it helps if you choose a name that tells you what the variable means or how it's supposed to be used. In the Hunt the Wumpus program, you'll use variable names like this:

```
player_name = "Bob"
wumpus_location = 2
```

NOTE   There are some restrictions on what your variable names can be; they can't start with a number, have spaces in them, or conflict with some of the names which Python uses for its own purposes. In practice, you won't run into these limitations if you're using meaningful names.

Table 2.1 gives you an overview of the variable types you'll be using in your Hunt the Wumpus program.

Table 2.1   Types of variable used in Hunt the Wumpus

Type	Overview
Numbers	Whole numbers like 3 or 527, or floating-point numbers like 2.0 or 3.14159. Python won't switch between them, so you'll need to be careful in some cases; for instance, 3 / 2 is 1 instead of 1.5. 3.0 / 2 will give the right answer.
Strings	A sequence of characters, including *a–z*, numbers, and punctuation. They can be used for storing words and sentences. Python has a few different ways of representing strings: you can use both single or double quotes— 'foo' or "foo"—as well as special versions with triple quotes that can run over multiple lines.
Lists	A collection of other variables, which can include other lists. Lists begin and end with a square bracket, and the items inside are separated with commas: ["foo", "bar", 1, 2, [3, 4, 5]].

Now that you have variables working, how do you get the player involved?

Asking the player what to do

The program also needs some way of asking the player what to do in certain situations. For Hunt the Wumpus, you'll use the raw_input command. When Python runs that command, it will prompt the player to type something in, and then whatever was typed can be stored in a variable:

```
player_input = raw_input(">")
```

Next, you need to figure out what to do with user input.

Making decisions

If that was all there was to programming, it would be kind of boring. All of the interesting stuff happens when the player has to make a choice in the game. Will they pick cave 2 or cave 8? Is the wumpus hiding in there? Will the player be eaten? To tell Python what you want to happen in certain situations, you use the `if` statement, which takes a *condition*, such as two variables being equal or a variable being equal to something else, and something to do if the condition is met:

```
if x == y:
    print "x is equal to y!"
if a_variable > 2:
    print "The variable is greater than 2"
if player_name == "Bob":
    print "Hello Bob!"
```

You can also use an `else` command, which tells Python what to do if the condition doesn't match, like this:

```
if player_name == "Bob":
    print "Hello Bob!"
else:
    print "Hey! You're not Bob!"
```

So that Python can tell the body of the `if` statement from the rest of your program, the lines which are part of it are indented. If you put an `if` statement within another `if` statement—usually referred to as *nesting*—then you need to indent again, for a total of eight spaces. Normally, you'll use four spaces for each level of indentation.

Some common conditions are listed in table 2.2.

Table 2.2 Common conditions

Condition	Overview
`name == "bob"`	True if the variable *name* stores the string "bob". Python uses two equal signs to distinguish it from assignment: `name = "bob"` means something completely different.
`name != "bob"`	True if the variable *name* is something other than the string "bob". `!=` is generally read as "not equals."
`a > 0`	True if the variable *a* stores a number that is greater than 0.
`0 <= a <= 10`	True if *a* is a number between 0 and 10, inclusive.

Table 2.2   Common conditions *(continued)*

Condition	Overview
"ab" in "abcde"	You can also tell whether a string is part of another string by using in.
not "bob" in "ab" "bob" not in "ab"	Python also has the not and not in commands, which reverse the sense of an expression.

Now that you have a handle on decision-making statements, let's see what you can do to keep the program going.

Loops

One of the great things about computers is not that they can do things, but that they can do things over and over and over and not get bored. Big lists of numbers to add? No problem. Hundreds of lines of files? Ditto. The program only needs to know what it's going to be repeating and when it should stop. In the Hunt the Wumpus program, you'll be using a structure called a *while loop*, which loops as long as a condition that you specify is true, and a break statement, which allows you to control when it stops. Here's an example:

```
while True:
    print "What word am I thinking of?"
    answer = raw_input(">")
    if answer == "cheese":
        print "You guessed it!"
        break
    else:
        print "No, not that word..."
```

We're almost to the end of the tour of Python's basic features; our last one is functions.

Functions

There are also a few statements called *functions* in the Wumpus program. They usually tell you useful things about your program, the player, or the variables, and they look like this:

```
range(1,21)
len(cave_numbers)
```

Normally, functions will tell you things by *returning* a value, which you can store in a different variable or use directly:

```
cave_numbers = range(1,21)
print "You can see", len(cave_numbers), "caves"
```

Now that we've covered some of the basics, let's see how you can use them to build a simple program. This doesn't do everything that the original Hunt the Wumpus program did, but for now we want to get something off the ground to see how it all fits together.

> **Incremental programming**
>
> In later sections of this chapter, you'll build on this program by adding features or refining ones that are already there, and tidy up as you go. This is how most programmers tend to work: start simply and build as you go. You can download this program from www.manning.com/hellopython, but I'd suggest following along and typing it in as you read it. That'll help you remember the individual statements more easily, but you'll also be establishing a key habit which will help you as you write larger programs—start with a small program and grow from there.

Table 2.3 lists the basic features that you'll learn in this chapter.

Table 2.3 Basic Python features

Feature	Overview
Statements	Usually one line in a program (but can be more) that tells Python to do something.
Variables	Used to refer to information so that a program can use it later. There are many different types of information that Python can refer to.

Table 2.3   Basic Python features *(continued)*

Feature	Overview
if–then–else	This is how you tell Python to make a decision. An `if` statement consists of at least a condition such as x == 2 or some_function() < 42 and something for Python to do if that expression is true. You can also include an `else` clause, which tells Python what to do if the expression is false.
Loops	Used to repeat certain statements multiple times. They can be either `while` loops, which are based on a condition like an if statement, or `for` loops, which run once for each element of a list. From within a loop, you can use the `continue` statement, which jumps to the next iteration of the loop, or a `break` statement, which breaks out of the loop entirely.
Functions	A series of statements that can be run to return a value to a separate part of your program. They can take input if necessary, or they can read (and sometimes write) other variables in your program.
Indenting	Because you can nest functions, loops, and if statements within each other, Python uses white space (normally four spaces per level) at the start of a line to tell which statements belong where.
Comments	Whenever Python encounters a # character at the start of a line, it will ignore that line and not run it. Additionally, if there's a # character that's not inside a string, it will ignore the rest of the line. Comments are used to explain parts of your program, either to other programmers or to yourself in a few weeks—when you've forgotten most of the details of what you were doing. You won't see too many in the book, because we use numbered comments for code listings.

You've learned a lot in this section, but in the next section you'll put this knowledge to good use and write your first program.

Your first program

Now that you have an understanding of the basics of Python, let's take a look at the program. It's difficult to see how a program works just by reading about individual features, because, in a working program, they all depend on each other. In this section, we'll explore the first version of Hunt the Wumpus and solve the first problem that comes up.

RUN!

RRRR!

NOTE   Experimentation is critical to developing an intuition for how Python works, and how all of the parts fit together. Without it, you'll be stuck cut and pasting other people's programs, and when you have a bug, it'll be impossible to fix.

The first version of Hunt the Wumpus

If you don't understand the next listing right away, don't worry. A good way to figure out what a program does is to experiment with it—change a few statements, run it again, and see what the differences are. Or, copy a few statements into another file so you can run them in isolation.

Listing 2.1   Your first version of Hunt the Wumpus

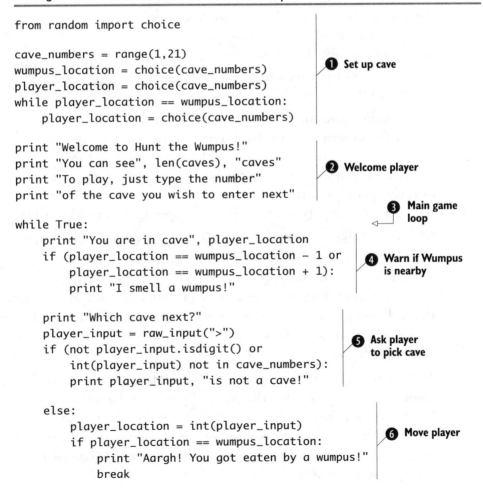

```
from random import choice

cave_numbers = range(1,21)
wumpus_location = choice(cave_numbers)
player_location = choice(cave_numbers)
while player_location == wumpus_location:
    player_location = choice(cave_numbers)

print "Welcome to Hunt the Wumpus!"
print "You can see", len(caves), "caves"
print "To play, just type the number"
print "of the cave you wish to enter next"

while True:
    print "You are in cave", player_location
    if (player_location == wumpus_location - 1 or
        player_location == wumpus_location + 1):
        print "I smell a wumpus!"

    print "Which cave next?"
    player_input = raw_input(">")
    if (not player_input.isdigit() or
        int(player_input) not in cave_numbers):
        print player_input, "is not a cave!"

    else:
        player_location = int(player_input)
        if player_location == wumpus_location:
            print "Aargh! You got eaten by a wumpus!"
            break
```

❶ Set up cave

❷ Welcome player

❸ Main game loop

❹ Warn if Wumpus is nearby

❺ Ask player to pick cave

❻ Move player

Let's start with the "setup" part of the program ❶. You're storing a list of numbers in the program, each of which represents a cave. Don't worry too much about the first line—you'll learn more about the import statement in chapter 3. The choice function will return one of the caves, picked at random, and you use it to place the wumpus and the player in their starting positions. Note the loop at the end that you use to tell if the player and the wumpus are in the same spot—it wouldn't be a fun game if the player got eaten right away!

The introductory text ❷ tells the player how the game works. You use the len() function to tell how many caves there are. This is useful because you may want to change the number of caves at a later point, and using a function like this means you only have to change things in one place when you define the list of caves.

Your main game loop ❸ is where the game starts. When playing the game, the program gives the player details of what the player can see, asks the player to enter a cave, checks to see whether the player has been eaten, and then starts over at the beginning. while loops will loop as long as their condition is true, so while True: means "loop over and over again without stopping" (you'll handle the stopping part in a minute).

The first if statement ❹ tells the player where the player is and prints a warning if the wumpus is only one room away ("I smell a wumpus!"). Note how you're using the player_location and wumpus_location variables. Because they're numbers, you can add to and subtract from them. If the player is in cave 3, and the wumpus is in cave 4, then the player_location == wumpus_location - 1 condition will be true, and Python will display the message.

You then ask the player which cave the player wants next ❺. You do some checking to see that the player has put in the right sort of input. It has to be a number, and it has to be one of the caves. Note also that the input will be a string, not a number, so you have to convert it using the int() function. If it doesn't match what you need, you display a message to the player.

If the input does match a cave number, it will trigger this else clause ❻. It updates the player_location variable with the new value and then checks to see if the player's location is the same as the wumpus's. If it is ... "Aargh! You got eaten by a wumpus!" Once the player has been eaten, the game should stop, so you use the break command to stop your main loop. Python has no more statements to execute, and so the game ends.

NO ONE'S QUITE SURE—
THEY'RE MASTERS OF
DISGUISE!

RRRR!

Debugging

If you've typed in listing 2.1 exactly as written and run it, you'll notice that it doesn't quite work as planned. In fact, it refuses to run at all. The exact results will depend on your computer's operating system and how you're running your Python program, but you should see something similar to what is shown in the following listing. If you don't, try running your program from the command line by typing python wumpus-1.py.

Listing 2.2   BANG! Your program explodes

```
Welcome to Hunt the Wumpus!
You can see
Traceback (most recent call last):
  File "wumpus-1.py", line 10, in ?
    print "You can see", len(caves), "caves"
NameError: name 'caves' is not defined
```

I AM TELLINK NOT TO BE
TOUCHING CODE! NOW
EXPERIMENT IS RUINED!

YOU LEFT YOUR
EXPERIMENTAL CODE
ON THE SERVER WHERE
ANYONE COULD
FIND IT?!

What's happened is that there's a *bug* in the program. There's a statement in listing 2.1 that Python doesn't know how to run. Rather than guess what you meant, it will stop and refuse to go any further until you've fixed it.

Luckily, the problem is easy to fix: Python tells you what line is at fault and the type of error that's been triggered, and it provides a rough description of the problem. In this case, it's line 10, and the error is `NameError: name 'caves' is not defined`. Oops—the program tried to access the variable `caves` instead of `cave_numbers`. If you change line 10 so that it reads

```
print "You can see", len(cave_numbers), "caves"
```

then the program should run.

Congratulations—your first real Python program! Next, let's see what else you can do to improve Hunt the Wumpus.

Experimenting with your program

Experimenting with programs is the most common way that most programmers learn how to deal with new programming problems and find solutions. You, too, can experiment with your new program and see what else you can get it to do. You're the one typing it in, so the wumpus program is yours. You can make it do whatever you want it to. If you're feeling brave, try the following ideas.

More (or fewer) caves

You might find 20 caves to be too many—or too few. Luckily, it's your program now, so you can change the line where you define `cave_numbers` to be smaller or larger. Question: what happens if you have only one cave?

A nicer wumpus

You haven't put a bow and arrow into the game yet, so all the player can do is wander aimlessly around the caves until the player bumps into the wumpus and gets eaten. Not a very fun game. How about if you change the line where the player finds the wumpus to read:

```
print "You got hugged by a wumpus!"
```

Aww, what a nice wumpus! (The author and publisher disclaim any and all responsibility for dry-cleaning your clothes to get out the wumpus smell should you choose this option.)

More than one wumpus

The wumpus must be awfully lonely down in the caves. How about giving it a friend? This is a bit trickier; but you already have the existing wumpus code to work from. Add a `wumpus_friend_location` variable, and check that wherever you check the first `wumpus_location` as shown here.

Listing 2.3   Adding a friend for the wumpus

```
wumpus_location = choice(cave_numbers)
wumpus_friend_location = choice(cave_numbers)
player_location = choice(cave_numbers)
while (player_location == wumpus_location or
        player_location == wumpus_friend_location):
        player_location = choice(cave_numbers)
...

if (player_location == wumpus_location - 1 or
    player_location == wumpus_location + 1):
    print "I smell a wumpus!"
if (player_location == wumpus_friend_location - 1 or
    player_location == wumpus_friend_location + 1):
    print "I smell an even stinkier wumpus!"
...

    if player_location == wumpus_location:
        print "Aargh! You got eaten by a wumpus!"
        break
    if player_location == wumpus_friend_location:
        print "Aargh! You got eaten by the wumpus' friend!"
        break
```

Now that's a more interesting game!

There's still more you can do to improve the Hunt the Wumpus game, starting with the cave structure.

AND THOSE WUMPUS
EXTERMINATORS ARE
EXPENSIVE!

AT LEAST WE'LL BE BACK
UP AND RUNNING SOON.
         NYET ...

Making the caves

The first thing that you might have noticed about listing 2.1 is that the "maze of caves" isn't a maze. It's more like a corridor, with the caves neatly placed in a line, one after the other. It's easy to figure out where the Wumpus is—move into the next cave in sequence until you smell it. Because figuring out the location of the wumpus is such an integral part of the game, this is the first thing to fix. While addressing this, you'll learn a bit more about Python's *lists* and for *loops*.

Lists

Assume for a second that you wanted to write a program to help you do your shopping. The first thing that you'd need is some way to keep track of what you wanted to buy. Python has a built in mechanism for exactly this sort of thing, called a *list*. You can create and use it like any other variable:

```
shopping_list = ['Milk', 'Bread', 'Cheese', 'Bow and Arrow']
```

If you want to find out what's on your shopping list, you can print it out or you can use an *index* to find out what's in a specific place. Lists will keep everything in the order in which you defined it. The only catch is that the index of an array starts at 0, rather than 1:

```
>>> print shopping_list
['Milk', 'Bread', 'Cheese', 'Bow and Arrow']
>>> print shopping_list[0]
Milk
```

A clever trick if you need it, is that an index of -1 gets the last item in your array:

```
>>> print shopping_list[-1]
Bow and Arrow
```

You can also check whether a particular thing is in your list:

```
if 'Milk' in shopping_list:
    print "Oh good, you remembered the milk!"
```

The other cool thing about lists is that they fulfill many purposes. You're not limited to strings or numbers—you can put anything at all in there, including other lists. If you had lists for two stores (say, the supermarket and Wumpus 'R' Us ("for all your Wumpus-hunting needs!"), you could store them in their own lists and then store those lists in one big list:

IS GREATER SIBERIAN WUMPUS—MUCH TOUGHER THAN PUNY AMERICAN WUMPUS!

RRRR!
AIEEEEE!

```
>>> supermarket_list = ['Milk', 'Bread',
    'Cheese']
>>> wumpus_r_us_list = ['Bow and Arrow',
    'Lantern', 'Wumpus B Gone']
>>> my_shopping_lists = [supermarket_list,
    wumpus_r_us_list]
```

You can also put things into a list and take them out again. If you forget to put rope on your list, that's easily fixed:

```
>>> wumpus_r_us_list.append('Rope')
>>> print wumpus_r_us_list
['Bow and Arrow', 'Lantern', 'Wumpus B Gone', 'Rope']
```

You want to catch a Wumpus instead of scaring it away, so perhaps the "Wumpus B Gone" isn't such a good idea:

```
>>> wumpus_r_us_list.remove('Wumpus B Gone')
>>> print wumpus_r_us_list
['Bow and Arrow', 'Lantern', 'Rope']
```

You can also cut out parts of a list if you need to, by giving two values separated with a colon. This is called *slicing* a list. Python will return another list starting at the first index, up to but not including the second index. Remember that list indexes start at zero:

```
first_three = wumpus_r_us_list[0:3]
```

If you give a negative value, then Python will measure from the end instead of the front:

```
last_three = wumpus_r_us_list[-3:]
```

Notice that that last example left out the last index. If you leave a value out of a slice like that, Python will use the start or end of the list. These two slices are exactly the same as the previous two:

```
first_three = wumpus_r_us_list[:3]
last_three = wumpus_r_us_list[1:]
```

Finally, once you've taken everything out of a list, you'll end up with an *empty list*, which is represented with two square brackets by themselves: [].

NOTE   One difference between Python and some other programs, such as C, is that Python's variables aren't variables in the classic sense. For the most part, they behave as if they are, but they're more like a label or a pointer to an object in memory. When you issue a command like a = [], Python creates a new list object and makes the a variable point to it. If you then issue a command like b = a, b will point to the same list object, and anything that you do via a will also appear to happen to b.

Now that you know about lists, let's tackle *for loops*.

For loops

Once you have all of your things in a list, a common way to use the list is to do something to each item in it. The easiest way to do this is to use a type of loop called a for *loop*. A for loop works by repeating some statements for every item in a list, and assigns that item to a variable so that you can do something with it:

```
print "Wumpus hunting checklist:"
for each_item in wumpus_r_us_list:
    print each_item
    if each_item == "Lantern":
        print "Don't forget to light your lantern"
        print "once you're down there."
```

Except for the variable, for loops are much the same as while loops. The break statement which you used in the while loop in listing 2.1 will also work in for loops.

NOTE   This is a common pattern in programming—get a bunch of stuff, and do something to everything in your bunch.

Coding your caves

In Hunt the Wumpus, each cave is only supposed to connect to a small number of other caves. For example, cave 1 might only have tunnels to caves 5, 7, and 12, and then cave 5 has tunnels to 10, 14, and 17. This limits the number of caves the player can visit at once, and navigating their way through the cave system to try and find the wumpus becomes the central challenge of the game.

A LIST OF LISTS? HOW DOES THAT WORK?

AH. I SEE—[2, 3, 7] IS A CAVE ...

AND THE NUMBERS TELL PYTHON WHICH CAVES THE TUNNELS GO TO:

In your first version of Hunt the Wumpus, you were already using a list of cave numbers to tell Python where the wumpus and player were. In your new version, you'll use a similar sort of list, but changed so that it can tell you which caves can be visited from a particular place. For each cave, you'll need a list of other caves, so what you're after is a list of lists. In Python, it looks like this:

```
caves = [ [2, 3, 7],
          [5, 6, 12],
          ...
        ]
```

What this tells you is that cave 0 (don't forget that lists start with their index at 0) links to caves 2, 3, and 7; cave 1 links to caves 5, 6, and 12; and so on. Because the caves are generated randomly, your numbers will be different, but the overall structure will be the same. The number of the cave is the same as its index in the list so that Python can easily find the exits later. Let's replace section 1 of listing 2.1 with the following listing so that it sets up your new and improved cave system.

Listing 2.4   Setting up your caves

```
from random import choice

cave_numbers = range(0,20)
caves = []
for i in cave_numbers:
    caves.append([])

for i in cave_numbers:
    for j in range(3):
        passage_to = choice(cave_numbers)
        caves[i].append(passage_to)
print caves
```

You're still using a range function to generate the list of caves, but you've changed the range so that it starts at 0 instead of 1, to match the indexes of your list. Then you make an empty list for each of the caves that you're supposed to have. At this point, it's a list of unconnected caves.

For each unconnected cave in your list, you pick three other caves at random and append them onto this cave's list of tunnels. To make things easier, you use another for loop inside the first one, so that if you need to change the number of tunnels later, you only need to change the number 3 to whatever you'd like.

When you're picking a cave to link to, you use a *temporary variable* to store it. The main advantage of this is that you can use a meaningful name to make the code much easier to read, because you know what that variable does. Note that you could have joined these two lines together by writing caves[i].append(choice(cave_numbers)) instead (using the choice(cave_numbers) function directly), but it's much harder to read.

So that you can check the program is working properly, you print out the list of caves. This is usually referred to as a *debug string*, because it's a handy technique when you're trying to debug a program. You can remove this line once the program is running properly, because the player shouldn't know the caves ahead of time.

Now, when you run your program, it should print out a list of caves, like this:

AH. YOU PROGRAMMINK WUMPUS GAME.

YEAH. EXCEPT MY WUMPUS IS STUCK, AND I CAN'T REACH IT.

IS FEATURE—NOT BEING EATEN BY WUMPUS.

```
[[8, 7, 14], [1, 18, 4], [4, 8, 15], [6, 6, 0],
 [5, 3, 6], [15, 9, 10], [2, 13, 5], [17, 18, 3],
 [4, 8, 15], [18, 17, 2], [1, 9, 15], [11, 4, 16],
 [16, 10, 6], [2, 10, 5], [13, 4, 6], [8, 14, 11],
 [16, 4, 10], [3, 12, 17], [18, 18, 0], [2, 8, 5]]
```

This is exactly what to expect. In this one, cave 0 links to caves 8, 7, and 14; cave 1 links to caves 1, 18, and 4; and so on. Now that you have the list, all that you have to do is alter the rest of your program to use it. Sections 4 and 5 of listing 2.1 should be replaced with the following listing.

Listing 2.5   Altering your program to use the new cave system

```
print "You are in cave", player_location
print "From here, you can see caves:", caves[player_location]
if wumpus_location in caves[player_location]:
    print "I smell a wumpus!"

print "Which cave next?"
player_input = raw_input(">")
if (not player_input.isdigit() or
    int(player_input) not in caves[player_location]):
    print player_input + "?"
    print "That's not a direction that I can see!"
    continue
```

Changes ❶
to the code

You're only using the cave list to find out which caves the player can enter next, so the changes to the code ❶ are pretty straightforward. Instead of checking whether the player's input is within the list of cave numbers, you check the list for the specific cave you're in.

There's a bug in the code you used to set up your caves. You may not believe me, especially if you've played a few games already, but there is. Let's get back into debugging mode.

Fixing a more subtle bug

What makes the bug hard to spot is that the code runs properly, but sometimes the game is impossible to win. In this section, we'll look at why the game can be unwinnable and how to fix it.

NOTE   These are the worst kind of bugs to hunt down—your program doesn't crash or spit out any obvious errors, but it's definitely wrong.

We'll start by examining how the caves are linked.

The problem

The trick is that all the cave tunnels are generated randomly, so they can be linked in any possible way. Let's think about an easier case, with a

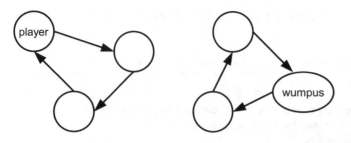

Figure 2.1
This isn't a very fun game.

small cave system. Suppose the tunnels happened to link like they do in figure 2.1.

The player wouldn't ever be able to catch the wumpus.

With lots of caves, it's less likely that you'll strand the player in an isolated corner of the map; but, ideally, you'd like the program to be as bulletproof as you can make it, so that it's *impossible*, rather than unlikely.

The solution

You need to make two changes to the map generation to solve the problem. The first is to make the tunnels two-way. If you can go from cave 1 to cave 2, then you should be able to move back from cave 2 to cave 1.

The second is to make sure that every cave is linked together and that there are no isolated caves (or networks of caves). This is called a *connected* structure. That way, no matter how you join up the rest of the passages, you can be sure players can reach every cave, because players can go back the way they came and choose a different passage. If players forget which way they came then they can still get lost, but that's their fault rather than yours.

Now, how do you use Python to link tunnels?

Coding connected caves

Connecting caves is straightforward—when you create a one-way tunnel, you add another one way tunnel back the way you came. Every time you say caves[a].append[b], you also say caves[b].append[a]. The program looks something like the following listing.

Listing 2.6   Creating a linked cave network

```
import random

cave_numbers = range(0,20)
caves = []
for i in cave_numbers:
    caves.append([])

unvisited_caves = range(0,20)
visited_caves = [0]                    ❶ Set up
unvisited_caves.remove(0)

                                       ❷ Main loop
while unvisited_caves != []:
    i = choice(visited_caves)
    if len(caves[i]) >= 3:             ❸ Pick random
        continue                          visited cave

    next_cave = choice(unvisited_caves)
    caves[i].append(next_cave)         ❹ Link it to an
    caves[next_cave].append(i)            unvisited one

    visited_caves.append(next_cave)    ❺ Mark cave
    unvisited_caves.remove(next_cave)     as visited

    for number in cave_numbers:
        print number, ":", caves[number]   ❻ Progress report
    print '----------'

for i in cave_numbers:
    while len(caves[i]) < 3:           ❼ Dig out rest of
        passage_to = choice(cave_numbers)    tunnels
        caves[i].append(passage_to)

    for number in cave_numbers:
        print number, ":", caves[number]   ❻ Progress report
    print '----------'
```

First, create a list of caves that you haven't visited, and visit cave 0 ❶. You loop until unvisited_caves is empty ❷; that is, there are no unvisited caves left. You pick one that has fewer than three tunnels to other caves ❸. If you link 1 cave to 10 others, the game will be too hard, because it will be difficult or impossible to work out which tunnel leads to the wumpus.

❹ is where you're building the cave. You pick a random unvisited cave, put a tunnel in the old cave to the new one, and then link from the new one back to the old one. This way you know that players can find their way back. In figure 2.2, you're adding cave 3 to your structure — it will get linked to one of either cave 0, 1, or 2.

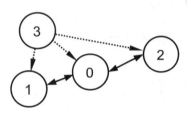

Figure 2.2 Adding cave 3 to your network

Once you're done with the cave, you can move it from the unvisited list to the visited list ❺. Steps ❸, ❹, and ❺ get repeated until you run out of caves (unvisited caves == []). Your cave structure will start to look like figure 2.3.

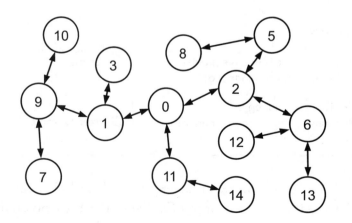

Figure 2.3
That's much better!

The progress report lines ❻ are optional, but if you include them you'll be able to see your caves in the process of being built, because every time Python goes through the loop it will print out the current cave structure. It also looks a bit nicer than print caves.

Now that all the caves are linked, the rest of the job requires adding some more one-way tunnels ❼. It's exactly the same as the previous example, except that you'll already have at least one tunnel in each cave. So that you don't add more than three tunnels, you change your for loop into a while loop.

With your cave problem solved, let's see how functions can improve the readability of your code.

Clean up your code with functions!

If you've been following along with the examples (you should!), you'll notice that your program is growing longer and longer. It's a relatively short example, but, even so, it's becoming hard to understand what's happening in the program. If you wanted to give a copy of your program to a friend for them to use, they might have a hard time figuring out what all the pieces do.

> **NOTE** Remember how we were talking about hiding complexity in chapter 1? Functions are one of the critical ways that Python can hide the complex parts of your program.

It's time for a spring-cleaning, and you're going to do that by designing your program to use some functions. You've been using a few functions so far; they're the choice(), len(), raw_input() parts of your code — so you have a rough idea of how they work. What you don't know (yet) is what they really are or how to create your own.

Function basics

Functions are a way of making a section of your program self contained, often referred to as *encapsulation*. It's an important way of breaking down a program into easily understood parts. A good rule of thumb is that each function "should do one thing and do it well." There should be as little overlap between your functions as possible. This is similar to the

way the parts of a car engine work; if a fan
belt breaks, you should replace the fan
belt—it wouldn't make much sense to have
to change your tires or spark plugs as well.

There are several advantages to using functions in your program:

- You only have to write that part of the
  program once, and then you can use it
  wherever you like. Later, if you don't like
  the way your program works or you find a bug, you only have to
  change your code in one place.

- In much the same way you can choose nice variable names that tell
  you what's going on in your program, you can also choose nice function names that describe what the function does.

- One of the reasons your code is hard to understand now is that it's
  all in one big piece and it's difficult to tell where parts begin and end.
  If it were broken into smaller parts, with a part for setting up the
  caves, a part for making a tunnel, a part for moving the player, and
  so on, you would only need to read (and understand) one small piece
  of the program instead of a large chunk.

Functions are one of the main units of encapsulation in Python. Even
advanced structures such as classes, which we cover in chapter 6, are
composed of functions. Python also has what are called *first-class functions*, which means that you can assign functions to variables and pass
them to other functions. You'll learn more about how to use functions
like this in chapter 7.

Functions have input and output, which you've seen already—when
you use a function, you send it some data and then get back some more
data as an answer. Some functions will do things themselves, but other
functions will return a value after performing some calculations. Here's
a simple function that will add two numbers together:

```python
def add_two_numbers(a, b):
    """ This function adds two numbers """
    return a + b
```

Let's look at the initial line of the function declaration. It starts with the reserved word def, followed by a name for your function, and then the parameters that the function will expect within brackets. When you call the function later in your program, you specify what these parameters are—they can be explicit values or variables.

The second line is called a *docstring*, and it's another useful way of making your programs easier to read when combined with good variable and function names. It should be a short description of the function and what it does—anything that someone might need to know in order to use the function properly. You've also used a special version of a Python string with three quotes, so that you can extend the docstring over more than one line if you need to.

The third line is where the function does its work. In this case it's easy—add *a* and *b* together. The return statement tells Python that the function has finished and to send the result of *a* + *b* back to whoever called it.

Variable scope

Python places some limits on functions so they can only affect a small part of your program, normally the function itself. Most variables that are set inside your functions are known as *local variables*, and you won't be able to use them outside of the function:

ACCORDING TO MY OLD PROFESSOR, THIS ONE'S BEEN HUNTING WUMPUSES IN THE ANDES FOR 20 YEARS ...

WUMPII, ACTUALLY.

```
def create_a():
    a = 42

create_a()
print a
```

When you try and run this program, you'll get an error like this one:

```
Traceback (most recent call last):
  File "<stdin>", line 5, in test.py
NameError: name 'a' is not defined
```

What happened? You set the *a* variable inside the create_a() function, didn't you? Actually, it was only created inside the function. You can think of it as "belonging" to create_a. As soon as Python has finished with a variable, it gets thrown away—in this case, as soon as the function exits.

Additionally, you won't be able to change most variables that have been defined outside the function. Instead, when you create a variable, you'll be creating a new one. The following code won't work:

```
a = 42
def add_to_a(b):
    a = a + b
add_to_a(42)
```

Unless you tell it otherwise, Python assumes that the a variable is supposed to be within the add_one_to_a function. Trying to access a variable inside of a function produces an error like this:

```
Traceback (most recent call last):
  File "<stdin>", line 1, in ?
  File "<stdin>", line 2, in add_to_a
UnboundLocalError: local variable 'a' referenced before assignment
```

The rule of thumb to remember is that the variables used in functions and the variables used in the rest of your program are different. Within a function, you should only use the variables that are passed into it as parameters, and, once back in the main part of your program, you should only use the variables that are returned from the function.

But, like most rules of thumb, there are exceptions. In your program, you're making one exception when you're modifying the list of caves. In Python, the lists of caves and cave networks are a special type of variable called an *object*, and behind the scenes you're sending messages to these objects instead of modifying them directly. You'll learn more about how that works in chapter 6. But, for now, think of lists as being a special exception to the rule that you can't modify external variables.

Shared state

When functions (or objects) work on a single copy of something, it's referred to as *shared state*. You can use shared state by making functions work on a list of caves, but, generally, shared state is a bad thing to have in your programs. If you have a bug in one of your functions, Python may *corrupt* your data (perhaps truncate it, or replace it with something odd). You won't notice this until a completely separate part of your program tries to read the garbled data and displays odd results. When that happens, your program will become much harder to fix, depending on the number of functions that access your shared state.

NOTE　　Shared data is a double-edged sword. You need to have some, but it's also a source of bugs — particularly if a lot of functions share the data.

In chapter 6, you'll learn how to limit the number of functions that have access to shared state by using another Python structure called a *class*. For now, though, you'll have to be careful; you'll only modify your caves when you set them up, and you'll leave them alone once you're playing the game.

Data and operations on data

Most programs can be thought of as a collection of information or data that also features rules about ways to interact with that data. The Hunt the Wumpus program is no exception. You have a cave structure and locations for the wumpus and the player, functions that make changes to that data, and then a main program that ties it all together using the functions.

Designing your programs this way makes them much easier to write and debug and gives you more opportunities to reuse your code than if you had thrown everything into one big program or function.

If you have a *data structure* that fits everything your program needs and makes it easy to retrieve the data you need, that's usually half the battle when it comes to writing your program.

Now that you know what functions are and why you'd want to use them, let's go ahead and see how to break up your wumpus game into individual functions.

Fixing the wumpus

In principle, encapsulating a program into functions isn't too hard: look for parts of your program that fit some of the following criteria, and try to pull them out into functions where they

⦿ Do one particular thing (*self contained*)

⦿ Are repeated several times

⦿ Are hard to understand

When considering the Hunt the Wumpus game, you should be able to see that it has three main sections. You'll start with the simplest functions first and then use them to build the rest of your program.

Interacting with the caves

When dealing with cave-related tasks, there are several simple actions that you perform quite often:

⦿ Create a tunnel from one cave to another.

⦿ Mark a cave as visited.

⦿ Pick a cave at random, preferably one that is ok to dig a tunnel to.

To make your life easier when working with the list of caves, you can create what are known as *convenience functions*. These are functions that perform a (potentially complicated) series of actions but hide that complexity when you're using the function in your program. The benefit is that you can perform the actions in one step in your main program, and you don't have to worry about the details once you've created the function. That makes your program easier to understand and helps to reduce bugs in your programs. The next listing introduces some convenience functions that you can use to make Hunt the Wumpus clearer and more comprehensible.

Listing 2.7   Adding convenience functions

```
def create_tunnel(cave_from, cave_to):
    """ Create a tunnel between cave_from
    and cave_to """
    caves[cave_from].append(cave_to)
    caves[cave_to].append(cave_from)

def visit_cave(cave_number):
    """ Mark a cave as visited """
    visited_caves.append(cave_number)
    unvisited_caves.remove(cave_number)
```

❶ Create tunnels and visit caves

❷ Choose cave

```
def choose_cave(cave_list):
    """ Pick a cave from a list, provided
    that the cave has less than 3 tunnels."""
    cave_number = choice(cave_list)
    while len(caves[cave_number]) >= 3:
        cave_number = choice(cave_list)
    return cave_number

def print_caves():
    """ Print out the current cave structure """
    for number in cave_numbers:
        print number, ":", caves[number]
    print '----------'
```

❸ Print caves

Creating tunnels and visiting caves are both obvious candidates for functions ❶. It's easy to make an error by using the wrong variable to refer to a cave, and using code like create_tunnel(cave1, cave2) makes your program much easier to read.

In the choose_cave function ❷, you can hide even more detail. When you choose a cave, you're normally only interested in caves that have fewer than three tunnels. Adding that check into the function will remove a lot of duplicated code from your main program. Note also that choose_cave accepts a list of caves as input so you can use it to pick a cave from either the visited or unvisited cave list.

It's not only the "final" versions of your code that can have convenience functions. You can also create convenience functions to help you while programming. If you want to debug your code at a later point, a function to print all of your caves ❸ comes in handy. .

Next let's turn our attention to how to create your caves.

Creating the caves

We've already talked about the data that a program uses. One good rule of thumb is to create functions that do particular things to your data or that tell you about your data, and then use only those functions to "talk" to your data. In programming terminology, this is normally referred to as an *interface.* With an interface to guide you, it's much harder to make a mistake or get confused about what the data means. To some extent, you've already started that process.

In Hunt the Wumpus, there are three tasks that you need to perform when creating caves that are ideal candidates for functions:

- Set up the cave list.
- Make sure all of the caves are linked.
- Make sure there are three tunnels per cave.

In listing 2.8, three functions do exactly that. These functions are the essential core of your program, so it will pay off to try to get them right. There are no hard and fast rules, but some signs that your program is well written include the following:

- It's easy to read and understand.
- It's easy to find and fix bugs.
- You only have to change limited parts of your program when you add new features.
- You can reuse some of your functions when modifying the program.

Ultimately, though, what "right" means will vary from program to program depending on the design and what that design is trying to achieve.

Listing 2.8 Cave-creation functions

```
def setup_caves(cave_numbers):                          Create list
    """ Create the starting list of caves """       ❶  of caves
    caves = []
    for cave in cave_numbers:
        caves.append([])
    return caves
                                                     ❷  Connect caves
def link_caves():
    """ Make sure all of the caves are connected
    with two-way tunnels """
    while unvisited_caves != []:
        this_cave = choose_cave(visited_caves)
        next_cave = choose_cave(unvisited_caves)
```

```
        create_tunnel(this_cave, next_cave)
        visit_cave(next_cave)

def finish_caves():
    """ Link the rest of the caves with          Three tunnels
    one-way tunnels """                       ❸ per cave
    for cave in cave_numbers:
        while len(caves[cave]) < 3:
            passage_to = choose_cave(cave_numbers)
            caves[cave].append(passage_to)
```

Creating the list of caves ❶ hasn't changed much from the previous listing, but it's still a good idea to put well-defined sections of code in their own functions for readability.

All the hard work of connecting the caves and tunneling is done in link_caves ❷. Did you notice how the convenience functions that you defined in the previous listing help to tidy things up even further? Even if you didn't know what this function was doing, it'd be pretty easy to guess.

With finish_caves, you haven't created a convenience function ❸. It's the only section of code where you create a one-way tunnel, so the benefit is a bit more limited than in the other cases. Whether you create a function in cases like this might depend on whether you were planning on adding more functionality later. Decisions like this can be something of a stylistic issue, so pick the option that feels best for you. You can always change it later if you need to repeat some code.

Finally, let's bring functions to how Hunt the Wumpus interacts with the player.

Interacting with the player

When running the program, there are two tasks that you perform regularly to find out what the player wants to do next:

⊙ Tell the player about where they are.

⊙ Get some input from the player.

Because the appearance of a program is likely to change substantially, either due to the feedback of the people using it or from adding new features, it often makes sense to keep the interface separated from the rest of the program and interact with the player through well-defined mechanisms. The next listing defines two functions you'll use for these two tasks in your user interface.

Listing 2.9 Player-interaction functions

```
def print_location(player_location):
    """ Tell the player about where they are """
    print "You are in cave", player_location
    print "From here, you can see caves:"
    print caves[player_location]
    if wumpus_location in caves[player_location]:
        print "I smell a wumpus!"

def get_next_location():                              ←──┐ Get next
    """ Get the player's next location """                 location
    print "Which cave next?"
    player_input = raw_input(">")
    if (not player_input.isdigit() or
        int(player_input) not in
                caves[player_location]):
        print player_input + "?"
        print "That's not a direction that I can see!"
        return None
    else:
        return int(player_input)
```

Here's the mechanism that I was talking about. It doesn't matter what the player enters; this function will always return either a special value of None (Python's version of null) if the input wasn't right, or the number of the cave that the player wants to enter. You can check this easily in the main part of your program.

The rest of the program

Once you have all of these functions, it doesn't leave much of your program that isn't a function. But this is a good thing, as you'll see shortly.

Listing 2.10 shows the final installment of the updated Hunt the Wumpus game. It behaves exactly the same way as the program in listing 2.6 as far as the player is concerned, but the structure has completely changed. All of your tasks are now stored within functions, and the main program uses those functions to do everything in the game—display the current cave, get input, move the player, and so on.

Listing 2.10   The refactored wumpus game

```
from random import choice

...function definitions...

cave_numbers = range(0,20)
unvisited_caves = range(0,20)
visited_caves = []
caves = setup_caves(cave_numbers)

visit_cave(0)
print_caves()
link_caves()
print_caves()
finish_caves()

wumpus_location = choice(cave_numbers)
player_location = choice(cave_numbers)
while player_location == wumpus_location:
    player_location = choice(cave_numbers)

while True:
    print_location(player_location)
    new_location = get_next_location()
    if new_location isn't None:
        player_location = new_location
    if player_location == wumpus_location:
        print "Aargh! You got eaten by a wumpus!"
        break
```

Notice how short and easy to follow the main part of the program is now. It's only 20 lines, and, because you've chosen useful function names, you could probably figure out what it does even if you didn't know anything about Python. That's the ideal that you should be aiming for. Clear, easy-to-understand code will save you a lot of time when reading and modifying it later on.

Simplify

You've seen how you refined and simplified the program as you went along, including going back and changing parts completely when necessary. If you can simplify your code, there's normally no reason not to. The simpler a program is, the easier it is to write, understand, debug, and modify. The refining process is typically along the lines that you've seen so far in this chapter:

- Use meaningful names for both variables and functions.
- Use white space to separate different sections of program.
- Store values in intermediate variables.
- Break up functions so that they do one thing well.
- Limit the amount of shared state that functions use, and be clear about what that shared state is.

Perfection is achieved not when there is nothing left to add, but when there is nothing left to take away.

—Antoine de Saint-Exupéry

Caves … check. Wumpus … check. Running around in the caves … check. A way to win the game… Hmm. There's no way to win the game. Better do something about that.

Bows and arrows

In the traditional wumpus game, you had a bow and one arrow, and when you thought that you knew which cave the wumpus was in, you could choose to fire an arrow into that cave. If you guessed wrong, too bad!

BOW AND ARROW? NOW WE'RE TALKING!

NOTE   One of the golden rules of game design is that the player has to be able to enjoy your game. Without a bow and arrow, you can still explore and have fun, but firing the bow and arrow is how you find out whether your exploration and understanding of the cave system is correct.

It should be easy to see how to add this sort of feature by now, because it's similar in style to the get_next_location() function. You'll add a total of three more functions:

- Ask whether the player wants to move or shoot.
- Find out where to move.
- Find out where to fire an arrow.

You'll also modify the get_next_location() function into a general function ask_for_cave(). That's what it is already, and you can call it from both your movement and firing functions. By writing it this way, your two input functions will be short, which helps keep your program manageable. If you add another feature later that needs to ask for a cave, then you'll already have a useful function to call on, which makes programming easier and faster.

Listing 2.11   Adding arrows

```python
def ask_for_cave():                                          ← ❶ Redefine
    """ Ask the player to choose a cave from                      player_input()
    their current_location."""
    player_input = raw_input("Which cave?")
    if (not player_input.isdigit() or
        int(player_input) not in caves[player_location]):
        print player_input + "?"
        print "That's not a direction that I can see!"
        return None
    else:
        return int(player_input)
                                              ❷ Get player action
def get_action():                             ←
    """ Find out what the player wants to do next. """
    print "What do you do next?"
    print "   m) move"
    print "   a) fire an arrow"
    action = raw_input("> ")
    if action == "m" or action == "a":
        return action
    else:
        print action + "?"
        print "That's not an action that I know about"
        return None
```

```
def do_movement():
    print "Moving..."
    new_location = ask_for_cave()
    if new_location is None:
        return player_location
    else:
        return new_location

def do_shooting():
    print "Firing..."
    shoot_at = ask_for_cave()
    if shoot_at is None:
        return False

    if shoot_at == wumpus_location:
        print "Twang ... Aargh! You shot the wumpus!"
        print "Well done, mighty wumpus hunter!"
    else:
        print "Twang ... clatter, clatter!"
        print "You wasted your arrow!"
        print "Empty handed, you begin the "
        print "long trek back to your village..."
    return True

...

while 1:
    print_location(player_location)

    action = get_action()
    if action is None:
        continue

    if action == "m":
        player_location = do_movement()
        if player_location == wumpus_location:
            print "Aargh! You got eaten by a wumpus!"
            break

    if action == "a":
        game_over = do_shooting()
        if game_over:
            break
```

❸ Functions for program actions, too

❹ Main program is clear

You don't need to make too many changes to your earlier `get_next_location` function; you just need a name change to make its intention clear and some cosmetic changes to how the program asks for input ❶. The fact that you don't need to make extensive changes is normally a good sign that a function is designed properly. If you had to significantly modify your function, it could be a sign that the original was trying to do too much at once.

WHAT'S WITH THE CRATE?

I'M GETTING TIRED OF THIS WUMPUS SMELL. SO I'M TAKING MATTERS INTO MY OWN HANDS.

The function `get_action()` ❷ is similar to the `ask_for_cave()` function, except that the valid input differs. Hmm … perhaps there's the possibility that you can create a clearer function, one that both of these can call. In chapter 6, you'll learn about a good way to do that.

It's not just input that can be made into its own function. Actions within the game can be functions too ❸. Perhaps *actions* is too strong a word—notice how the action functions don't *do* anything (that is, set any variables); they only return what should happen, and then the main program takes action based on what the functions tell it to do.

The main part of your program is still as clear as it was previously ❹, even though you've added a major new piece of functionality. If it's much more complicated, that's usually a sign that you might need to create a new function for some parts of your program and simplify the core of what you're doing.

More atmosphere

Congratulations! You now have a fully functional Hunt the Wumpus program, which you can play over and over again and use to impress your friends. Well, sort of. It works, but a number for each cave isn't atmospheric or impressive. It makes your program easier to think about, but it needs that extra bit of polish. How about changing the program so that instead of numbers, it uses descriptive names for each cave?

NOTE   The core game mechanics are what make Hunt the Wumpus fun, but the final bits of polish like this are what distinguish good games from *great* games.

One way to do that is to reference a list of cave names stored in your program based on the cave number. Instead of displaying the raw cave number, display cave_names[cave_number]. When you ask the player for a cave, they should instead pick a number from 1 to 3, with the name of the cave after the number. You're aiming for something similar to what's shown in the following listing.

Listing 2.12   An interface for Hunt the Wumpus

```
Black pit
From here, you can see:
    1 - Winding steps
    2 - Old firepit
    3 - Icy underground river
I smell a wumpus!

What do you do next?
    m) move
    a) fire an arrow
>
```

I'VE PUT ALL OF OUR OLD DUST PUPPY MASCOTS IN HERE. ALONG WITH SOME OF PITR'S OLD SOCKS.

WHAT'S THAT GOING TO DO?   / RRRR!

The list of cave names is relatively easy. You can borrow mine or create your own. Notice that, in the following listing of cave names, you can break a list over multiple lines at the commas between items. This is to make the program easier to read and modify.

Listing 2.13   A list of cave names

```
cave_names = [
    "Arched cavern",
    "Twisty passages",
    "Dripping cave",
    "Dusty crawlspace",
    "Underground lake",
    "Black pit",
    "Fallen cave",
    "Shallow pool",
    "Icy underground river",
```

```
    "Sandy hollow",
    "Old firepit",
    "Tree root cave",
    "Narrow ledge",
    "Winding steps",
    "Echoing chamber",
    "Musty cave",
    "Gloomy cave",
    "Low ceilinged cave",
    "Wumpus lair",
    "Spooky Chasm",
]
```

The only other changes that you need to make are to what you're displaying, and what input you'll accept, as shown in the following listing.

Listing 2.14   Hunt the Wumpus—now with 40% more atmosphere!

```
def print_location(player_location):
    """ Tell the player about where they are """
    print
    print cave_names[player_location]
    print "From here, you can see:"
    neighbors = caves[player_location]                    Changes to  ❶
    for tunnel in range(0,3):                             player's view
        next_cave = neighbors[tunnel]
        print "   ", tunnel+1, "-", cave_names[next_cave]
    if wumpus_location in neighbors:
        print "I smell a wumpus!"


def ask_for_cave():
    """ Ask the player to choose a cave from
    their current_location."""
    player_input = raw_input("Which cave? ")
    if player_input in ['1', '2', '3']:
        index = int(player_input) - 1               ❷ Simplify player
        neighbors = caves[player_location]            input
        cave_number = neighbors[index]
        return cave_number                        Nothing else
    else:                                       ❸ has changed
        print player_input + "?"
        print "That's not a direction that I can see!"
        return False
```

Here's where you print out the current caves and the list of caves the player can see ❶. They're all using the printable cave name from your list of cave names, rather than the number. Instead of printing the cave list, you're using a for loop, with tunnel as an index into the list of tunnels. You're also adding one to it to get 1, 2, or 3 rather than the 0, 1, or 2 indexes, to make it extra friendly.

Now that you know there are only three valid choices, you can check directly for those ❷ rather than needing the user to enter the number of the cave. You're also subtracting one from the result, because you need 0, 1, or 2 for your list index, rather than 1, 2, or 3.

Even though you're using 1, 2, and 3 as choices, you still return the cave number as an index. All of your changes are contained within the print_location and ask_for_cave functions and use the interface that we talked about earlier, so nothing else in your program needs to be changed at all ❸.

Where to from here?

You don't have to stop with the program as listed. There are a number of features you can add, including some that were in the original version of Hunt the Wumpus. Feel free to invent your own—this is your program now, and you can make it do whatever you like.

Bats and pits

In the original Hunt the Wumpus, there were other hazards: bats, which carried the player to another cave, and pits, which worked in a similar way to the wumpus ("I feel a draft!").

Making the wumpus move

One wumpus variant made the wumpus move to a different, random cave if the player missed with their arrow—instead of causing the player to lose the game.

Different cave structures

The original Hunt the Wumpus had a static cave structure, in which the caves were vertices of a dodecahedron. You don't necessarily have to follow this format, but experimenting with different cave structures could make for a more fun game. For example, perhaps you don't like one-way tunnels; that should be easy to fix. Also, in the current version, caves can tunnel to themselves. I happen to like that sort of layout, but you may not. Being able to write your own programs means that you're not stuck with my design choices; you're free to make your own.

Summary

This chapter covered a lot of material. Not only did you learn the basics of Python and how to fit them together to make a program, but we also covered possible ways to design your programs and took a look at why certain design choices might be better than others.

The best way to *start* writing a program is to choose something simple that either does part of what you need or describes the core of your program; then, build it from there. In Hunt the Wumpus, the first step was to create the initial game loop of choosing a cave and allowing the player to move to a different one. From there, you were able to develop a proper cave system; after making sure that the caves were connected properly, your program became a fully fledged game that can be played and won (or lost).

The best way to *continue* to develop your program is to refine it as you go, by breaking commonly used parts into functions and trying to develop an interface between different sections of your program. Because it's easy to lose track of the overall structure in low-level details, such as adding items to lists or making sure that caves have three tunnels, a large part of your interfaces will often entail hiding superfluous details or making sections of your program easier to work with.

3

Interacting with the world

This chapter covers

- *What libraries are*
- *How to use libraries, including Python's standard library*
- *An example program that uses Python's* os *and* sys *libraries*
- *Python's dictionary data type*

One of the key strengths of Python is its standard library. Installed along with Python, the standard library is a large suite of program code that covers common tasks like finding and iterating over files, handling user input, downloading and parsing pages from the web, and accessing databases. If you make good use of the standard library, you can often write programs in a fraction of the time that it would take you otherwise, with less typing and far fewer bugs.

GUIDO'S TIME MACHINE   The standard library is so extensive that one of the running jokes in the Python community is that Guido (the inventor of Python) owns a time machine. When someone asks for a module that performs a particular task, Guido hops in his time machine, travels back to the beginning of Python, and— "poof!"—it's already there.

In chapter 2, you used the choice function in Python's random module to pick something from a list, so you've already used a library. In this chapter, we'll go in depth and find out more about how to use libraries, what other libraries exist, and how to use Python's documentation to learn about specific libraries. In the process, you'll also pick up a few other missing pieces of Python, such as how you can read files, and you'll discover another of Python's data types—the dictionary.

The program in this chapter solves a common problem that you've probably faced before: you have two similar folders (perhaps one's a backup of your holiday photos), and you'd like to know which files differ between the two of them. You'll be tackling this program from a different angle than in chapter 2, though. Rather than write most of your own code, you'll be using Python to glue together several standard libraries to get the job done.

Let's start by learning more about Python libraries.

"Batteries included": Python's libraries

What are libraries used for? Normally, they're geared toward a single purpose, such as sending data via a network, writing CSV or Excel files, displaying graphics, or handling user input. But libraries can grow to cover a large number of related functions; there's no hard or fast rule.

LIBRARY   Program code that is written so that it can be used by other programs.

Python libraries can do anything that Python can, and more. In some (rare) cases, like intensive number crunching or graphics processing, Python can be too slow to do what you need; but it's possible to extend Python to use libraries written in C.

In this section, you'll learn about Python's standard library, see which other libraries you can add, try them out, and get a handle on exploring a single library.

Python's standard library

GREG, HAVE YOU SEEN MY FILE?

FILE? WHAT FILE?

Python installs with a large number of libraries that cover most of the common tasks that you'll need to handle when programming.

If you find yourself facing a tricky problem, it's a good habit to read through the modules in Python's standard library to see if something covers what you need to do. The Python manuals are installed with the standard Windows installer, and there's normally a documentation package when installing under Linux. The latest versions are also available at http://docs.python.org if you're connected to the internet. Being able to use a good library can save you hours of programming, so 5 or 10 minutes up front can pay big dividends.

The Python standard library is large enough that it can be hard to find what you need. Another way to learn it is to take it one piece at a time. The Python Module of the Week blog (www.doughellmann.com/PyMOTW/) covers most of Python's standard library and is an excellent way to familiarize yourself with what's available, because it often contains far more explanation than the standard Python documentation.

Other libraries

You're not limited to the libraries that Python installs. It's easy to download and install extra libraries to add the additional functionality that you need. Most add-on libraries come with their own installers or installation script; those that don't can normally be copied into the library folder of your Python directory. You'll find out how to install libraries in later chapters, Once the extra libraries are installed, they behave like Python's built-in ones; there's no special syntax that you need to know.

Using libraries

Once installed, using a library is straightforward: just add an import line at the top of the script. There are several ways to do it, but here are the three most common.

INCLUDE EVERYTHING

You can include everything from a library into your script by using a line like

```
from os import *
```

This will read everything from the os module and drop it straight into your script. If you want to use the access function from os, you can use it directly, like access("myfile.txt"). This has the advantage of saving some typing, but with serious downsides:

IT'S AN IMPORTANT REPORT THAT I'M WORKING ON. I HAD IT SAVED ON THE SERVER YESTERDAY. BUT NOW IT'S GONE!

I'LL HAVE A LOOK IN YOUR SHARED FOLDER ...

- You now have a lot of strange functions in your script.
- Worse, if you include more than one module in this way, then you run the risk of functions in the later module overwriting the functions from the first module—ouch!
- Finally, it's much harder to remember which module a particular function came from, which makes your program difficult to maintain.

Fortunately, there are much better ways to import modules.

INCLUDE THE MODULE

A better way to handle things is with a line like import os. This will import everything in os but make it available only through an os object. Now, if you want to use the access function, you need to use it like this: os.access("myfile.txt"). It's a bit more typing, but you won't run the risk of overwriting any other functions.

INCLUDE ONLY THE BITS THAT YOU WANT

If you're using the functions from a module a lot, you might find that your code becomes hard to read, particularly if the module has a long name. There's a third option in this case: you can use a line like from os import access. This will import directly so that you can use access ("myfile.txt") without the module name, but only include the access function, not the entire os module. You still run the risk of overwriting with a later module, but, because you have to specify the functions and there are fewer of them, it's much less likely.

What's in a library, anyway?

Libraries can include anything that comes with standard Python—variables, functions, and classes, as well as Python code that should be run when the library is loaded. You're not limited in any way; anything that's legal in Python is fine to put in a library. When using a library for the first time, it helps to know what's in it, and what it does. There are two main ways to find out.

> **TIP**   dir and help aren't only useful for libraries. You can try them on all of the Python objects, such as classes and functions. They even support strings and numbers.

READ THE FINE MANUAL

Python comes with a detailed manual on every aspect of its use, syntax, standard libraries—pretty much everything you might need to reference when writing programs. It doesn't cover every possible use, but the majority of the standard library is there. If you have internet access, you can view it at http://docs.python.org, and it's normally installed alongside Python, too.

EXPLORATION

One useful function for finding out what a library contains is dir(). You can call it on any object to find out what methods it supports, but it's particularly useful with libraries. You can combine it with the __doc__ special variable, which is set to the docstring defined for a function or method, to get a quick overview of a library's or class's methods and what they do. This combination is so useful that there's a shortcut called help() that is defined as one of Python's built-in functions.

"BIG_BAZONGAS.JPG"?! IS THAT IT?

HEY! THAT'S LEGITIMATE MARKETING MATERIAL!

I'LL BET IT IS ...

For the details, you're often better off looking at the documentation; but if you only need to jog your memory, or if the documentation is patchy or confusing, dir(), __doc__, and help() are much faster. The following listing is an example of looking up some information about the os library.

Listing 3.1   Finding out more about the os.path library

```
>>> import os                                    ◁——① Import os
>>> dir(os.path)
['__all__', '__builtins__', '__doc__', '__file__',
 '__name__', '__package__', '_getfullpathname',
 'abspath', 'altsep', 'basename', 'commonprefix',
 'curdir', 'defpath', 'devnull', 'dirname', 'exists',
 'expanduser', 'expandvars', 'extsep', 'genericpath',
 'getatime', 'getctime', 'getmtime', 'getsize',
 'isabs', 'isdir', 'isfile', 'islink', 'ismount',
 'join', 'lexists', 'normcase', 'normpath', 'os',
 'pardir', 'pathsep', 'realpath', 'relpath', 'sep',
 'split', 'splitdrive', 'splitext', 'splitunc',
 'stat', 'supports_unicode_filenames', 'sys',
 'walk', 'warnings']
>>> print os.path.__doc__
Common pathname manipulations, WindowsNT/95 version.

Instead of importing this module directly, import os
and refer to this module as os.path.

>>> print os.path.isdir.__doc__
Return true if the pathname refers to an existing
directory.
>>> print os.path.isdir('c:/')
True
>>> print os.path.isdir('c:/windows/system.ini')
False

>>> help (os)
Help on module os:

NAME
    os - OS routines for Mac, NT, or Posix depending
    on what system we're on.

FILE
    c:\python26\lib\os.py
```

② Explore os.path

③ Docstring for os.path module

④ Docstring for the isdir function

⑤ Test functions

⑥ help() function

```
DESCRIPTION
    This exports:
      - all functions from posix, nt, os2, or ce,
        e.g. unlink, stat, etc.
      - os.path is one of the modules posixpath,
        or ntpath
      - os.name is 'posix', 'nt', 'os2', 'ce' or
        'riscos'
      - os.curdir is a string representing the
        current directory ('.' or ':')
      - os.pardir is a string representing the
        parent directory ('..' or '::')
```

6 help() function

First, you need to import the os module ❶. You can import os.path directly, but this is the way that it's normally done, so you'll have fewer surprises later. Next, you call the dir() function on os.path, to see what's in it ❷. The function will return a big list of function and variable names, including some built-in Python ones like __doc__ and __name__.

Because you can see a __doc__ variable in os.path, print it and see what it contains ❸. It's a general description of the os.path module and how it's supposed to be used.

If you look at the __doc__ variable for a function in os.path ❹, it shows much the same thing—a short description of what the function is supposed to do.

Once you've found a function that you think does what you need, you can try it out to make sure ❺. Here, you're calling os.path.isdir() on a couple of different files and directories to see what it returns. For more complicated libraries, you might find it easier to write a short program rather than type it all in at the command line.

Finally, the output of the help() function ❻ contains all the same information that __doc__ and dir() do, but printed nicely. It also looks through the whole object and returns all of its variables and methods without you having to look for them. You can press space or page up and down to read the output, and Q when you want to go back to the interpreter.

In practice, it can often take a combination of these methods before you understand enough about the library for it to be useful. A quick overview of the library documentation, followed by some experimenting at the command line and a further read of the documentation, will provide you with some of the finer points once you understand how it all fits together. Also, bear in mind that you don't necessarily have to understand the entire library at once, as long as you can pick and choose the pieces you need.

Now that you know the basics of Python libraries, let's see what you can do with them.

Another way to ask questions

There's one thing that you need to know before you can start putting your program together. Actually, there are a couple of other things, but you can pick those up on the way. What you'd like to be able to do in order to begin is tell the computer which directories you want to compare. If this were a normal program, you'd probably have a graphical interface where you could click the relevant directories. But that sounds hard, so you'll pick something simpler to write: a command-line interface.

Using command-line arguments

Command-line arguments are often used in system-level programs. When you run a program from the command line, you can specify additional parameters by typing them after the program's name. In this case, you'll be typing in the names of the two directories that you want to compare; something like this:

```
python difference.py directory1 directory2
```

If you have spaces in your directory name, you can surround the parameters with quotation marks; otherwise, your operating system will interpret it as two different parameters:

```
python difference.py "My Documents\directory1" "My Documents\directory2"
```

Now that you have your parameters, what are you going to do with them?

Using the sys module

In order to read the parameters you've fed in, you'll need to use the sys module that comes with Python's standard library. sys deals with all sorts of system-related functionality, such as finding out which version of Python a script is running on, information about the script, paths, and so on. You'll be using sys.argv, which is an array containing the script's name and any parameters that it was called with. Your initial program is listing 3.2, which will be the starting point for the comparison script.

Listing 3.2   Reading parameters using **sys**

```
import sys

if len(sys.argv) < 3:
        print "You need to specify two directories:"          ① Check
        print sys.argv[0], "<directory 1> <directory 2>"         parameters
        sys.exit()

directory1 = sys.argv[1]          ② Store parameter
directory2 = sys.argv[2]             values

print "Comparing:"
print directory1          ③ Debug strings
print directory2
print
```

First, you check to make sure that the script has been called with enough parameters ①. If there are too few, then you return an error to the user. Note also that you're using sys.argv[0] to find out what the name of your script is and sys.exit to end the program early.

Because you know now that there are at least two other values, you can store them for later use ②. You could use sys.argv directly, but this way, you've got a nice variable name, which makes the program easier to understand.

Once you have the variables set, you can print them out ❸ to make sure they're what you're expecting. You can test it out by trying the commands from the section "Using command-line arguments." The script should respond back with whatever you've specified.

NOTE   File objects are an important part of Python. Quite a few libraries use file-like objects to access other things, like web pages, strings, and the output returned from other programs.

If you're happy with the results, it's time to start building the program in the next section.

Reading and writing files

The next thing you'll need to do in your duplicate checker is to find your files and directories and open them to see if they're the same. Python has built-in support for handling files as well as good cross platform file and directory support via the os module. You'll be using both of these in your program.

Paths and directories (a.k.a. dude, where's my file?)

Before you open your file, you need to know where to find it. You want to find all of the files in a directory and open them, as well as any files in directories within that directory, and so on. That's pretty tricky if you're writing it yourself; fortunately, the os module has a function called os.walk() that does exactly what you want. The os.walk() function returns a list of all of the directories and files for a path. If you append listing 3.3 to the end of listing 3.2, it will call os.walk() on the directories that you've specified.

Listing 3.3   Using os.walk()

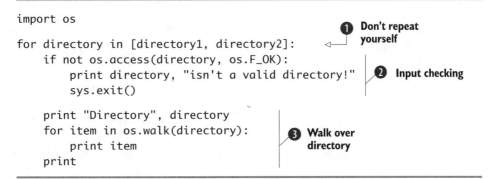

```
import os

for directory in [directory1, directory2]:          ❶ Don't repeat
    if not os.access(directory, os.F_OK):              yourself
        print directory, "isn't a valid directory!"  ❷ Input checking
        sys.exit()

    print "Directory", directory
    for item in os.walk(directory):                  ❸ Walk over
        print item                                     directory
    print
```

THERE. THAT SHOULD DO IT.
>CLICK<
YES MASTER.
FINDING REPORT ...
DID THE LIGHTS
JUST DIM?

You're going to be doing the same thing for both directory1 and directory2 ❶. You could repeat your code over again for directory2, but if you want to change it later, you'll have to change it in two places. Worse, you could accidentally change one but not the other, or change it slightly differently. A better way is to use the directory names in a for loop like this, so you can reuse the code within the loop.

It's good idea to check the input that your script's been given ❷. If there's something amiss, then exit with a reasonable error message to let the user know what's gone wrong.

❸ is the part where you walk over the directory. For now, you're printing the raw output that's returned from os.walk(), but in a minute you'll do something with it.

I've set up two test directories on my computer with a few directories that I found lying around. It's probably a good idea for you to do the same, so you can test your program and know you're making progress.

If you run the program so far, you should see something like the following output:

```
D:\code>python difference_engine_2_os.py . test1 test2
Comparing:
test1
test2

Directory test1
('C:\\test1', ['31123', 'My Music', 'My Pictures', 'test'], [])
('C:\\test1\\31123', [], [])
('C:\\test1\\My Music', [], ['Desktop.ini', 'Sample Music.lnk'])
('C:\\test1\\My Pictures', [], ['Sample Pictures.lnk'])
('C:\\test1\\test', [], ['foo1.py', 'foo1.pyc', 'foo2.py', 'foo2.pyc',
    'os.walk.py', 'test.py'])

Directory test2
('C:\\test2', ['31123', 'My Music', 'My Pictures', 'test'], [])
('C:\\test2\\31123', [], [])
('C:\\test2\\My Music', [], ['Desktop.ini', 'Sample Music.lnk'])
```

```
('C:\\test2\\My Pictures', [], ['Sample Pictures.lnk'])
('C:\\test2\\test', [], ['foo1.py', 'foo1.pyc', 'foo2.py', 'foo2.pyc',
'os.walk.py', 'test.py'])
```

In Python strings, some special characters can be created by using a backslash in front of another character. If you want a tab character, for example, you can put \t into your string. When Python prints it, it will be replaced with a literal tab character. If you do want a backslash, though—as you do here—then you'll need to use two backslashes, one after the other.

The output for each line gives you the name of a directory within your path, then a list of directories within that directory, then a list of the files ... handy, and definitely beats writing your own version.

Paths

If you want to use a file or directory, you'll need what's called a *path*. A path is a string that gives the exact location of a file, including any directories that contain it. For example, the path to Python on my computer is C:\python26\python.exe, which looks like "C:\\python26\\python.exe" when expressed as a Python string.

If you wanted a path for foo2.py in the last line of the previous listing, you can use os.path.join('C:\\test2\\test', 'foo2.py'), to get a path that looks like 'C:\\test2\\test\\foo2.py'. You'll see more of the details when you start putting your program together in a minute.

TIP   One thing to keep in mind when using paths is that the separator will be different depending on which platform you're using. Windows uses a backslash (\) character, and Linux and Macintosh use a forward slash (/). To make sure your programs work on all three systems, it's a good idea to get in the habit of using the os.path.join() function, which takes a list of strings and joins them with whatever the path separator is on the current computer.

Once you have the location of your file, the next step is opening it.

File, open!

To open a file in Python, you can use the file() or open() built-in function. They're exactly the same behind the scenes, so it doesn't matter which one you use. If the file exists and you can open it, you'll get back a file object, which you can read using the read() or readlines() method. The only difference between read() and readlines() is that readlines() will split the file into strings, but read() will return the file as one big string. This code shows how you can open a file and read its contents:

```
read_file = file(os.path.join("c:\\test1\\test", "foo2.py"))
file_contents = list(read_file.readlines())
print "Read in", len(file_contents), "lines from foo2.py"
print "The first line reads:", file_contents[0]
```

First, create a path using os.path.join(), and then use it to open the file at that location. You'll want to put in the path to a text file that exists on your computer. read_file will now be a file object, so you can use the readlines() method to read the entire contents of the file. You're also turning the file contents into a list using the list() function. You don't normally treat files like this, but it helps to show you what's going on. file_contents is a list now, so you can use the len() function to see how many lines it has, and print the first line by using an index of 0.

Although you won't be using it in your program, it's also possible to write text into a file as well as read from it. To do this, you'll need to open the file with a write mode instead of the default read-only mode, and use the write() or writelines() function of the file object. Here's a quick example:

```
write_file = file("C:\\test2\\test\\write_file.txt", "w")   ← ❶ Open file
write_file.write("This is the first line of the file\n")    ←      Write
write_file.writelines(                                           ❷ one line
    ["and the second\n",              ❸ Write multiple lines
     "and the third!\n"])
write_file.close()                                               ❹ Close file
```

You're using the same file() function you used before, but here you're feeding it an extra parameter, the string "w", to tell Python that you want to open it for writing ❶.

Once you have the file object back, you can write to it by using the .write() method, with the string you want to write as a parameter ❷. The "\n" at the end is a special character for a new line; without it, all of the output would be on one line. You can also write multiple lines at once, by putting them into a list and using the .writelines() method instead ❸.

Once you're done with a file, it's normally a good idea to close it ❹, particularly if you're writing to it. Files can sometimes be buffered, which means they're not written onto the disk straight away—if your computer crashes, it might not be saved.

That's not all you can do with files, but it's enough to get started. For your difference engine you won't need to write files, but it will help for future programs. For now, let's turn our attention to the last major feature you'll add to your program.

Comparing files

We're almost there, but there's one last hurdle. When you're running your program, you need to know whether you've seen a particular file in the other directory, and if so, whether it has the same content, too. You could read in all the files in and compare their content line by line, but what if you have a large directory with big images? That's a lot of storage, which means Python is likely to run slowly.

> **NOTE** It's often important to consider how fast your program will run, or how much data it will need to store, particularly if the problem that you're working on is open ended—that is, if it might be run on a large amount of data.

Fingerprinting a file

Fortunately, there's another library to help you, called hashlib, which is used to generate a hash for a particular piece of data. A hash is like a fingerprint for a file: from the data it's given, it will generate a list of numbers and letters that's virtually guaranteed to be unique for that data. If even a small part of the file changes, the hash will be completely different, and you'll be able to detect the change. Best of all, the hashes are relatively small, so they won't take up much space. The following listing features a small script that shows how you might generate a hash for one file.

Listing 3.4   Generating a hash for a file

```
import hashlib
import sys

file_name = sys.argv[1]
read_file = file(file_name)
the_hash = hashlib.md5()
for line in read_file.readlines():
    the_hash.update(line)
print the_hash.hexdigest()
```

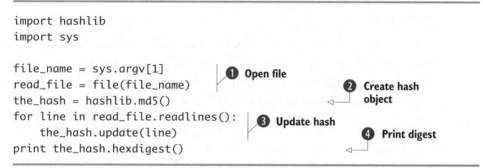

❶ **Open file**

❷ **Create hash object**

❸ **Update hash**

❹ **Print digest**

After importing your libraries, you read a file name from the command line and open it ❶. Next, you create a hash object here ❷, which will handle all of the hash generation. I'm using md5, but there are many others in hashlib.

Once you have an open file and a hash object, you feed each line of the file into the hash with the update() method ❸.

After you've fed all the lines into the hash, you can get the final hash in hexdigest form ❹. It uses only numbers and the letters *a–f*, so it's easy to display on screen or paste into an email.

An easy way to test the script is to run it on itself. After you've run it once, try making a minor change to the script, such as adding an extra blank line at the end of the file. If you run the script again, the output should be completely different.

Here, I'm running the hash-generating script on itself. For the same content, it will always generate the same output:

```
D:\test>python hash.py hash.py
df16fd6453cedecdea3dddca83d070d4
D:\test>python hash.py hash.py
df16fd6453cedecdea3dddca83d070d4
```

These are the results of adding one blank line to the end of the hash.py file. It's a minor change (most people wouldn't notice it), but now the hash is completely different:

```
D:\test>hash.py hash.py
47eeac6e2f3e676933e88f096e457911
```

Now that your hashes are working, let's see how you can use them in your program.

Mugshots: storing your files' fingerprints in a dictionary

Now that you can generate a hash for any given file, you need somewhere to put it. One option is to put the hashes into a list, but searching over a list every time you want to find a particular file is slow, particularly if you have a large directory with lots of files. There's a better way to do it, by using Python's other main data type: the dictionary.

You can think of dictionaries as a bag of data. You put data in, give it a name, and then, later, when you want the data back, you give the dictionary its name, and the dictionary will return the data. In Python's terminology, the name is called a *key* and the data is called the *value* for that key. Let's see how you use a dictionary by taking a look at the following listing.

Listing 3.5   How to use a dictionary

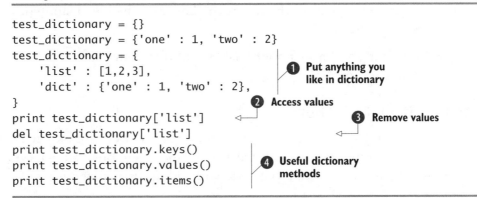

```
test_dictionary = {}
test_dictionary = {'one' : 1, 'two' : 2}
test_dictionary = {
    'list' : [1,2,3],
    'dict' : {'one' : 1, 'two' : 2},
}
print test_dictionary['list']
del test_dictionary['list']
print test_dictionary.keys()
print test_dictionary.values()
print test_dictionary.items()
```

❶ Put anything you like in dictionary

❷ Access values

❸ Remove values

❹ Useful dictionary methods

Dictionaries are fairly similar to lists, except that you use curly braces instead of square brackets, and you separate keys and their values with a colon.

The other similarity to lists is that you can include anything that you like as a value ❶, including lists, dictionaries, and other objects. You're not limited to storing simple types like strings or numbers, or one type of thing. The only constraint is on the key: it can only be something that isn't modifiable, like a string or number.

To get your value back once you've put it in the dictionary, use the dictionary's name with the key after it in square brackets ❷. If you're finished with a value, it's easy to remove it by using del followed by the dictionary and the key that you want to delete ❸.

Dictionaries are objects, so they have some useful methods ❹ as well as direct access. keys() returns all of the keys in a dictionary, values() will return its values, and items() returns both the keys and values. Typically, you'll use it in a for loop, like this:

```
for key, value in test_dictionary.items(): ...
```

When deciding what keys and values to use for a dictionary, the best option is to use something unique for the key, and the data you'll need in your program as the value. You might need to convert the data somehow when building your dictionary, but it normally makes your code easier to write and easier to understand. For your dictionary, you'll use the path to the file as the key, and the checksum you've generated as the value.

Now that you know about hashes and dictionaries, let's put your program together.

Putting it all together

"Measure twice, cut once" is an old adage that often holds true. When programming, you always have your undo key, but you can't undo the time you spent writing the code you end up throwing away.

When developing a program, it often helps to have some sort of plan in place as to how you'll proceed. Your plan doesn't have to be terribly detailed; but it can help you to avoid potential roadblocks or trouble spots if you can foresee them. Now that you think you have all of the parts you'll need, let's plan out the overall design of your program at a high level. It should go something like

- Read in and sanity-check the directories you want to compare.
- Build a dictionary containing all the files in the first directory.
- For each file in the second directory, compare it to the same file in the first dictionary.

That seems pretty straightforward. In addition to having this overall structure, it can help to think about the four different possibilities for each file, as shown in the following figure.

Case 1	The file doesn't exist in directory 2.	Case 2	The file exists, but is different in each directory.
Case 3	The files are identical in both.	Case 4	The file exists in directory 2, but not in your first directory.

Figure 3.1 The four possibilities for differences between files

Given this rough approach, a couple of issues should stand out. First, your initial plan of building all the checksums right away may not be such a good idea after all. If the file isn't in the second directory, then you'll have gone to all the trouble of building a checksum that you'll never use. For small files and directories it might not make much difference, but for larger ones (for example, photos from a digital camera or MP3s), the extra time might be significant. The solution to this is to put a placeholder into the dictionary that you build and only generate the checksum once you know you have both files.

CAN'T YOU USE A LIST? If you're putting a placeholder into your dictionary instead of a checksum, you'd normally start by using a list. Looking up a value in a dictionary is typically much faster, though; for large lists, Python needs to check each value in turn, whereas a dictionary needs a single lookup. Another good reason is that dictionaries are more flexible and easier to use than lists if you're comparing independent objects.

Second, what happens if a file is in the first directory but not the second? Given the rough plan we just discussed, you're only comparing the second directory to the first one, not vice versa. You won't notice a file if it's not in the second directory. One solution to this is to delete the files from the dictionary as you compare them. Once you've finished the comparisons, you know that anything left over is missing from the second directory.

Planning like this can take time, but it's often faster to spend a little time up front working out potential problems. What's better to throw away when you change your mind: five minutes of design or half  an hour of writing code? Listings 3.6 and 3.7 show the last two parts of your program based on the updated plan. You can join these together with listings 3.2 and 3.3 to get a working program.

Listing 3.6   Utility functions for your difference program

```python
import hashlib

def md5(file_path):
    """Return an md5 checksum for a file."""
    read_file = file(file_path)
    the_hash = hashlib.md5()
    for line in read_file.readlines():
        the_hash.update(line)
    return the_hash.hexdigest()

def directory_listing(dir_name):
    """Return all of the files in a directory."""
    dir_file_list = {}
    dir_root = None
    dir_trim = 0
    for path, dirs, files in os.walk(dir_name):
        if dir_root is None:
            dir_root = path
```

❶ MD5 function

❷ Directory listing function

❸ Finding root of directory

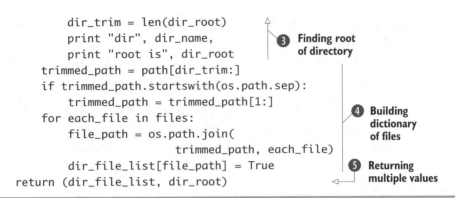

```
        dir_trim = len(dir_root)
        print "dir", dir_name,
        print "root is", dir_root
    trimmed_path = path[dir_trim:]
    if trimmed_path.startswith(os.path.sep):
        trimmed_path = trimmed_path[1:]
    for each_file in files:
        file_path = os.path.join(
                    trimmed_path, each_file)
        dir_file_list[file_path] = True
    return (dir_file_list, dir_root)
```

3 Finding root of directory

4 Building dictionary of files

5 Returning multiple values

This is the program from listing 3.5, rolled up into a function. Notice how a docstring has been added as the second line **1** so it's easy to remember what the function does.

Because you'll be building a list of files for two directories, it makes sense to have a function that returns all the information you need about a directory **2**, so you can reuse it each time. The two things you need are the *root*, or lowest-level directory (the one typed in at the command line) and a list of all the files relative to that root so you can compare the two directories easily. For example, C:\test\test_dir\file.txt and C:\test2\test_dir\file.txt should both be entered into their respective dictionaries as \test_dir\file.txt.

Because os.walk() starts at the root of a directory by default, all you need to do is remember the first directory that it returns **3**. You do that by setting dir_root to None before you enter the for loop. None is a special value in Python that means "not set" or "value unknown." It's what you use if you need to define a variable but don't know its value yet. Inside the loop, if dir_root is None, you know it's the first time through the loop and you have to set it. You're setting a dir_trim variable too, so that later you can easily trim the first part of each directory that's returned.

Once you have your directory root, you can chop off the common part of your directories and path separators from the front of the path returned by os.walk() ❹. You do that by using string slices, which will return a subsection of a string. It works in exactly the same way as a list index, so it starts at 0 and can go up to the length of the string.

When you're done, you return both the directory listing and the root of the directory ❺ using a special Python data type called a *tuple*. Tuples are similar to lists, except that they're immutable—you can't change them after they've been created.

Now that you've checked your inputs and set up all of your program's data, you can start making use of it. As in chapter 2, when you simplified Hunt the Wumpus, the part of the program that does stuff is fairly short, clear, and easy to understand. All the tricky details have been hidden away inside functions, as you can see in the next listing.

Listing 3.7   Finding the differences between directories

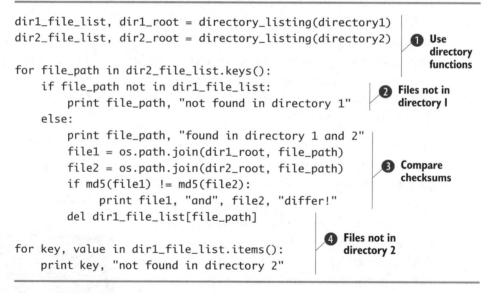

```
dir1_file_list, dir1_root = directory_listing(directory1)
dir2_file_list, dir2_root = directory_listing(directory2)
```
❶ **Use directory functions**

```
for file_path in dir2_file_list.keys():
    if file_path not in dir1_file_list:
        print file_path, "not found in directory 1"
```
❷ **Files not in directory 1**

```
    else:
        print file_path, "found in directory 1 and 2"
        file1 = os.path.join(dir1_root, file_path)
        file2 = os.path.join(dir2_root, file_path)
        if md5(file1) != md5(file2):
            print file1, "and", file2, "differ!"
        del dir1_file_list[file_path]
```
❸ **Compare checksums**

❹ **Files not in directory 2**

```
for key, value in dir1_file_list.items():
    print key, "not found in directory 2"
```

To assign both of the variables you get back from your function, you separate them with a comma ❶. You've already seen this when using dictionary.items() in a for loop.

Here's the first comparison ❷: if the file isn't in directory 1, then you warn the user. You can use in with a dictionary in the same way that you would for a list, and Python will return True if the object is in the dictionaries' keys.

If the file exists in both directories, then you build a checksum for each file and compare them ❸. If they're different, then you know the files are different and you again warn the user. If the checksums are the same then you keep quiet, because you don't want to overwhelm people with screens and screens of output—they want to know the differences.

Once you've compared the files in section 3, you delete them from the dictionary. Any that are left over you know aren't in directory 2 and you tell the user about them ❹.

That seems to about do it for your program, but are you sure it's working? Time to test it.

Testing your program

If you haven't already, now's probably a good time to create some test directories so you can try your script and make sure it's working. It's especially important as you start working on problems that have real-world consequences. For example, if you're backing up some family photos and your program doesn't report that a file has changed (or doesn't exist), you won't know to back it up and might lose it if your hard drive crashes. Or it might report two files as the same when they're actually different.

You can test your script on directories that you already have, but specific test directories are a good idea, mainly because you can exercise all the features you're expecting. At a minimum, I'd suggest

- Adding at least two directory levels, to make sure paths are handled properly
- Creating a directory with at least one space in its name

◉ Using both text and binary files (for example, images)

◉ Setting up all the cases you're expecting (files missing, file differences, files that are the same)

By thinking about all the possible cases, you can catch bugs in your program before you run it over a real directory and miss something or, worse, lose important data. The following figure shows the initial test directory (called test) that I set up on my computer.

Figure 3.2   A test directory for the difference engine

This test directory doesn't get all the possible failures, but it does check for most of them. The next step was to copy that directory (I called it test2) and make some changes for the difference engine to work on, as shown in figure 3.3. I've used the numbers 1 to 4 within the files to represent each of the possible cases, with 1 and 4 being missing files, 2 for files that have some differences, and 3 for files that are identical in both directories.

Figure 3.3   test2, an almost identical copy of the first test directory

You can see the output of running your script over these directories:

```
D:\>python code\difference_engine.py test test2
Comparing:
test
test2
dir test root is test
dir test2 root is test2
test\test 2\test2.txt and test2\test 2\test2.txt differ!
image4.gif not found in directory 1
test 2\test4.txt not found in directory 1
test\image2.gif and test2\image2.gif differ!
test4.txt not found in directory 1
test\test2.txt and test2\test2.txt differ!
test1.txt not found in directory 2
test 2\test1.txt not found in directory 2
image1.gif not found in directory 2
```

That seems to be pretty much what you were expecting. The script is descending into the test 2 directory in each case and is picking up the differences between the files—1 and 4 are missing, 2 is different, and 3 isn't reported because the files are identical.

Now that you've tested out your script, let's see what you can do to improve it.

Improving your script

Your script so far works, but it could do with a few improvements. For a start, the results it returns are out of order. The files that are missing from the second directory appear right at the end. Ideally, you'd have them appear next to the other entries for that directory, to make it easier to see what the differences are.

NOTE   Does this strategy look familiar? It's exactly what you did when developing Hunt the Wumpus. You start by writing a program that's as simple as you can make it and then build on the extra features that you need.

Putting results in order

It initially might be difficult to see how you might go about ordering the results, but if you think back to chapter 2, one of the strategies that you used with Hunt the Wumpus was to separate the program from its interface. In your difference engine, you haven't done so much of that so far—now might be a good time to start. You need two parts to your program: one part that does the work and stores the data it generates, and another to display that data. The following listing shows how you generate your results and store them.

Listing 3.8   Separating generated results from display

```
dir1_file_list, dir1_root = directory_listing(directory1)
dir2_file_list, dir2_root = directory_listing(directory2)
results = {}                                                    ◁──── ❶ Results
                                                                        dictionary
for file_path in dir2_file_list.keys():
    if file_path not in dir1_file_list:
        results[file_path] = "not found in directory 1"        ◁────
    else:
        file1 = os.path.join(dir1_root, file_path)                   Store  ❷
        file2 = os.path.join(dir2_root, file_path)                   results
        if md5(file1) != md5(file2):
            results[file_path] = "is different in directory 2"  ◁────
        else:
            results[file_path] = "is the same in both"         ◁────

for file_path, value in dir1_file_list.items():
    if file_path not in results:
        results[file_path] = "not found in directory 2"        ◁────
```

Here's the trick. Rather than try to display the results as soon as you get them, which means you're trying to shoehorn your program structure into your display structure, you store the results in a dictionary to display later ❶.

The result of each comparison is stored in result ❷, with the file path as the key and a description of the result of the comparison as the value.

That should take care of storing the results; let's take a look at how you display them:

```
print                                                   ❶ Sort results
for file_path, result in sorted(results.items()):       ◁────
```

```
    if os.path.sep not in file_path and "same" not in result:
        print path, result                              Check in strings  ❷
```

```
for path, result in sorted(results.items()):
    if os.path.sep in file_path and "same" not in result:  ❸  Other
        print path, result                                       directories
```

sorted() is a built-in Python function that sorts groups of items ❶. You can give it lists, dictionary keys, values or items, strings, and all sorts of other things. In this case, you're using it to sort result.items() by file_path, the first part of result.items().

ALL STEF'S "MARKETING MATERIAL" WAS PUT ON A SEPARATE DRIVE AFTER LAST TIME. I JUST ... REMOVED IT.

WHAT ARE YOU GOING TO DO WITH IT?

MASTER HELP ME! AAGH! NO FILES!

Within the body of the loop, you're using in to check the contents of the strings ❷. You want to know whether this path is part of a directory, in which case it will have os.path.sep somewhere within it, and you also want to know whether the result shows that the files are the same.

Now that you've displayed everything within the root of the directory, you can go ahead and show everything within the subdirectories ❸. You're reversing the sense of the if statement to show everything that wasn't shown the first time around.

In hindsight, that was relatively easy. Following the pattern you established in Hunt the Wumpus, separating data from its display is a powerful tactic that can make complicated problems easy to understand and program.

Comparing directories

The other thing your program should probably handle is the case where you have empty directories. Currently it only looks for files, and any empty directories will be skipped. Although unnecessary for your initial use case (checking for missing images before you back up), it will almost certainly be useful somewhere down the track. Once you've added this feature, you'll be able to spot any change in the directories, short of permission changes to the files—and it requires surprisingly little code. The next listing shows how I did it.

Listing 3.9   Comparing directories, too

```
def md5(file_path):
    if os.path.isdir(file_path):            ❶ Don't try to checksum
        return '1'                             directories
    read_file = file(file_path)

...

    for path, dirs, files in os.walk(directory_name):
        ...                                   ❷ Include directory
        for each_file in files + dirs:           and file paths
            file_path = os.path.join(trimmed_path, each_file)
            dir_file_list[file_path] = True
```

The first thing to do is to include directory paths as well as files when generating a listing ❷. To do that, you join the dirs and files lists with the + operator.

OH, I'LL JUST PUT IT IN WITH THE NEGATIVES FROM THE LAST OFFICE XMAS PARTY—I'M PRETTY SURE I HAVE A PAY REVIEW COMING UP SOON ...

If you try to open a directory to read its contents, you'll get an error ❶; this is because directories don't have contents the same way files do. To get around that, it's ok to cheat a little bit. You alter the md5 function and use os.path.isdir() to find out whether it's a directory. If it is, you return a dummy value of '1'. It doesn't matter what the contents of a directory are, because the files will be checked in turn, and you only care whether a directory exists (or not).

Once you've made those changes, you're done. Because the directories follow the same data structure as the files, you don't need to make any changes to the comparison or display parts of your program. You'll probably want to add some directories to both your test directories to make sure the program is working properly.

You've improved your script, but that doesn't mean there isn't more you can do.

Where to from here?

The program as it stands now is feature-complete based on your initial need, but you can use the code you've written so far for other purposes. Here are some ideas:

- If you're sure you won't have any different files, you can extend the program to create a merged directory from multiple sources. Given a number of directories, consolidate their contents into a third, separate location.

- A related task would be to find all the identical copies of a file in a directory—you might have several old backups and want to know whether there are any sneaky extra files you've put in one of them.

- You could create a change monitor—a script that notifies you of changes in one directory. One script would look at a directory and store the results in a file. The second script would look at that file and directory and tell you if any of the output has changed. Your storage file doesn't have to be complicated—a text file containing a path and checksum for each file should be all you need.

- You can also use your os.walk functions as a template to do something other than check file contents. A script to check directory sizes could be useful. Your operating system will probably give you information about how much space a particular directory takes up, but what if you want to graph usage over time, or break your results down by file type? A script is much more flexible, and you can make it do whatever you need.

You'll need to avoid the temptation of reinventing the wheel. If a tool has already been written that solves your problem, it's generally better to use that, or at least include it in your script if possible. For example, you might consider writing a program that shows you the changes between different versions of files as well as whether they're different—but that program's already been written; it's called diff. It's widely available as a command-line program under Linux, but it's also available for Windows and comes in graphical versions, too.

One of the other programming tricks is knowing when to stop. Gold-plating your program can be fun, but you could always be working on your next project instead!

Summary

In this chapter, you learned about some of the standard library packages available with every installation of Python, as well as how to include and use them and how to learn about unfamiliar ones. You built what would normally be a fairly complex application, but, because you made good use of several Python libraries, the amount of code you had to write was minimal.

In the next chapter, we'll look at another way of organizing programs, as well as other uses for functions and some other Python techniques that can help you to write clearer, more concise code. The program in this chapter was fairly easy to test, but not all programs will be that straightforward, so we'll also look at another way of testing programs to make sure they work.

4

Getting organized

This chapter covers

- *How to plan programs more thoroughly*
- *Testing programs using unit tests*

Until now, you've been learning how to use Python, and programming has been "by the seat of your pants." Hunt the Wumpus didn't have much in the way of planning and no tests at all, and, although you tested in the last chapter, you did so only fairly lightly. Now, you'll change tactics and focus on how to plan and test programs more thoroughly. You'll also do some more tricky things with functions and learn about `pickle` and `textwrap`, two more of Python's standard libraries.

The major change in this chapter is that you'll start learning how to test programs automatically. *Unit tests* are a relatively recent idea and help offload a lot of the grunt work of testing and debugging your programs onto the computer. You'll also be turning development practice on its head by using Test-Driven Development, writing tests before the program. It sounds odd, but it can be enlightening to see how unit testing can make tricky problems easy, and how writing tests first can help shape the design of your program for the better.

Because the theme for this chapter is "getting organized," the program you'll be writing is a productivity application to help manage to-do lists. You'll be making it a command line application so you can focus on the important parts, namely, getting the to-do list functionality right. Later, in chapter 8, we'll take a look at how you can extend the core of this program and give it a web interface.

Let's start by figuring out what you'd like to accomplish.

Planning: specifying your program

The first thing you need to do is try to figure out ahead of time what your program needs to do, as well as what would be nice to have. That way, you'll have the advantage of knowing in advance what you're trying to do, and you'll have had time to think about the best way to approach a problem.

You'll be using a top-down approach to design, where you break down your program and describe each part. You'll also want to think about how each part fits together and how they'll communicate and store data—commonly referred to as the *architecture* of your program. If you have enough detail to start programming: great. If not, you can repeat it by breaking down your parts into other parts until each is detailed enough for you to start work (or, for your customer to sign off). Different projects will require different levels of detail depending on what they are and who the final customer is. The finished product of this process is known as a *specification*, or *spec*, and it's similar to a blueprint for a building.

In the case of the to-do list program, you can use the popular computer industry acronym *CRUD* to help guide your spec. 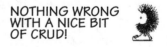 NOTHING WRONG WITH A NICE BIT OF CRUD!

CRUD isn't a statement on the quality of your program; it stands for create, retrieve, update, and delete, which are the four basic things you generally need to be able to do with your data:

1 Add a to-do item (create).

2 View the to-dos you've already created (retrieve).

3   Edit the information in a to-do (update).

4   Delete a to-do from your list (delete).

The program will also need to handle input from the user, in addition to saving the current to-dos so they're accessible later, and searching for specific to-dos (or at least displaying a list of the ones which match certain criteria, such as "due today").

In terms of architecture, you'll reuse the route featuring functions plus shared data that you put together for Hunt the Wumpus, but you'll enhance the user interface so you can ask the user for more detailed information.

How do you know your program works?

Before we dive into coding, let's first talk a little about unit tests and how to test your programs more thoroughly. Testing properly sounds boring, but it's actually the opposite. If you don't test, you'll invariably end up debugging your program instead—if you think testing is boring, debugging is ten times worse. Let's see how automated tests can help make programming more fun.

Testing manually—boring!

In the Hunt the Wumpus program, you had no automatic testing at all. Any changes you made to the program were verified manually; whenever you made a change, you'd run the program and type some input, and, if everything looked good, then you could assume your change was good. This can have some downsides, as you've seen. Your program can *look* ok but have errors you can't see.

NOTE   Why the emphasis on testing? The simple answer is that creating a program is much more fun than trying to debug it. Testing thoroughly, particularly with automatic tests, helps to nip errors in the bud, and will keep your programming fun!

HMM. I WONDER IF
THIS WILL WORK?

The other problem is that it's boring. That means, as you develop your program further, you're more likely to assume something's working when it may be broken, particularly as you ask old parts of your program to do new things. An "easy fix" can end up seriously damaging your program.

Functional testing

When writing your difference engine, you used some simple *functional testing* to make sure the program worked properly. You set up two directories, ran the program, and checked that it output the right results; that is, you tested its functionality directly. That's a lot better than manually testing, because it's easier and faster and you're not likely to get too bored, but the downside is that it only finds bugs in your program. You still need to go through the arduous process of debugging in order to find out what's causing the error.

The other problem is that if you change how your program works, then you might need to change your tests, which could potentially be a lot of work. In that case, you might be tempted to ignore your tests and go back to testing manually.

Unit testing: make the computer do it

Luckily, there's an easier way to deal with repetitive, boring tasks: make the computer do it. The mechanism you'll use in this chapter is called *unit testing*. Unit testing works by testing small parts, or units, of your program. In the same way you've been breaking down programs to make them easier to write, unit testing breaks down the program into units—such as functions—and makes sure they work for a range of inputs. Unit tests also help to isolate the code you're testing, which means any errors that occur when running your tests can be quickly tracked down to individual functions and fixed.

Test-Driven Development

The key way to use unit testing when developing your programs is to write your tests first. That seems backward, but it forces you to focus on the higher-level design of your code instead of the details. The way it works is this: if you want to add a feature, you write a test and run it. You won't have written the code the test needs yet, so it will break. You

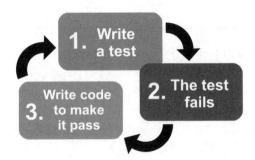

Figure 4.1
The Test-Driven Development cycle

then add enough code so your test passes and starts to work; then you think of another test, and repeat the process. Figure 4.1 is a handy three-step chart you can follow if you get lost.

As you work, you'll be building a suite of tests that will help keep your program on the right track. Your unit tests will also act as a low-level specification for how your program should work. It will answer questions such as, exactly what input should Python expect from this function? What should it do when you give it some input it's not expecting, or if the input is wrong?

Writing the program

Let's get started with writing the first test. There are libraries that can help you to test your programs, but, for now, you'll keep things simple and use Python's built-in `assert` statement. `assert` takes the following format:

```
assert something == something_else, "Message if assert is triggered!"
```

Python will test the first condition, exactly like an `if` statement, and, if it's false, then an error is raised with the message you've specified in the second part. You'll test each part of the program with a function that tries a particular section of the program then uses `assert` to make sure the results are what you expect.

AWOOOOGAH!

BUG DETECTED
IN CODE!!
NO TEST CASE
WRITTEN!!
FIX IMMEDIATELY!!
IMMEDIATELY!!

Type the program from the following listing into a file called test_todo.py. This test specifies how one function from your program should behave.

Listing 4.1 Your first unit test

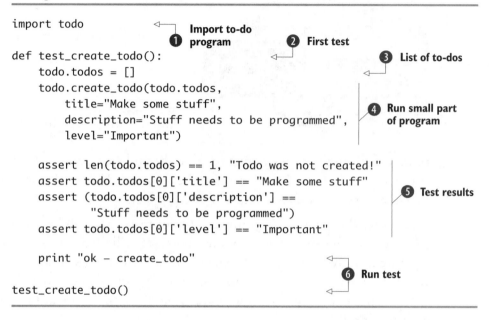

```
import todo                              ◁──┐  Import to-do
                                         ❶   program      ❷  First test
def test_create_todo():              ◁──────                        ❸  List of to-dos
    todo.todos = []                                      ◁──┐
    todo.create_todo(todo.todos,
        title="Make some stuff",                            ❹  Run small part
        description="Stuff needs to be programmed",             of program
        level="Important")

    assert len(todo.todos) == 1, "Todo was not created!"
    assert todo.todos[0]['title'] == "Make some stuff"
    assert (todo.todos[0]['description'] ==                 ❺  Test results
            "Stuff needs to be programmed")
    assert todo.todos[0]['level'] == "Important"

    print "ok - create_todo"                         ◁──┐
                                                     ❻  Run test
test_create_todo()                                   ◁──
```

This is the program you'll write, which will be called todo.py ❶. Don't create the file just yet; you'll do that in the next section.

The first test is a simple function ❷. Note that you should follow the same rules for your unit tests that you do for the functions in the rest of your program. If they're confusing, then you'll have trouble finding errors or fixing things when your tests fail.

todos will be where your program will store its list of to-dos ❸. Note that you're overriding whatever the current list of to-dos is by making it an empty list. This helps you write your tests faster—if you had a shared to-do list, then you'd have to worry about what other tests had done to it before you'd run the tests. The other thing to note is that you're referring to the module's version of todos. If you were to only use a local todos variable, you'd have two versions: one in the module and another you'd created, and you might confuse the two.

The test runs one small part of the to-do program ❹, creating a to-do. It might be tempting to do more in one test, but the larger your test is, the more difficult it is to track down errors when they happen.

Now you use Python's assert command to test that create_todo has done the right thing ❺. It should have created a to-do item with the right details and added it into your to-do list.

Once you've set up the test, you can call it to run it and test the program ❻. You've also added a print statement so you know when the test has been run successfully.

NOTE   It's not just your tests that should be simple. Unit testing also forces you to make your *code* simple. Large, clumsy functions are hard to test—and, by extension, hard to understand.

The main thing to notice about listing 4.1 is that it's short and simple. Unit tests shouldn't be long, complicated, and hard to understand—if they are, then there's something wrong with either your tests or your code.

Making your tests pass

You have a unit test, but what does it do? Let's run it and see what happens:

```
Traceback (most recent call last):
  File "D:/Documents and Settings/Anthony/.../test_todo.py",
      line 2, in <module>
    import todo
ImportError: No module named todo
```

COOL, ISN'T IT? THAT'S "ORWELL," OUR NEW TESTING AND PERFORMANCE FRAMEWORK!

WHA? HUH?

Uh-oh, what's gone wrong? Well, nothing. That's pretty much what you were expecting. Because you haven't written the program yet, your test doesn't have a todo module to work with. From here, you'll be adding bits to the program to fix the errors you'll get from your unit tests, so go ahead and create a file called todo.py in the same directory and run the test again:

```
Traceback (most recent call last):
  File "D:/Documents and Settings/Anthony/.../test_todo.py",
      line 18, in <module>
    test_create_todo()
  File "D:/Documents and Settings/Anthony/.../test_todo.py",
```

```
    line 6, in test_create_todo
  todo.create_todo(
AttributeError: 'module' object has no attribute 'create_todo'
```

Another error, but it's different this time and on line 6 rather than line 2, so you're making progress. Your test is now complaining that it can't find the create_todo function, so let's go ahead and add that to todo.py. As input, it will need to have your to-do list, plus a title, description, and level, because that's what you've specified in the test:

```
def create_todo(todos, title, description, level):
    pass
```

It's a simple program that uses Python's pass statement to do nothing at all. It doesn't pass your test either, but you're making progress. You're starting to test the functionality of the program rather than whether a function exists:

```
Traceback (most recent call last):
  File "D:/Documents and Settings/Anthony/.../test_todo.py",
      line 18, in <module>
    test_create_todo()
  File "D:/Documents and Settings/Anthony/.../test_todo.py",
      line 10, in test_create_todo
    assert len(todo.todos) == 1, "Todo was not created!"
AssertionError: Todo was not created!
```

Now your test is complaining that the to-do wasn't added to the to-do list. The code to make your test pass is pretty obvious now, so fix it all in one fell swoop:

```
def create_todo(todos, title, description, level):
    todo = {
        'title' : title,
        'description' : description,
        'level' : level,
    }
    todos.append(todo)
```

The test passes. When you run the test against this program, you should see ok - create_todo printed to the screen. Fantastic—the test passes, so you know the function is working. Now, let's have a look at how you'll be calling this function within your program.

Putting your program together

You'll follow the same strategy you did for Hunt the Wumpus: get something simple up and running quickly, and then build from there. The simplest usable program you can create will be something that's only able to create to-dos—but that should be enough. To get there, you'll have to think about how you want to be able to input to-dos, as well as how to get from that input to running the relevant function in the program, and then

how to return output to the screen. More important, you want to think about an easy way for you to write tests to make sure everything is working properly.

Testing user interfaces

One of the big problems with unit testing is that it's not so good at testing user interfaces. For example, there's no Python command that will let you type information into raw_input. Things get even harder when it comes to testing graphical interfaces, with mouse positions and pop-up windows.

The solution is to make your user interface as simple as possible, so it's easy to test. Ideally, it should be possible to make sure your code is correct just by looking at it. In your to-do list application, you'll use the following snippet to run everything in the program. Go ahead and add it to todo.py at the bottom of the file.

Listing 4.2   One part of the program you can't test

```
def main_loop():
    user_input = ""
    while 1:
        print run_command(user_input)
        user_input = raw_input("> ")
```

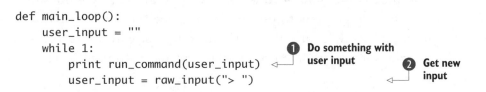

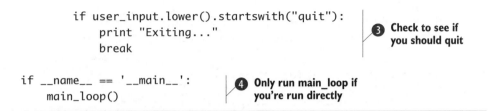

```
        if user_input.lower().startswith("quit"):
            print "Exiting..."
            break
```
3 Check to see if
you should quit

```
if __name__ == '__main__':
    main_loop()
```
4 Only run main_loop if
you're run directly

First, you do something with the command the person using the program has typed in **1**. Initially, you're not accepting input, which might seem a bit backward, but it will let you print a welcome/help screen when the program is first run. run_command is the meat of the program, but it takes whatever input has been typed in; that will make it easier for you to test in a minute.

Once you've run with the input you've been given, tell Python to ask for some more input **2**.

The one command that's outside the run_command function is quit. You check here for any command that starts with the word *quit* **3**. If you see it, you break out of the while loop right away; this will end the program.

When you're importing your program as part of your tests, you don't want to run the main_loop function, but you do if you run it directly as a program **4**. The solution is this if statement, which is common in Python programs. __name__ is the current namespace, or the name of the module you're running in. If a program is run directly, it will be called __main__, and you can catch it with the if statement. Usually, this if block will go at the end of your program to make sure all the functions it uses are defined.

NOTE   This type of structure is called an *event loop*; it tells Python to wait for input from the person using the program—or some other source, like the network—and then takes action based on what it finds.

The other thing you need is some way to get multiple lines of input. If you're adding a new to-do, then you'll need to ask for its title, description, and level. That's also fairly hard to test without resorting to drastic measures, like modifying the raw_input function. The following function goes in todo.py too and prompts the person using the program for an entry into a list of fields.

Listing 4.3   The other part of the program you can't test

```python
def get_input(fields):
    user_input = {}
    for field in fields:
        user_input[field] = raw_input(field + " > ")
    return user_input
```

Again, this is a straightforward part of the program. We're keeping it as simple as possible so you have little to debug manually. If there's an error your tests can't pick up, it should be obvious where that error is.

What do you do with your input?

Now you can start writing the run_command script in earnest. The first thing you'll want the program to do is to pick a Python function to run based on what the user types in, so let's do that part first. It's fairly easy, but you'll need to use a new Python trick. You should put the next section in `test_todo.py`. All the testing code will go in that file, and the program code itself will go in todo.py:

I AM HAVING EMAILS WITH DESCRIPTION!

I DIDN'T TELL YOU TO DO THAT! BESIDES—IF ORWELL SAYS IT'S A BUG, IT MUST BE A BUG!

```python
def test_get_function():
    assert todo.get_function('new') == todo.create_todo
    print "ok - get_function"
...
test_get_function()
```

You're planning on setting up a function that tells you what to run for a given command. Then, when you call it with a new command, you expect it to return the create_todo function — not the results of the function, but the function itself. In Python, you can assign functions to variables the same way you can assign strings, numbers, lists, and dictionaries. You'll see how to make use of it shortly.

Now that you have your test, add the code to call it beneath the
`test_create_todo()` one and run the tests again. The new test you've just
added should fail.

Here's some code that fixes it and allows room for you to expand to
include other functions:

```
commands = {
    'new' : create_todo,
}

def get_function(command_name):
    return commands[command_name]
```

`commands` is a dictionary with all your commands in it. The key is the
name of the command, and the value of the dictionary is the function
that will be called.

Given the name of the command you want to run, `get_function` will
return the function you need to call.

Running commands

That's one piece of the puzzle. The next piece is how you get the input
from your `get_input` function into your final function. Well, you'll need
to know what fields a particular function needs, so let's start with that:

```
def test_get_fields():
    assert (todo.get_fields('new') ==
            ['title', 'description', 'level'])
    print "ok - test_get_fields"
```

That's pretty easy, because it's much the same thing you did to find the
command function. Add the test function at the bottom as before, run
your tests, and make sure your new test fails; then you can write your
code. My version is featured in the following listing.

Listing 4.4 **Finding command fields**

```
commands = {
    'new' : [create_todo, ['title', 'description', 'level']],
}
```

```
def get_function(command_name):
    return commands[command_name][0]

def get_fields(command_name):
    return commands[command_name][1]
```

Notice that the commands dictionary has changed as well as the code you wrote to find the function. It makes more sense to keep the command function and the fields it's expecting in the same place so they're easier to change and don't get mixed up. That's completely normal and perfectly ok — as long as your tests still pass.

Now that you've created and tested those two low-lying functions, you're ready to try to create the run_command function. That will complete the user interface section of the program, and you can work on the rest of the code that does the work. There are a few more unit-testing techniques you'll need to use first, though.

The following listing is a new test that makes sure your run command works.

Listing 4.5 Testing run_command

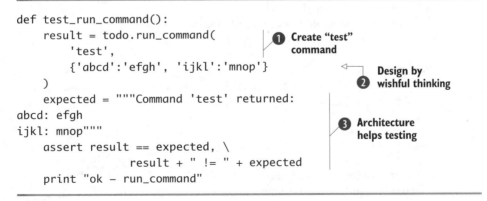

```
def test_run_command():
    result = todo.run_command(
        'test',
        {'abcd':'efgh', 'ijkl':'mnop'}
    )
    expected = """Command 'test' returned:
abcd: efgh
ijkl: mnop"""
    assert result == expected, \
            result + " != " + expected
    print "ok - run_command"
```

❶ Create "test" command

❷ Design by wishful thinking

❸ Architecture helps testing

Ideally, when you're unit testing, you'd like to test exactly one aspect of the program. If you have tests that combine results from lots of functions and one of those functions fails, you still have to debug the program. You only want to test run_command, so let's create a dummy test program ❶ that only returns its input, rather than forcing the tests to use (and then interpret the results from) the create_todo function.

The other thing you need to test is that data is fed into the command function properly. But how do you do that without forcing someone to enter the data every time you test? The solution is to use a Python default variable to mimic the data entry ❷. When the program runs normally, it will ask the user via the get_input function; but if you feed in a dictionary, it will use that instead.

Because the architecture is only moving text around ❸, your function is easy to test—feed in some input dictionary, and check that you get the right output back. Note that I've broken up the line here in a different way, by using a backslash character (\) instead of braces. If you choose to use this too, make sure it's the very last character on the line; otherwise it won't work.

Let's see what the code looks like that will make your test pass. Again, once you've written the test, the code is relatively straightforward—and you generally don't have to debug functions you've already written. My version looks like the following listing.

Listing 4.6   Writing **run_command**

```python
def test(todos, abcd, ijkl):
    return "Command 'test' returned:\n" + \
        "abcd: " + abcd + "\nijkl: " + ijkl

commands = {
    'new' : [create_todo, ['title', 'description', 'level']],
    'test' : [test, ['abcd', 'ijkl']],
}

todos = []

def run_command(user_input, data=None):            ❶ Default
    user_input = user_input.lower()                   variable
    if user_input not in commands:
        return user_input + "?" \               ❷ Figure out
                " I don't know what that command is."     which command
                                                          function you
                                                          need to run
```

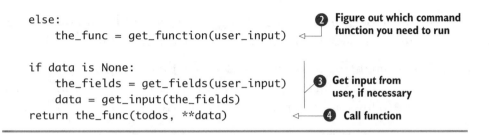

```
    else:
        the_func = get_function(user_input)
```
2 Figure out which command function you need to run

```
    if data is None:
        the_fields = get_fields(user_input)
        data = get_input(the_fields)
    return the_func(todos, **data)
```
3 Get input from user, if necessary

4 Call function

First, you use a default variable **1**. You set data to None for most cases, but, when testing, you can feed in data as a dictionary to mimic user input.

You use the lower() method to make the command lowercase, and then you look it up in your dictionary **2**. If you can't find it, then you return an error.

When running the program normally, data will be None. When you see this, you know you need to read some input from the user, and you can call get_fields so you know what to ask **3**.

Now that you know which function to call and what data to call it with, you can go ahead and pass control over **4**. The command function will do whatever it's supposed to and feed the results back as a string, which you hand back to the user. The ** in front of your input dictionary looks a bit weird—what it does is pass in the dictionary arguments as keyword arguments. This way, you can see what values a particular function is expecting in the function definition, rather than having one big value.

Great—now you have a straightforward way to assign text input from the person using the program and pass that on to a particular function. The rest of the chapter will deal with adding to that framework by writing other functions that fit into it.

Running your program

You might've noticed something odd by this stage; you haven't actually run the program yet to make sure it works. In previous chapters, you've been writing your program, running it to make sure it works, and then writing a bit more. Because

BATHROOM BREAK DETECTED!! YOU HAVE 4 MINUTES AND 59 SECONDS TO RETURN TO YOUR SEAT!

you've been unit testing, though, you haven't had to do that once—the unit tests pass, so the code must be working, right?

You might be a bit skeptical about that, but your program is pretty functional at this stage, and you can run it if you want to make sure. The following listing shows a sample run.

Listing 4.7 Your program so far

```
D:\Documents and Settings\Anthony>python  todo.py
? I don't know what that command is.
> test
abcd > qwer
ijkl > uiop
Command 'test' returned:
abcd: qwer
ijkl: uiop
> new
title > Test Todo
description > This is a test
level > Very Important
None
> quit
Exiting...
```

There are still a few loose ends to tidy up, but you can already create a to-do item from the user interface on your program, which means all of your infrastructure is working. You're on a roll!

Taking stock

So far, you've made a good start on your program, and you have most of the core of it working. Additionally, you have tests you can run to make sure the program *stays* working. Your unit tests have also had another benefit; because you've only been testing small parts of the program, your program is already broken down into small functions, and there's no need to tidy it up or refactor it. At least, not yet.

FIVE MINUTES FOR A BATHROOM BREAK? YOU'VE GOT TO BE KIDDING ME!

PROGRAMMER INSUBORDINATION NOTED!

What to do next?

The next important part of your application is showing what's in the to-do list; there's not much point in adding to your list if you can't see what's in it later. To get started, you'll write a test for a function that will show you all your to-dos. Then, you'll look at streamlining it to hide those that aren't as important. After you've done that, we'll look at how you can save your lists and reload them, so you don't have to reenter everything when you restart the program.

This next listing makes sure a to-do is shown properly when you view it in your program.

Listing 4.8 Testing your to-do list view

```
def test_show_todos():
    todo.todos = [
        { 'title' : 'test todo',
          'description' : 'This is a test',      ❶ Set up data
          'level' : 'Important'
        }
    ]
    result = todo.show_todos(todo.todos)           ❷ Run show_todos
    lines = result.split("\n")                        function

    first_line = lines[0]
    assert "Item" in first_line
    assert "Title" in first_line
    assert "Description" in first_line
    assert "Level" in first_line
                                                   ❸ Test results
    second_line = lines[1]
    assert "1" in second_line
    assert "test todo" in second_line
    assert "This is a test" in second_line
    assert "Important" in second_line

    print "ok - show_todos"
```

First, you set up a to-do list ❶. Because your to-do list is in a known state, this will make it easier to test. It's tempting here to reuse your creation test to set up the to-do list, but that's a trap. Even though it might save some code, you're creating a dependency between your tests. Later, if there was a bug in the creation function, you'd have two (or more) test failures, and the bug would be much harder to track down.

You run the view function over the to-do list ❷ and get the results back. To make life easier, you split the result into lines by using the split() method of the result string to split on line endings. I'm imagining that the list of to-dos will look something like the following:

```
Item    Title          Description              Level
1       test todo      This is a test           Important
```

YOU HAVE 4 MINUTES AND 42 SECONDS TO RETURN TO YOUR SEAT!

Next, you test that the words you're expecting exist in each line ❸. The first line should be the headers for the columns, and the second should have the values you're expecting. Notice that you're specifying each value individually in the test—you could generate a string for the exact result you're expecting from the function, but that's another trap. Specifying the results too strictly makes the test fragile, and the slightest change to how the results are formatted or the order of the columns can make your test fail when it shouldn't. In practice, you should only test what's important and leave out as much of the rest as you can.

Now that you know what you're expecting of your function, you can go ahead and write it. Python strings have several methods you can use to format the output; let's see how you can use them. The show_todos() function in the following listing shows you how a few of them work.

Listing 4.9   Displaying to-do items

```python
def show_todos(todos):
    output = ("Item    Title           "
              "Description             Level\n")
    for index, todo in enumerate(todos):
        line = str(index+1).ljust(8)
        for key, length in [('title', 16),
                            ('description', 24),
                            ('level', 16)]:
```

```
            line += str(todo[key]).ljust(length)
        output += line + "\n"
    return output

commands = {
    'new' : [create_todo, ['title', 'description', 'level']],
    'show' : [show_todos, []],
    'test' : [test, ['abcd', 'ijkl']],
}
```

First, you initialize the output as a list of headers. You'll be copying each line onto the end of the output as you go. Notice how the string is placed on two lines and wrapped within brackets? This makes it easier to read on the page. Python automatically joins strings like this, so there'll only be one big string when it's assigned to output.

Next, you go through each of the to-dos and add numbers. I've added an index to make it easier to see how many to-dos you have. enumerate() takes a list or iterable and returns the next item along with its index in the list—handy for situations like this.

In order to format the results, you start the line by printing the number of the to-do. So that the rest of the columns line up, you convert it to a string and use the .ljust() string method to space it out to eight columns. Python strings have many other methods like this, such as .rjust() and .center().

Next, you print each part of your to-do in a column. Here I've been a bit tricky and pulled out the key you're printing and its width into a list, which you're looping over. That way, you can pull out each value from the to-do and make it the right width.

Finally, don't forget to add the show command into the list of commands so you can use it when you're running your program. It doesn't take any arguments, so it has an empty list instead.

The code you've added is straightforward, but if you were developing this using "code and bugfix" as you did for Hunt the Wumpus, you'd have to go back and forth several times to get the code working. With unit testing, you can specify exactly what your output should be and then add it directly to your program.

I'm very busy and important

The other thing you'd like to check is that your view function displays your to-dos in the right order. Ideally, important

HOW ABOUT WE PUT EVERYTHING MARKED AS UNIMPORTANT IN THE ROUND FILE?

things should be displayed differently depending on how important they are. You'll put the important items at the top and unimportant ones at the bottom. The problem is that, so far, you've been putting the level of importance as a text field, which would appear to make your list a bit hard to sort. Luckily, there are tools in Python to deal with this sort of thing.

But we're getting ahead of ourselves. First you need a test to make sure your program sorts your to-dos properly! The test in the following listing should do the trick.

Listing 4.10   Testing the order of your view

```python
def test_todo_sort_order():
    todo.todos = [
        { 'title' : 'test unimportant todo',
          'description' : 'An unimportant test',
          'level' : 'Unimportant'
        },
        { 'title' : 'test medium todo',
          'description' : 'A test',
          'level' : 'Medium'
        },
        { 'title' : 'test important todo',
          'description' : 'An important test',
          'level' : 'Important'
        },
    ]
    result = todo.show_todos(todo.todos)
    lines = result.split("\n")
```

❶ Sample list of to-dos

```
assert "IMPORTANT" in lines[1]
assert "Medium" in lines[2]
assert "Unimportant" in lines[3]
```

Test they're in right order

```
print "ok - todo sort order"
```

Here's your sample list of to-dos ❶. They're in reverse order (unimportant to important), to make sure the sorting is working.

The to-dos should be in order from important to unimportant ❷. You also display the important statuses in capitals, so they stand out more.

BUG DETECTED! THE PROGRAM AS ENTERED DEVIATES FROM MANDATE #973: "THE SITE MUST BE GREEN"! RECTIFY IMMEDIATELY!

OK. IT'S HALF BLUE AND ... HALF GREEN. HAPPY NOW?

This covers what you're expecting. How do you get there? In practice, you'll still be entering them as text strings, so how about if you put all the important fields first, all the ones marked "unimportant" at the bottom, and everything else in between?

The standard way you'd do that would be with three for loops one after the other, each for a separate case—but I'd like to show you a faster way, which is also clearer once you get used to it.

List comprehensions

List comprehensions are a powerful built-in Python tool for making sense of lists of things. They're a general solution to a common programming problem: handling groups of items. Perhaps you want to get the total of every item in a list, or filter out the ones that aren't important, or only include the ones that have been open for too long. List comprehensions will let you do all these things.

What you're trying to ask for when you want to display important to-dos is something like this: "Python, please give me every to-do in the to-do list that is marked as 'Important.'"

You can use a list comprehension to get exactly that and more. The following listing gives you a look at some common types of list comprehension and a feel for what they can do.

Listing 4.11   Lots of things you can do with list comprehensions

```python
important_todos = [todo for todo in todos
                   if todo['level'].lower() == 'important']
```
❶ Basic version

```python
def capitalize(todo):
    todo['level'] = todo['level'].upper()
    return todo

important_todos = [capitalize(todo) for todo in todos
                   if todo['level'].lower() == 'important']
```
❷ You can use functions

```python
squares = [x**2 for x in range(10)]
names   = [name.title() for name in list_of_names]
```
❸ You can also use numbers

```python
coordinates = [(x,y) for x in range(10)
               for y in range(10)]
```
❹ You're not limited to using one list

Here's a list comprehension that gives you what you're after ❶. Python will go through each to-do in your list and collect the ones that match your `if` statement (that is, have a level of "important"). You add a `.lower()` call so the level will get converted to lowercase; *important*, *Important*, and IMPORTANT will all match.

PROGRAMMER INSUBORDINATION DETECTED! YOU HAVE 4 MIN 59 SEC TO ATTEND PERFORMANCE REVIEW!

That's not all list comprehensions can do. You can also apply functions to each member of the final result to get a different list ❷. Here, you're writing a function to capitalize the level and then calling it on each to-do that's marked as "important".

If you have a list of numbers, you can perform other operations on them as well ❸. If they're an object, you can call any method of that object, and so on. Anything you can do to the original value you can do within a list comprehension.

Finally, you have a list comprehension that uses two lists of numbers to generate a list of coordinates ❹.

Given all that, your final code listing could look something like the following.

Listing 4.12   Code to sort your list of to-dos

```
def capitalize(todo):
    todo['level'] = todo['level'].upper()
    return todo

def show_todos(todos):
    output = ("Item    Title            "
             "Description               Level\n")
    important = [capitalize(todo) for todo in todos
                if todo['level'].lower() == 'important']
    unimportant = [todo for todo in todos
                  if todo['level'].lower() == 'unimportant']          ❶ Filter
    medium = [todo for todo in todos                                    to-dos
             if todo['level'].lower() != 'important' and
                todo['level'].lower() != 'unimportant']
    sorted_todos = (important +
                   medium +                                           ❷ Join to-dos
                   unimportant)                                         back up

    for index, todo in enumerate(sorted_todos):
        line = str(index+1).ljust(8)
        for key, length in [('title', 16),
                            ('description', 24),
                            ('level', 16)]:
            line += str(todo[key]).ljust(length)
        output += line + "\n"
    return output                              ◄———— ❸ Debug
```

Here are three list comprehensions ❶, each for a separate level of to-do: "Important", "unimportant", and "everything else." You capitalize the important ones to make them stand out a bit more.

Once you have the to-do lists separated, you can join them back up by using a + ❷.

If you want to see what the output looks like when running your tests, you can print the output here, right before it's sent back. Your program will print exactly what the function returns, so you'll see what the end user will see ❸. Alternatively, you can put the print statements in your tests. If you're having trouble with a failing test, printing out some of the variables you're working with can save a lot of time.

Finally, if you run your tests again, you'll notice that one of your earlier tests, `test_show_todos`, is now failing. In this case it's nothing to worry about—you wrote that test before you'd really thought about how the program should look. Just change the "Important" in the test to "IMPORTANT", and the test should pass.

Now, you can sort to-dos into a specific order by using some list comprehensions, a powerful tool that's easy to understand. Often, you'll find you can replace complicated for loops with a simple function and a list comprehension.

Oops, a bug!

If you look at the output in listing 4.13, you'll notice the columns don't quite display properly. The `show_todos` test looks ok, but the second one has all its fields squashed together—where an item is too long, it's pushing the other columns out.

Listing 4.13   Output from your tests

```
C:\Documents and Settings\Anthony>python test_todo.py
ok - create_todo
ok - get_function
ok - get_fields
ok - run_command
Item    Title           Description             Level
1       test todo       This is a test          IMPORTANT

ok - show_todos
Item    Title           Description             Level
1       test important todoThis is an important testIMPORTANT
2       test medium todoThis is a test          Medium
3       test unimportant todoThis is an unimportant testUnimportant

ok - todo sort order
```

That doesn't look nice. Isn't unit testing supposed to make sure code is bug-free? Unfortunately, not entirely. You can test for things you've thought of, but if there's something you haven't considered, then you might still have bugs in your program. If you're using unit testing and you notice a bug in your program like this, the solution is relatively easy: write a test that covers the behavior you *do* expect, make sure it fails, and then fix your program.

It's also possible you might have made a mistake in one of your tests. Again, unit testing is a useful tool, but not a complete solution. It's still possible to test the wrong thing, or to have bugs in your unit tests. In practice, that's a lot less likely than having errors in your program because the unit tests are easier to follow.

The question still remains, though: what do you want the program to do when a line is too long? If you don't have a clear answer for that, then it's hard to write a test! You could trim the string down to a fixed width if it was too long—but you'd like all the information to still be visible. A better way to do it would be to wrap each to-do.

Listing 4.14   A better way to display your to-dos

Item	Title	Description	Level
1	test important todo	This is an important test	IMPORTANT
2	test medium todo	This is a test	Medium
3	test unimportant todo	This is an unimportant test	Unimportant

From a visual point of view, that looks a lot better. But how on earth are you going to program it? The short answer is … exactly the way you've been programming it so far: write a test first! I came up with test_todo_wrap_long_lines, which you can see in the next listing.

Listing 4.15   Testing that your to-dos wrap lines

```
def test_todo_wrap_long_lines():
    todo.todos = [
        { 'title' : 'test important todo',
          'description' : ('This is an important '       ❶ Set up data
              'test. We\'d really like '
              'this line to wrap '
```

```
            'several times, to '
            'imitate what might '
            'happen in a real '
            'program.'),
        'level' : 'Important'
    },
]
result = todo.show_todos(todo.todos)
lines = result.split("\n")

assert "test important" in lines[1]
assert "This is an important" in lines[1]

assert "todo" in lines[2]
assert "test. We'd really like" in lines[2]

assert "this line to wrap" in lines[3]
assert "several times, to" in lines[4]
assert "imitate what might" in lines[5]
assert "happen in a real" in lines[6]
assert "program." in lines[7]

print "ok — todo wrap long lines"
```

❶ Set up data

❷ Test that lines wrap

First, you set up a to-do with long lines that should be wrapped ❶. In this example, I've made it look as close as I can to what a real to-do might look like to make sure wrapping works when you have to wrap over several lines, as well as only one. Notice that I've broken up the description so the lines are less than 24 characters long, which is the width of the description column. That helps when you're writing the test, because you can see what you need to check for.

Then you test that the correct parts of the lines appear when the to-do is viewed ❷. The test for the description goes for several lines, but this way you're sure the program is wrapping properly for larger descriptions.

Well, the test was easy; but I suspect that writing the code might be a bit harder. Fortunately, you've been testing thoroughly so far, so if you make a mistake, your tests should catch you.

NOTE What would you do if the code was too hard to write? In that case, the answer is usually that you're trying to do too much at once, and you need to break the problem into smaller, easier parts.

The problem is that you're wrapping the lines, but within other lines, so you can't rely on Python's built-in printing mechanisms. Python does have a `textwrap` module available, which doesn't quite do what we'd like, but it's a start. The overall plan would then be to write a function to generate the lines for each to-do. Within that, you can split each section of the to-do (the title, description, and so on) into lines using the `textwrap` module, and then somehow knit them together into the final output. Let's try that. The following listing features the new function, `show_todo`, and the changes you'll need to make to `show_todos`.

Listing 4.16 A function to show a to-do

```python
import textwrap
...
def show_todo(todo, index):                                      ◁──┐  Wrap title and ❶
    wrapped_title = textwrap.wrap(todo['title'], 16)             ◁──┤  description
    wrapped_descr = textwrap.wrap(todo['description'], 24)       ◁──┘

    output = str(index+1).ljust(8) + "   "
    output += wrapped_title[0].ljust(16) + "   "                      ❷ Output
    output += wrapped_descr[0].ljust(24) + "   "                        first line
    output += todo['level'].ljust(16)
    output += "\n"

    max_len = max(len(wrapped_title),
                  len(wrapped_descr))
    for index in range(1, max_len):
        output += " " * 8 + "   "
        if index < len(wrapped_title):
            output += wrapped_title[index].ljust(16) + "   "
        else:                                                          ❸ Output
            output += " " * 16 + "   "                                   any
        if index < len(wrapped_descr):                                  remaining
            output += wrapped_descr[index].ljust(24) + "   "            lines
        else:
            output += " " * 24 + "   "
        output += "\n"

    return output
```

```
def sort_todos(todos):
    important = [capitalize(todo) for todo in todos
                 if todo['level'].lower() == 'important']
    unimportant = [todo for todo in todos
                   if todo['level'].lower() == 'unimportant']
    medium = [todo for todo in todos
              if todo['level'].lower() != 'important' and
                 todo['level'].lower() != 'unimportant']
    todos = important + medium + unimportant
    return todos
```

❹ **Sort to-dos**

```
def show_todos(todos):
    output = ("Item        Title                "
              "Description                Level\n")
    sorted_todos = sort_todos(todos)
    for index, todo in enumerate(sorted_todos):
        output += show_todo(todo, index)
    return output
```

❺ **New version of show_todos**

First, you use the `textwrap` module's `wrap()` function to wrap the title and description to the right number of characters ❶. You'll also need `import textwrap` at the top of your script.

You start by building the first line with the index and level, which you assume don't wrap, plus the first wrapped line of the title and description ❷. You're using the `+=` operator, which is shorthand for `output = output + ...`. (You're also adding two spaces between each column, to make it easier to read.)

If there are any lines left in your title or description, you print them here and put in placeholders for the index and importance ❸. You're using a slightly different version of range, where you specify the starting index as well as the ending one. If there's only one line, `max_len` will be 1 as well, enumerate will be empty, and no extra lines will be printed. The other catch is that before you print out each line in the title and description, you need to make sure you still have something to print; otherwise, Python will crash with a "list index out of range" error. You use the multiplier operation on a single blank space so it's obvious how long the strings are.

Although it isn't strictly necessary, you break the sorting of to-dos out into its own function ❹. You can do this because you have unit tests to catch any breakages, and it makes the program nicer to look at.

The new version of show_todos calls on both show_todo and sort_todos and is much shorter and easier to follow ❺. That tells you you're moving in the right direction; if it were longer and more complicated, you'd be doing the wrong thing.

The last thing you'll need to do is update the test_todo_sort_order test case so it references the new line numbers in the output. If you run your tests after that change, they should all pass, and you now have a much prettier view of your to-dos. Ta-da! Next feature!

Saving your work

The last essential thing you need to be able to do is save the to-do list to a file. Without that, the person using the program would have to reenter all their work. Well, they probably wouldn't—they would instead find a program that could save their data. Because you'll be using this program yourself, that's not an option.

To save your to-do list, you'll be using a Python module called pickle, which is designed for writing Python objects to a file. There are some limitations on the sorts of objects you can pickle, but all the basic Python types such as strings, lists, and dictionaries are supported, so it's ideal for your program. Using pickle has the advantage of being quick to implement and easy to test, but it won't be editable in a plain-text editor. Writing your own functions to read and write a custom format is possible, but it's harder to program and difficult to get completely right. Here you'll take the easy option, but you can always write your own format at a later stage if you need it.

How do you test your saving function? The easiest option is to use what's called a *round-trip*: create a to-do list and save it, and then reload it from the same file and compare it to the original. If it's the same, then your test passes; but the downside is that you're testing both the load and save functionality in one go. If your test doesn't pass, then it's hard to tell whether it's the load function or the save function (or both) that is at fault. The way around that is to create a *known good* file from a successful save. But that implies you've already saved properly.

Let's pick the first option and see how it goes. You'll be using a built-in Python module in a pretty straightforward way, so you're not likely to run into any major problems. The next listing is your round-trip test, `test_save_todo_list`.

CAREFUL NOT TO DO
TOO MANY ROUND-TRIPS.
YOUR DATA MIGHT
GET DIZZY!

Listing 4.17   Testing that your application saves properly

```
import os
...
def test_save_todo_list():
        todos_original = [
          { 'title' : 'test todo',
          'description' : 'This is a test',
          'level' : 'Important'
          }
        ]
        todo.todos = todos_original
        assert "todos.pickle" not in os.listdir('.')

        todo.save_todo_list()
        assert "todos.pickle" in os.listdir('.')

        todo.load_todo_list()
        assert todo.todos == todos_original
        os.unlink("todos.pickle")
                print "ok - save todo list"
```

❶ Create to-do list

❷ Test saving

❸ Test loading

Here you're creating your to-do list ❶ exactly the same way you've been doing in previous tests. The only difference is that you're keeping another copy so you can refer back to it once you've reloaded the to-do list. You also make sure you don't have an existing to-do list; otherwise the tests would fail or overwrite someone's to-do list.

First, you run the save command ❷. Although you can't test the contents of the save file directly, you can test that the file has been created by using the `os.listdir()` function. `'.'` is shorthand for whatever the current directory is.

Next, you clear the to-do list out and then call the `load_todo_list()` function to reload it ❸. At the end, you'll have two lists of dictionaries that should be exactly the same.

Run your tests, make sure the new one fails, and then you can add the following code to create your save file and reload it.

Listing 4.18   Loading and saving your to-dos

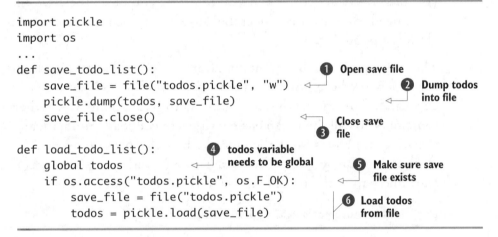

```python
import pickle
import os
...
def save_todo_list():
    save_file = file("todos.pickle", "w")        ❶ Open save file
    pickle.dump(todos, save_file)                ❷ Dump todos
    save_file.close()                               into file
                                                 ❸ Close save
                                                    file
def load_todo_list():        ❹ todos variable
    global todos                needs to be global
    if os.access("todos.pickle", os.F_OK):       ❺ Make sure save
        save_file = file("todos.pickle")            file exists
        todos = pickle.load(save_file)           ❻ Load todos
                                                    from file
```

`pickle` needs an open file to work with, so you first open your save file ❶, which you've called `"todos.pickle"`, with a mode of `"w"`, which means open it and overwrite whatever's already there.

The pickle syntax is straightforward—just call the `pickle.dump()` function ❷ with the object you want to pickle and the file where you want it to be pickled.

Next, you close the file ❸. You don't have to do this step, because Python will close the file once it leaves the `save_todo_list()` function, but it's a good habit to get into and helps to keep things tidy.

Because you're replacing your to-do list when you load it, you'll need to declare it as a global variable ❹. This means the changes you make to the todos variable will be visible outside your function.

One thing you need to check before you do anything is that the file exists ❺. If you try to open a non-existent file, then Python will raise an error and the program will crash.

Once you're ready to load from your save file, it should be opened in read mode ❻. The pickle.load() method will then read the to-do list you previously saved. When you're done, you close the save file. You don't need to return the object, because it's a global variable and you've already updated it.

The only question that remains after you've added the load and save functions is where you call them. You could make the user call them explicitly, but they'd have to know the functions were there and remember to call them. An easier way is to call load automatically when the program starts, and then save when the program exits. You can easily add that by calling load_todo_list() and save_todo_list() at the start and end of the main loop, as in the listing that follows.

Listing 4.19   Automatic loading and saving

```
def main_loop():
    user_input = ""
    load_todo_list()
    while 1:
        print run_command(user_input)
        user_input = raw_input("> ")
        if user_input.lower().startswith("quit"):
            print "Exiting..."
            break
    save_todo_list()
```

Before you start accepting any user input, you first look for a pre-existing save file, and, if it exists, you load the to-dos from that.

Once the user issues a quit command, you break out of the loop and the program will automatically save its to-do list. If you want to be even more cautious, you can call save_todo_list() at the end of each function that might cause a change: create_todo(), edit_todo(), and delete_todo().

You can add, view, and save your to-do lists (that's the C and R in CRUD for those of you who remember the first part of the chapter) and store all the to-dos entered to date, so all you have to do now to have completed all the absolutely essential features is to handle the editing and deleting of the existing to-dos.

Editing and deleting

For this particular application they're not quite as essential, which is why we've left them until last, but it'd be pretty annoying to have to do without deletion or editing.

A quick fix

First, there's one problem which you should deal with before you start. When you sorted the to-dos earlier, you didn't update the stored list, and sorted your list every time you viewed it. When the user wants to tell you which to-do they want to edit or delete—say, with the index number— you'll have to rebuild the list again to know which one they mean. It'd be much easier to have the to-do list sorted already. Let's do that

DO YOU THINK WE LAID THAT ON A BIT THICK?

NYET—TIE IS INTERFERING WITH DETECTION OF SARCASM.

now. It will mean calling the sort_todos function every time a to-do is added to the to-do list. The user might've changed the importance of a to-do when editing it, so you'll need to call it then, too, but you won't need to call it for deletion because it will already be in order then.

As you've done so far, start by writing a unit test.

Listing 4.20   Adding a to-do sorter

```
def test_todo_sort_after_creation():
    todo.todos = [
        { 'title' : 'test unimportant todo',
          'description' : 'This is an unimportant test',
```

❶ Set up initial data

```
                'level' : 'Unimportant'
            },
            { 'title' : 'test medium todo',
              'description' : 'This is a test',       ➊ Set up
              'level' : 'Medium'                        initial data
            },
        ]

    todo.create_todo(todo.todos,
        title="Make some stuff",                     ➋ Create another
        description="Stuff needs to be programmed",     to-do
        level="Important")

    assert todo.todos[0]['level'] == "IMPORTANT"
    assert todo.todos[1]['level'] == "Medium"        ➌ Check to-do order
    assert todo.todos[2]['level'] == "Unimportant"

    print "ok - todo sort after creation"
```

AWOOOGAH!
TIE IS 12
DEGREES FROM
VERTICAL!
INSUFFICIENT
PERSONAL
GROOMING
DETECTED!

This should be pretty familiar by now. For this test, you're only setting up two to-dos, in the reverse order ➊.

➋ is where the action takes place. You create an important to-do. With the code as it currently stands, this will only append the important to-do at the bottom.

Now you check that all the to-dos are in the right order ➌. Important ones come first, unimportant at the bottom, and everything else in the middle.

Run your tests now, and the newest one should fail. Time to write some code!

Listing 4.21   New sort_todos

```
def sort_todos():                                    ➊ Alter sort_todos
    global todos
    important = [capitalize(todo) for todo in todos
                if todo['level'].lower() == 'important']
    unimportant = [todo for todo in todos
                    if todo['level'].lower() == 'unimportant']
    medium = [todo for todo in todos
```

```
            if todo['level'].lower() != 'important' and
                todo['level'].lower() != 'unimportant']
        todos = important + medium + unimportant
```
❶ Alter sort_todos

```
def create_todo(todos, title, description, level):
    todo = {
        'title' : title,
        'description' : description,
        'level' : level,
    }
    todos.append(todo)
    sort_todos()
    return "Created '%s'." % title

def show_todos(todos):
    output = ("Item        Title                    "
            "Description             Level\n")
    for index, todo in enumerate(todos):
        output += show_todo(todo, index)
    return output
```
❷ Move sort_todos from show_todos to create_todo

Ideally, you'd like to be able to call sort_todos() from anywhere in the program, but that's a bit hard in its current state. The easiest way forward is to make todos a global variable ❶. Note that once you've done this, you don't have to return todos from sort_todos(). Now you can call it from any function you want to.

Now that sort_todos() is easier to use, you can remove it from show_todos() and put it wherever the order of todos is likely to be changed ❷. In the next section, you'll also call it when changing to-dos in the to-do list.

You'll find that you have test failures once show_todos() doesn't sort the to-dos any more, but they're easy to fix. In test_todo_sort_order() and test_show_todos(), just call todo.sort_todos() once you've set up your list of to-dos, to make sure they're in the right order and have the correct formatting.

That should be enough to get you going for the next section. What you've done is

CHAINSAW CODING ...
WITH A SAFETY NET!

to ensure that the to-do list is always sorted in the same order, whether that's behind the scenes or when displayed on the screen. It's a major change to the way the program stores its data, but because you have a suite of unit tests, you can be confident that making major changes like this won't have broken anything in the program. Let's press on and put the final pieces in place.

Deleting to-dos

Now you're ready to starting deleting to-dos from your list. The code to do this is pretty straightforward, but because you're starting on destructive functions that can potentially delete user data, you'll step up the unit testing a notch. Up until now you've mainly been testing the "happy path," by making sure the code works for normal usage. It's equally important to make sure your program notices input or data which is wrong and generates an appropriate error message. Let's take a look now at how you test that in the following listing.

Listing 4.22   *Testing deletion*

```
def test_delete_todo():
    todo.todos = [
        { 'title' : 'test important todo',
          'description' : 'This is an important test',
          'level' : 'IMPORTANT'
        },
        { 'title' : 'test medium todo',
          'description' : 'This is a test',
          'level' : 'Medium'
        },
        { 'title' : 'test unimportant todo',
          'description' : 'This is an unimportant test',
          'level' : 'Unimportant'
        },
    ]

    response = todo.delete_todo(todo.todos, which="2")

    assert response == "Deleted todo #2"
    assert len(todo.todos) == 2
    assert todo.todos[0]['level'] == 'IMPORTANT'
    assert todo.todos[1]['level'] == 'Unimportant'
```

❶ Test "happy path"

```
def test_delete_todo_failure():
    todo.todos = [
        { 'title' : 'test important todo',
          'description' : 'This is an important test',
          'level' : 'IMPORTANT'
        },
    ]

    for bad_input in ['', 'foo', '0', '42']:
        response = todo.delete_todo(
            todo.todos, which=bad_input)
        assert response == ("'" + bad_input +
            "' needs to be the number of a todo!")
        assert len(todo.todos) == 1

    print "ok - test delete todo failures"
```

 **2** **Test for bad input**

For the deletion test, you set up three to-dos and delete the middle one. This tests that you don't delete the wrong to-do, as well as that the right one is deleted **1**. You're also checking that delete_todos gives back a reasonable message to tell you what it's done.

One of the things you've been able to skip over so far is checking user input. For your deletion script, that's no longer possible, because you might put in a wrong number or something that isn't a number. Here, you check that all the possible types of bad input generate an error message and don't delete any to-dos **2**.

That covers all the potential things I can think of can go wrong, but it's important to note that testing failures like this is an ongoing process. In other words, the failure tests aren't final. Especially with more complex functions, there may be bad input or data which will cause errors you haven't considered. When you find input like that, you should consider it a bug in your program. But the fix is easy: add either another unit test or an extra case to your failure test that will cover the failure, and then fix your code so the test passes.

The following listing is the code I wrote to make the two deletion tests pass.

Listing 4.23   Deleting to-dos

```python
def delete_todo(todos, which):
    if not which.isdigit():
        return ("'" + which +
            "' needs to be the number of a todo!")
    which = int(which)
    if which < 1 or which > len(todos):
        return ("'" + str(which) +
            "' needs to be the number of a todo!")
    del todos[which-1]
    return "Deleted todo #" + str(which)

commands = {
    ...
    'delete' : [delete_todo, ['which']],
```

Here's where you do your checking to make sure the input you're fed matches a to-do in your list. It has to be a number, so you first use the .isdigit() method to make sure of that. Then, you turn it into a number by using int(), and check to see if it corresponds to an entry in the to-do list. If your input fails any of these checks, you do nothing except return an informative error message.

Now you can delete the to-do. Notice that you're converting the number you're given into a list index by subtracting one from it.

The person using the program probably wants to know what you've done, so you tell them here ❸. Whatever string you return will be printed on the screen as a result.

MARKETING
INSUBORDINATION
DETECTED!
PREPARING
ATTITUDE
READJUSTMENT
PROBE!

Because you've added a new command, you'll also need to add it to the commands dictionary too. The only argument it takes is 'which', which is the id of the to-do you want to delete.

That's all you need to do to make sure deleting to-dos works properly. All your tests should pass now, and you're ready to move on to the next section.

Editing to-dos

Editing to-dos is also fairly straightforward. Because, in many ways, editing is a cross between deletion and editing, you can combine code from your previous unit tests and program code to create an `edit_todo()` function. There's nothing in principle that we haven't already covered in this chapter.

PREDICTING STEF COMING TO HIS SENSES IN 5 ... 4 ... 3 ...

AAAAIIIIEEE!!

The only catch is that you're running into a limitation of Python's `raw_input()` function. Because you can't pre-populate the text that's entered into the function, you can't make it as easy as you'd like to edit an existing entry. Unfortunately, you'll need to work around it. The easiest way is to make a blank entry not overwrite an existing field; rather, for any field you want to edit, you'll need to either reenter the data or cut and paste it from earlier on in the output. It's annoying, but there's not a lot you can do about it. In chapter 8, you'll extend your to-do list and give it a web interface with Django, so proper editing will have to wait until then.

Let's go ahead and write a test that covers the functionality you can add.

Listing 4.24   Testing to-do editing

```
def test_edit_todo():
    todo.todos = [
        { 'title' : "Make some stuff",
          'description' : 'This is an important test',
          'level' : 'IMPORTANT'
        },
    ]

    response = todo.edit_todo(todo.todos,
        which="1",
        title="",
        description="Stuff needs to be programmed properly",
        level="")
```

❶ Edit to-do

```
assert response == "Edited todo #1", response
assert len(todo.todos) == 1
assert todo.todos[0]['title'] == "Make some stuff"
assert (todo.todos[0]['description'] ==
        "Stuff needs to be programmed properly")
assert todo.todos[0]['level'] == "IMPORTANT"

print "ok — edit todo"
```

❷ **Test that correct fields were edited**

Here's a function call that should edit a to-do ❶. You're simulating blank entries with blank strings in the input arguments.

Now you test that the to-do has the right fields ❷. Those that were blank should be unchanged, and those that weren't should be set to the correct values. You're also checking that you still have only one to-do and that you get the right response.

The other thing you need to test is that editing the level of a to-do will result in it being reordered. If a to-do suddenly becomes important, you want it to appear at the start of the list, rather than still being half-way down. The following listing shows how to test that.

Listing 4.25   Testing sort order after editing

```
def test_edit_importance():
    todo.todos = [
        { 'title' : 'test medium todo',
          'description' : 'This is a medium todo',
          'level' : 'medium'
        },
        { 'title' : 'test another medium todo',
          'description' : 'This is another medium todo',
          'level' : 'medium'
        },
    ]
    response = todo.edit_todo(todo.todos,

        which="2",
        title="",
        description="",
        level="Important")
```

❶ **Set up two medium to-dos**

❷ **Edit last to-do in list**

```
assert todo.todos[0]['level'] == "IMPORTANT"
assert todo.todos[1]['level'] == "medium"

print "ok - edit importance"
```

❸ **Important to-do should now appear first**

First, you set up two Medium level to-dos ❶. You edit the last to-do and set its level to Important but leave the other fields unchanged ❷.

Now that the importance of the second to-do has been changed, it should appear first in the list rather than second ❸.

That covers the behavior you're expecting from editing a to-do. Let's see how you go about implementing it in your program.

Listing 4.26   *Code to edit a to-do*

```
def edit_todo(todos, which, title, description, level):
    if not which.isdigit():
        return ("'" + which +
            "' needs to be the number of a todo!")
    which = int(which)
    if which < 1 or which > len(todos):
        return ("'" + str(which) +
            "' needs to be the number of a todo!")

    todo = todos[which-1]
    if title != "":
        todo['title'] = title
    if description != "":
        todo['description'] = description
    if level != "":
        todo['level'] = level

    sort_todos()
    return "Edited todo #" + str(which)

commands = {
    ...
    'edit': [edit_todo,
            ['which', 'title', 'description', 'level']],
```

❶ **Check user input**

❷ **Update to-do**

❸ **Tidy up**

You use exactly the same code you're using in `delete_todo()` to check user input ❶. You could probably pull it out and make it a function, but because you're only using it in two places, whether you do so or not is a line call. If you add a third function that uses this code, then it should definitely be separated.

Now you update the to-do ❷. For any non-blank input, you override the field of the to-do with what's been entered.

The final step is to sort the to-dos (because the level might have changed) and return a message to let the user know what's happened ❸. Don't forget to add the `edit_todo()` function to the `commands` dictionary with the arguments it needs.

You're done! All the essential features you set out at the start of the chapter have been completed, and you have a usable to-do list program.

NOTE   The definition of "essential" will vary from person to person, but getting the core of your application in place will definitely help put the finishing touches on the rest of the essential parts.

Better yet, you have a comprehensive test suite that covers all the major functionality of the application, so if you make any changes further down the line, you can easily check to make sure the program still works.

Where to from here?

Like all the programs in this book, the to-do list program is now yours, and you can extend and enhance it to suit your own needs. Although it's usable, there are some things that could dramatically improve it, and adding them would be a useful exercise. Here are some ideas for features you could add.

A help command

If you're getting confused about what each of the commands does, a help command would probably make things clearer. To make it even easier, you might want to bind it to multiple commands such as ? and help, and possibly add it to the error message given if the program doesn't understand the command given.

Undo

When deleting or editing to-do items, there's no way out if you make a mistake. You're only human, and it makes sense to try to allow for errors as much as possible, especially when deleting to-do items. When you've deleted one, there's no way to get it back.

One way to get around this would be to mark deleted to-dos instead of removing them from the list, and not display them under normal circumstances. If necessary, you could use another command to display the to-dos that were deleted (perhaps showdeleted?) and restore them (restore).

Different interface

You might find the fact that this interface requires you to click prompt, then click response, then prompt, then response, and so on, to be a bit annoying. The interface was designed to be as easy to program as possible, but that doesn't mean it's as easy to use as possible. One alternative is to allow arguments after commands the user types in. For example, instead of typing delete <enter> 3 <enter>, you could instead type delete 3 <enter> and have the program do the same thing. How essential this is will depend on whether you prefer the existing interface or not, but if you decide to add this type of interface, the shlex module will be extremely useful.

Time management and estimation

Another useful feature would be to record an estimate of how long you think a task will take to complete and then, later, mark items as done and record the time you spent on them. At the end, you could generate a report showing where you've spent your time, and discover how accurate your initial estimates were. Being able to estimate the time it will take to complete a task can be a useful skill, but it improves only if you practice and get feedback on how accurate your estimates were.

Study one of the unit-testing frameworks

Unit testing in itself isn't particularly difficult, which is why you developed your own method in this chapter. But there are a number of unit testing modules you can use, and using them offers two key advantages. First, they can help you organize your tests into test suites and classes and run them all automatically from multiple files, as well as run setup and tear-down code before and after each test. Second, they allow you to test a lot more than you can with only simple assert statements, and they'll give you more detailed information when things go wrong. The three unit-testing modules you'll initially want to look at are unittest and doctest, both included with Python, and py.test, which is a lighter-weight version of unittest, available from http://pytest.org/.

Summary

In this chapter, you learned about unit testing, saw firsthand how to use it to write programs, and developed a large suite of unit tests so you could extend your application without worrying about how you might break it if you change something. You also learned about some aspects of the program (mainly user input) that were harder to unit test, and you discovered how to work around that by keeping the untested sections of code as small and simple as possible.

You also learned that Python has first-class functions that can be assigned to variables in the same way as more basic types, such as integers and strings, and that one good way to make use of functions is by assigning them as values in a dictionary. You'll learn more about first-class functions in chapter 7. You used two more Python libraries, pickle and textwrap, and also discovered how you could filter the to-do lists using list comprehensions, a simple but powerful way of filtering and processing lists.

The final thing we covered was how to work around problems that arise in development. Sometimes, as with editing to-do items, there's not much that can be done beyond finding a reasonable workaround. In other cases—for example, when wrapping the text of to-dos—some patience and persistence (and a decent suite of tests) can pay off.

5

Business-oriented programming

This chapter covers

- *Writing programs for the real world*
- *Interacting with existing systems*
- *How to handle errors in your program*

In this chapter, we're going to take a look at how Python can be used in the real world to help you to do your job better and faster. As a sample project, you'll take some stock data from a web page on the internet, extract the figures you're interested in, and then see how you can make use of that data, report on it, and send those reports to interested parties. To make your life easier, all of this will be written so it's easy to automate.

One of the critical tasks facing many programmers and system administrators is to make many different systems talk to each other. You might need to do the following:

- Read some data from one system
- Compare it with the results from a second

- Check that both of them make sense (often referred to as a *sanity check*)
- Save the results for later use
- Email relevant people with a report about what you found or any problems you encountered

People are depending on the information from these systems, so whatever you write has to be robust. You can't try something and hope for the best. Sound daunting? Don't worry—Python is at its heart a practical language, and has a number of features and library modules to make interfacing with the real world and all of its quirks much easier.

WHY AUTOMATE? The more selfish reason for wanting to automate is that once you've set up your program, you don't have to worry about it anymore, which frees you up to think about more important and interesting things.

You'll start by building your reporting program, and then we'll look at what steps you can take to anticipate errors and make the program bulletproof.

Making programs talk to each other

How do you make programs talk to each other? Typically, programs will have some sort of data input and output, so integrating two programs is normally a question of taking the output of one program, reading its data, and then presenting that data in a format that the second program will understand. Ultimately, you can chain lots of different programs together with Python acting as an interpreter. The system you'll be building looks something like figure 5.1.

Programs for tasks like this are normally referred to as *glue code*, because you're gluing two or more programs together into one system.

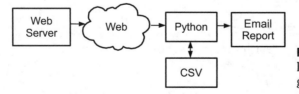

Figure 5.1 Python as a glue language, helping other programs "talk" to each other

CSV to the rescue!

The process of gluing programs together is much easier if you have a common data format—a data "language" that all of the programs in question speak. The format that's closest to being a lingua franca of data exchange is the humble comma-separated value (CSV) file, which is a simple spreadsheet format consisting of a header line and a number of rows afterward. The items on the

rows are separated by commas, hence the term *comma-separated value*. Some CSV files will use other character values, such as tabs, to separate their values, but the principle is the same.

There are many advantages to using CSV files. CSV is a simple and straightforward format, which is important when developing or debugging your system. If you run into problems, you can read the file in a text editor. Most programming languages will have a library to read and write CSV, and a lot of programs also use CSV as an import or export format, so you can reuse all the routines you write for one program on the next one. Finally, it also maps reasonably well onto most data—you can even think of it as an SQL table—so it's generally useful in most cases.

A nice feature of using CSV is that most spreadsheet programs, such as Excel, can import it easily, and you can then use them to generate graphs or color-coded charts. An important warning, though: many

spreadsheet programs will convert data into their internal formats when they import, which means your data may get silently corrupted. This is particularly important for anything that looks like a date, or a string that looks like a number. An employee ID of 00073261, for example, would get converted to the number 73,261. Wherever possible, it's best to use Excel to view data and consider any data

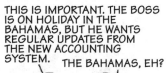

that it outputs as tainted. Don't use it for any further work—just the original CSV file.

TIP   If you need to get work done quickly, it's often quicker to build on systems that already exist. Python will let you email a report from one system to your program, along with some data from a web page, and dump it into a CSV file or database.

Other formats

In addition to CSV, Python has libraries to read many other formats, all of which can be used in data exchange in some way. Here's a quick list of the most common ones; many others are available either in Python's standard library or as add-on packages you can install.

HTML

You might not realize it, but HTML is a data format, and most programming languages have libraries that let you write programs that behave as if they were web browsers, reading HTML and posting data back via HTTP, POST, or GET requests. Python has several libraries available to download and interpret web pages and send data back in this way. In the next section, we'll look at how you can download a web page using Python's built-in urllib library and then extract stock prices from it using an add-on module called Beautiful Soup.

JSON, YAML, AND MICROFORMATS

If you need more structured data, such as a nested tree or a network of object, then CSV might not be the best fit. Other formats, such as JSON and YAML, are more general.

SQLITE

If you might be upgrading your data storage to a database or you need your data access to be fast, then you might want to consider SQLite, which is included in the Python standard library as of version 2.6. It provides a subset of the SQL commands that you would expect to find in databases such as MySQL or PostgreSQL, and saves its data to a local file. Many programs such as Mozilla, Skype, and the iPhone use SQLite as a data-storage format.

MAILBOXES (MBOX)

Python is also capable of reading most common mailbox formats, such as mbox and maildir, and parsing the messages within them, including extracting attachments and reading multipart MIME messages. Anything you receive via email can be read, interpreted, and acted on. Python is also capable of acting as a normal mail reader, via add-on libraries like getmail, and can send emails back out via SMTP.

I'M TOLD THAT IT'S POSSIBLE FOR YOU TO WRITE AN EMAIL PROGRAM TO DO THIS FOR US …

FINE. I'LL GET PITR AND GREG TO LOOK AT IT.

XML

Python supports reading, writing, and parsing XML files, as well as XML Remote Procedure Call (XMLRPC) services. The latest version of Python, version 2.6, includes ElementTree, which is an easy and powerful library for dealing with XML.

Any program you need to interface with will have its own way of doing things, so it's important to know what libraries are available to output the formats the program wants, and, conversely, to read in the formats it outputs. Fortunately, Python can handle a wide variety of formats very easily. Let's move on and take a look at the tools you'll be using in this chapter.

Getting started

Your first task is to look at the data that's exported by the program you want to interface with. In this case, you'd like to interface with Yahoo's stock-tracking site, which you can access at http://finance.yahoo.com/q?s=GOOG, and report on some of the statistics of the stock price over time. That link gives you the results for Google, but feel free to pick a different one, such as IBM or AAPL (Apple). You might be called on to interface with an entirely different site, but the general principles here will hold. You'll be using two main tools when parsing: Beautiful Soup, to let Python read HTML, and Firebug, to help you inspect the site's HTML and figure out which elements you want to extract.

Installing Beautiful Soup

Beautiful Soup is a Python library that's designed to be easy to use, but it also handles a wide variety of HTML markup, including "pathologically bad" markup. Often, you won't have a choice about which page you want to scrape, so it pays to pick a library like Beautiful Soup that isn't too fussy about the HTML it's given.

Beautiful Soup is available from www.crummy.com/software/BeautifulSoup/. To install it, download the file to your desktop and unzip it; then, from within a command prompt window, `cd` into the directory and run `python setup.py install`. If you're on Linux or Mac, you'll need to prefix this with `sudo`; and if you use Windows, you'll need to run the terminal application with administrator privileges. Beautiful Soup will then install itself into Python's site-packages folder so you can use it from anywhere. To make sure it's installed properly, open a Python command prompt and type `import BeautifulSoup`. If there's no error, you're good to go!

Installing Firefox and Firebug

The other tool you need is Firefox, which is a more open and standards-compliant browser than Internet Explorer. That will help you when you're looking at the code of web pages. You can get Firefox from http://getfirefox.com/.

Firebug provides a lot of extra development features for the Firefox web browser. It isn't essential for your task, but it does make interacting with the HTML of web pages a lot easier. You can download it by visiting http://getfirebug.com/ in Firefox and clicking the big Install Firebug button. You might need to change your settings to allow Firefox to install from that particular site, but other than that, everything should be automatic. When you're done and Firefox has restarted, you'll see a small bug icon in the lower-right corner of your Firefox window, and you'll have extra options when you right-click some elements of your page.

Examining the page

Now that you've got Firebug installed, you can look at the elements you'd like to be able to export in your Python script. If you right-click a section of one of Yahoo's finance pages, such as the title of the stock, and select Inspect Element, the bottom half of the window should open and show you the HTML corresponding to the title. It will be something like

```
<div class="yfi_quote_summary">
    <div class="hd">
[<div class="title">]
<h2>Google Inc.</h2>
        <span>(NasdaqGS: GOOG)</span>
    </div>
    ...
<div>
```

Figure 5.2 shows what it looks like in my browser.

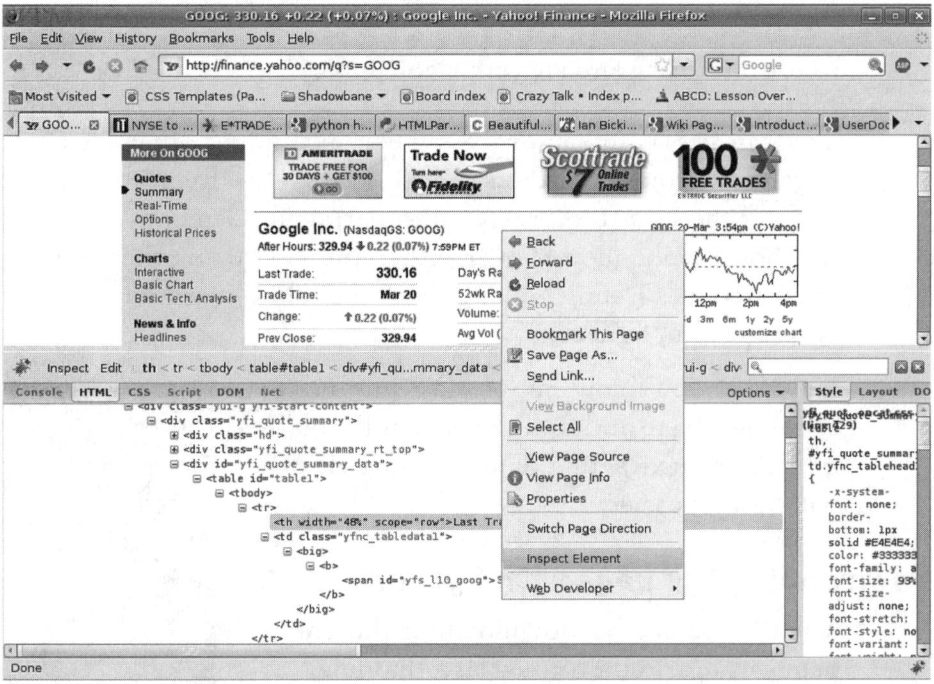

Figure 5.2 Examining elements using Firebug

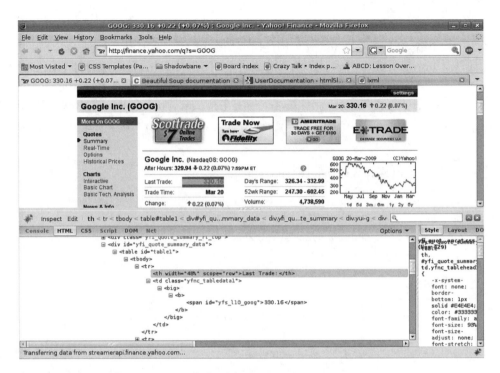

Figure 5.3 Using Firebug with highlighting

You can use a similar process when examining other elements of the page to find out what their HTML looks like. If you're not sure which parts of the HTML correspond to particular elements of the page, you can hover your mouse over either the HTML or the element you're interested in. Firebug will highlight the relevant sections of the page, as you can see in figure 5.3.

Now that you know how to use Firebug to examine a page and find the elements you're looking for, extracting data from the HTML will be a lot easier.

Downloading the page with Python

You'll start out by downloading the entire page using Python's `urllib2` module, as shown in the following listing. You'll do this

by writing a function that will return the HTML code for any stock page you name. This will be an easily reusable function that you can paste directly into the final script.

Listing 5.1   Downloading a web page

```python
import urllib2

def get_stock_html(ticker_name):
    opener = urllib2.build_opener(
            urllib2.HTTPRedirectHandler(),
            urllib2.HTTPHandler(debuglevel=0),
        )
    opener.addheaders = [
        ('User-agent',
         "Mozilla/4.0 (compatible; MSIE 7.0; "
         "Windows NT 5.1; .NET CLR 2.0.50727; "
         ".NET CLR 3.0.4506.2152; .NET CLR 3.5.30729)")
    ]

    url = "http://finance.yahoo.com/q?s=" + ticker_name
    response = opener.open(url)
    return ''.join(response.readlines())

if __name__ == '__main__':
    print get_stock_html('GOOG')
```

① Create opener object

② Add headers to request

③ Read web page with opener

④ Call function

urllib uses opener objects to read web pages. Here, you're creating one **①** and feeding it two handlers, which are objects that handle certain types of HTTP responses from the web server. HTTPRedirectHandler will automatically follow redirects, so if a page has moved temporarily, you don't have to worry about writing code to follow it. HTTPHandler will read any web pages that are returned.

Unfortunately, some websites like to block automated agents like this, so to be on the safe side you're being sneaky here and setting the user agent you send to the server so you appear to be a completely different web browser ❷. In this case, you're pretending to be Internet Explorer 7 running on Windows XP. You can find other user agent strings by doing a web search for "user agent strings."

Now all you need to do to be able to read a web page is call the opener's open() method with a URL ❸. That method returns a file-like object that which responds exactly like an open file, so you can get the text of the web page by calling readlines() and joining its response together.

It's easy to call the function now ❹, and all the tricky urllib parts are hidden away. If you run this script, it will print out the entire contents of the http://finance.yahoo.com/q?s=GOOG page on the screen.

NOTE   In Python 3.0, the urllib, urllib2, urlparse, and robotparse modules have all been merged into urllib, and several improvements have been made. The methods you're using here have been moved into the urllib.request module, but other than that, they're the same.

The entire content of the page is a little much for what you're trying to do. You're only interested in the part that has the stock price. You need to limit the result to the section of the page you're interested in.

Chopping out the bit you need

Let's get your feet wet with Beautiful Soup and parse out only the quote element you're interested in and print it. Once you've done that, you can start pulling out individual elements for the final output.

Most of the time, you can simplify your parsing by looking for landmarks in the web page's HTML. Normally there will be ID and class attributes that you can use to pinpoint a particular section and then narrow down your search from there. In this case, it looks like there's a <div> element with a class of yfi_quote_summary that contains all the information you need. The following listing features a function that uses Beautiful Soup to pull only that section out of your stock page.

Listing 5.2   Finding the quote section

```
from BeautifulSoup import BeautifulSoup
...
def find_quote_section(html):
```

```
    soup = BeautifulSoup(html)     ←——● Create parse object
    quote = soup.find('div',                    ❷ Find yfi_quote_
            attrs={'class': 'yfi_quote_summary'})    summary element
    return quote

if __name__ == '__main__':
    html = get_stock_html('GOOG')      ❸ Print
    print find_quote_section(html)        quote_section
```

The first thing you need to do when parsing HTML is to create a Beautiful Soup object ❶. This object looks at all of the HTML it's fed and provides lots of methods for you to examine, search through, and navigate it.

The soup object provides a find() method, which can quickly search through the HTML. Here, you're finding all the <div> elements that also have a class of yfi_quote_summary ❷. The find() command returns the first element it finds that matches the criteria, but as another soup object, so you can perform further searching if you need to.

As a shortcut, if you print a soup object ❸ it will return a string containing its HTML. In your case, this is exactly what you're looking for—the HTML of the yfi_quote_summary <div>.

If you run this script, it should print out a much shorter piece of HTML, which is the quote section you're looking for. You should be able to see some sections like the stock name and price, and some of the other <div> elements. Let's now add another function that will take the soup object for the summary <div> and produce more meaningful data.

Adding extra information

Now that you have the smaller section of HTML, you can examine it further and pull out the specific parts you need. The find() command will return another soup object, so you don't have to worry about parsing it again—you can call the find() method on the results to extract the data you need. The following listing shows a function that uses a number of find() calls to build a dictionary of data from your stock page.

Listing 5.3   Extracting the data for the stock

```
def parse_stock_html(html, ticker_name):
    quote = find_quote_section(html)
    result = {}
    tick = ticker_name.lower()

    # <h2>Google Inc.</h2>
    result['stock_name'] = quote.find('h2').contents[0]

    ### After hours values
    # <span id="yfs_l91_goog">329.94</span>
    result['ah_price'] = quote.find('span',
        attrs={'id': 'yfs_l91_'+tick}).string

    # <span id="yfs_z08_goog">
    #     <span class="yfi-price-change-down">0.22</span>
    result['ah_change'] = (quote.find(
        attrs={'id': 'yfs_z08_'+tick}).contents[1])

    ### Current values
    # <span id="yfs_l10_goog">330.16</span>
    result['last_trade'] = quote.find(
        'span', attrs={'id': 'yfs_l10_'+tick}).string

    # <span id="yfs_c10_goog" class="yfi_quote_price">
    #     <span class="yfi-price-change-down">1.06</span>
    def is_price_change(value):
        return (value is not None and
            value.strip().lower()
                .startswith('yfi-price-change'))

    result['change'] = (
        quote.find(attrs={'id': 'yfs_c10_'+tick})
            .find(attrs={'class': is_price_change})
            .string)

    return result

if __name__ == '__main__':
    html = get_stock_html('GOOG')
    print parse_stock_html(html, 'GOOG')
```

① Include elements as comments

② Simple find

③ More involved find

④ Differences between Beautiful Soup and Firebug

⑤ Function to locate elements

⑥ Use function

Does this look familiar? It's the old divide-and-conquer strategy again: write something simple that works, and then refine it a bit at a time until you have the data you need.

You might find it helpful to include the HTML you're trying to match as comments, like ❶. It saves switching back and forth between your editor window and your web browser to remind yourself what the HTML looks like.

Next, you run a simple find over your quote summary to find the first h2 element ❷. Once you've done that, you get the first element from the .contents attribute, which in this case will be the name of your stock. The .contents attribute returns all the sub-elements within a particular element as a list of soup objects.

Notice that in the HTML, the IDs you're looking for are named after the company. That's not much of a problem, because you can pass in the ticker name and make it low-ercase ❸. You're also using the .string method. If you're certain there will only ever be one text node within your search results, you can use the .string shortcut, which will return that node as text.

SO NOW THAT WE HAVE THAT, ALL WE NEED TO DO IS PASS IT TO EXCEL FOR CALCULATIONS, THEN WRITE IT OUT TO PLAIN TEXT, AND EMAIL IT OFF TO THE BOSS'S IPHONE.

I'M SURE PITR WILL BE HAPPY IT'S ALMOST OVER.

If you have a close look at the search here and the corresponding HTML in Firebug ❹, you might notice they're different. The code seems to be ignoring the extra span you can see in the browser. The answer is that sometimes, when HTML is invalid, Firebug will insert extra elements to make the HTML code valid. That's not a problem for Beautiful Soup, though, which returns both the image and text as two elements. If in doubt, you can always view the source of the page from the browser itself and search for the ID or class of the element to see the HTML exactly as you received it from the server.

If you need more flexibility in how you search, then another way you can use Beautiful Soup's find() method is to use a function instead of a string ❺. Beautiful Soup will feed the function the attribute name—if the function returns True, then the element is included.

Using the function from ❺ when searching is easy: just use the function ❻ instead of the string. In this section you're also chaining find() calls together. The first find() looks for elements with an ID of yfs_c10_goog and returns another Beautiful Soup object, which you use to immediately run another find() command. The whole set of calls is contained in brackets so you can wrap it over multiple lines and make it easier to understand.

You can continue in this vein until you've extracted all the data you need from the page. Be careful that your parsing doesn't grow too unwieldy. If it does, you may want to consider breaking parse_stock_html into functions, one per data value, and looping over a dictionary of data value names and functions when you're parsing:

```
parse_items = {'stock_name': parse_stock_name,
               'ah_price':   parse_ah_price, ... }
```

Caveats for web scraping

Although reading data directly from the web is a useful tool, it's not without its drawbacks. The main issue is that web pages change frequently, and your parsing code may need to change with it. You can lessen the risk somewhat by focusing on the elements of the page least likely to change, such as ID or class variables, but you're still at the mercy of whoever creates the page. If at all possible, it's usually much better in the long term if you can rely on official channels, such as a published API for accessing data, rather than doing it all yourself. Later, we'll look at strategies for dealing with failures in your script and how you can mitigate them.

But first, you need to add some complexity to your tool.

Writing out to a CSV file

An individual stock price isn't useful. To make any recommendations about whether it's good to buy or sell, or what the stock is likely to do in the future, you'd like some history of the stock price and its movement. That means you need to save the data you've just read so you can use it again in future. As we said in the section "CSV to the rescue!," the most common data format is a CSV file. The following listing will save your results dictionary to a row in a CSV file.

Listing 5.4   Writing a CSV file

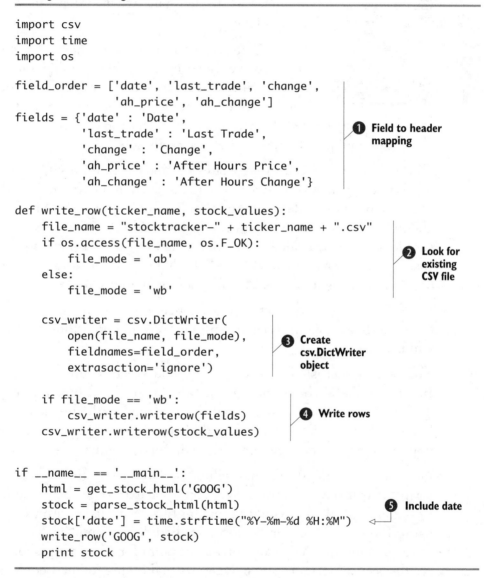

```
import csv
import time
import os

field_order = ['date', 'last_trade', 'change',
               'ah_price', 'ah_change']
fields = {'date' : 'Date',
          'last_trade' : 'Last Trade',
          'change' : 'Change',
          'ah_price' : 'After Hours Price',
          'ah_change' : 'After Hours Change'}

def write_row(ticker_name, stock_values):
    file_name = "stocktracker-" + ticker_name + ".csv"
    if os.access(file_name, os.F_OK):
        file_mode = 'ab'
    else:
        file_mode = 'wb'

    csv_writer = csv.DictWriter(
        open(file_name, file_mode),
        fieldnames=field_order,
        extrasaction='ignore')

    if file_mode == 'wb':
        csv_writer.writerow(fields)
    csv_writer.writerow(stock_values)

if __name__ == '__main__':
    html = get_stock_html('GOOG')
    stock = parse_stock_html(html)
    stock['date'] = time.strftime("%Y-%m-%d %H:%M")
    write_row('GOOG', stock)
    print stock
```

❶ **Field to header mapping**

❷ **Look for existing CSV file**

❸ **Create csv.DictWriter object**

❹ **Write rows**

❺ **Include date**

Before you start creating your CSV file, you need to know which key-value pairs in the dictionary correspond to which headers in the CSV

ANY PROGRESS ON THE EXPORT PROGRAM?

WELL, THE CS-XML PARSER THINKS THAT WE EARNED $öbýnø LAST MONTH, SO WE'RE HAVING TO PARSE THE INTERNAL HTML REPORTS INSTEAD.

file ❶. Storing them in a dictionary means you can easily access them later. Dictionaries aren't guaranteed to be in a specific order, though, so there's another list to tell you what order the columns should be in.

When you write the file, you'll name it after the stock you're tracking so it's easier to find and so any other scripts will be able to easily access it. You also need to know whether you've written to this file before, so you can add the headers to it if necessary. os.access does the trick, and you need to know whether it exists ❷.

csv.DictWriter is a class that writes dictionaries into a CSV file ❸. It needs two arguments to function: a file opened in binary mode and a list of the fields in the order that they should appear in the CSV file. I've also added an extrasaction argument, which tells DictWriter whether it should ignore extra values in the dictionary or raise an exception. In this case, you have an extra stock_name field that you'd rather not have appear over and over again in the CSV file, so you'll ignore it.

Once the DictWriter object is created, using it to write a row is easy ❹: feed it a dictionary to write. If any keys are missing, though, an error will be raised.

You're also interested in when a particular stock record was retrieved. In Python, here's how you output the current local time and date ❺. The %Y %H parts of the string will be replaced with the current year, hour, and so on. You can arrange them in any order you like, as long as you keep the % signs together with their corresponding character.

Now you have a CSV file that will be updated every time you run your script. If you run it several times, you'll see extra lines being appended to the end. Typically, you'd automate this script using cron (if you're using Linux or Mac), or Windows Scheduler or similar if you're running on Windows. You can stop at this point for some scripts, but if the results are important, you'll want to make sure other people know about them.

Next, let's figure out how to create an email with your CSV file.

Emailing the CSV file

If you need to do anything with email, the email module is normally the place to start. It contains classes and functions for parsing email and extracting their information as well as tools for creating and encoding emails, even the creation of multipart emails containing HTML, text (if the recipient can't read HTML), and attachments. Normally you'd start with a simple section and build up, but when creating an email it's easier to remove the sections you don't need.

Creating an email is straightforward, but it definitely helps if you have some background knowledge of how emails work. Let's take a look at that first, and then you'll see how to put it into practice in your program.

Email structure

Most emails, other than the simplest plain-text emails, are composed of containers, with parts within them. These parts can be text, HTML, or any other part that can be described with a MIME type. When the email is sent, the email structure will be converted into a plain text format that can be reassembled when it reaches its destination.

Normally, there will be at least two parts: one that contains your email in HTML, and another that contains a text version—but an email can in theory contain as many different parts as you need. The structure I've found most useful, and that displays the best across a variety of email programs, is in figure 5.4.

This structure has two containers. The outside one contains the message part and any number of attachments, and the inside container has the two versions of your email. If you need extra attachments, attach them to the outside container.

I SEE. AND THEN?

WELL, THEN WE'LL BE ABLE TO SEND IT OUT TO THE SPREADSHEET, THEN TEXT FILES ...

AND THEN OFF TO THE BOSS? OK. LET ME KNOW HOW IT GOES ...

Figure 5.4 The structure of a HTML email

Outside Container

Outside Container

Text Body

HTML Body

CSV File

Creating an email

Now that you know how MIME messages are constructed, let's take a look at the corresponding program in the following listing. This function will take an email address and a stock ticker name, such as "GOOG," and construct an email ready to be sent.

Listing 5.5   Creating a MIME email

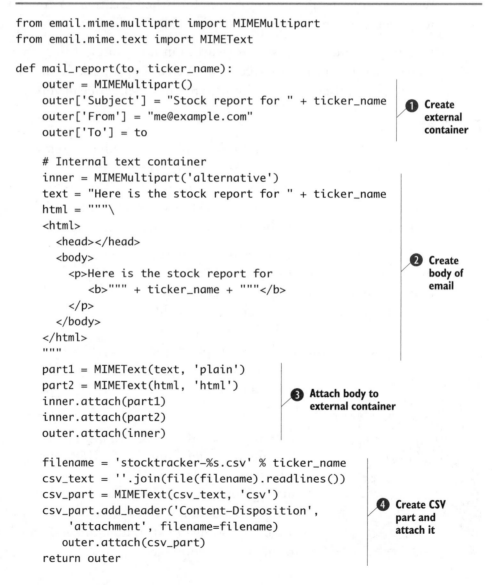

```python
from email.mime.multipart import MIMEMultipart
from email.mime.text import MIMEText

def mail_report(to, ticker_name):
    outer = MIMEMultipart()
    outer['Subject'] = "Stock report for " + ticker_name      ❶ Create
    outer['From'] = "me@example.com"                              external
    outer['To'] = to                                             container

    # Internal text container
    inner = MIMEMultipart('alternative')
    text = "Here is the stock report for " + ticker_name
    html = """\
<html>
  <head></head>
  <body>
    <p>Here is the stock report for                          ❷ Create
        <b>""" + ticker_name + """</b>                          body of
    </p>                                                         email
  </body>
</html>
"""
    part1 = MIMEText(text, 'plain')
    part2 = MIMEText(html, 'html')                            ❸ Attach body to
    inner.attach(part1)                                         external container
    inner.attach(part2)
    outer.attach(inner)

    filename = 'stocktracker-%s.csv' % ticker_name
    csv_text = ''.join(file(filename).readlines())
    csv_part = MIMEText(csv_text, 'csv')
    csv_part.add_header('Content-Disposition',               ❹ Create CSV
        'attachment', filename=filename)                        part and
      outer.attach(csv_part)                                    attach it
    return outer
```

```
if __name__ == '__main__':
    email = mail_report('youremail@example.com', 'GOOG')  ❺  Email object
    print email.as_string()
```

The first thing you need to do is to create the external container ❶ that will contain all the other parts. It's also where you put all the message headers—the Subject, To, and From lines.

Next up is the body of the email ❷, the HTML and text parts. Normally an email program will display the last part of this container as the body, and fall back on the others if it can't handle it, so you put the HTML last.

GREG, YOU AND PITR HAVE BEEN UP FOR 36 HOURS STRAIGHT NOW—WHAT'S GOING ON?

WE FOUND OUT THAT THE INTERNAL HTML THINKS THAT OUR INCOME FOR LAST YEAR IS BIGGER THAN BELGIUM'S ...

Now you can create MIMEText objects to hold the email body. They'll automatically be of type text/something, and the second argument tells what that something will be. Once you have those objects, you call attach to insert them into the inner container, and then attach the inner container to the outer one ❸.

You do the same thing for the CSV section that you did for the body of the email. Once you've read in the CSV file, you create a text/csv part and insert it into the outer section ❹. The only extra thing you need to do is add a Content-Disposition header to say that it's an attachment, and give it a file name. Without a file name, you'll get a default name like "Part 1.2," which doesn't look friendly or professional.

If you want to see what you've created, use the as_string() method on your outer message object, and it will print out the email exactly as it will be sent ❺. You'll be writing a send_message() function in the next section, which you'll use to send the email via an SMTP server.

That's all you need to do with the report email; it's ready to be sent. If you'd like to reuse this function, there are a number of things you can do to extend it. The first obvious one is to pass in the subject, and text and HTML content, as arguments, instead of hard-coding them in the body. Another is to be able to pass in more than one attachment, as a list. An important function for this second part is mimetypes.guess_type, which will give you a MIME type and an encoding (such as zip, gzip, or compress) based on the filename of the attachment. From there, you can create the right type of MIME object, such as `MIMEApplication` or `MIMEImage`, and attach it to the email.

By the way, if you're attaching images, you can link to them from within the HTML body by using a `cid:` URL, like this: `<img src="cid:image_name.gif">`.

Sending email

The last thing you need to do with your email is send it. This is the most straightforward part of the email sending process and only needs a From address, a list of To addresses, and the email itself.

Listing 5.6 Sending an email

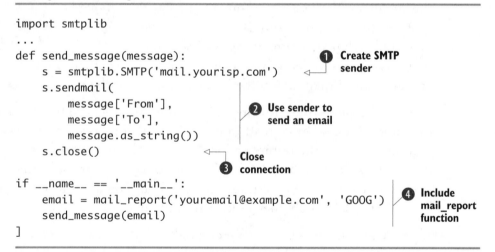

```
import smtplib
...
def send_message(message):
    s = smtplib.SMTP('mail.yourisp.com')          ❶ Create SMTP
    s.sendmail(                                       sender
        message['From'],
        message['To'],                             ❷ Use sender to
        message.as_string())                          send an email
    s.close()                                      ❸ Close
                                                      connection
if __name__ == '__main__':
    email = mail_report('youremail@example.com', 'GOOG')   ❹ Include
    send_message(email)                                       mail_report
]                                                             function
```

First you create an SMTP object, which will handle the sending of your email ❶. This will normally be enough if you're connecting to your internet service provider's mail server, normally something like mail.yourisp.com or smtp.yourisp.com—you can get it from the "sending email" section of your email program if you don't know what it is. Some ISPs require a username and password for SMTP that you can include with a line like `s.login('user', 'password')`.

Once you have an SMTP object, you can call its sendmail() method to send email ❷. You're pulling the email addresses as well as the body of the email out of the message; that way, you don't have to specify them as separate arguments, and your code stays neater. You can call the sendmail() method multiple times if you need to.

When you're done you can close the connection ❸. This saves some load on the SMTP server, because it will have one less connection to keep track of—but if you have multiple email messages to send, it's better to reuse the connection.

To create an email to send, you use your mail_report() function and feed it your email address and the name of the stock . Then you pass it to the send_message() function to send it ❹. If you prefer a weekly report, then you can run this on a separate schedule to the script, which reads the web page. If you'd like to email multiple people at once, then you still feed one string to mail_report()—but with commas separating the email addresses.

That's all you need to do for your script. It scrapes data from a web page, posts it into a CSV file, and then emails a report to someone who can make use of the information. A surprisingly large amount of business programming boils down to a roughly similar process: gather some data, process it, and then send or store the results somewhere, either to a human who needs the information, or to another program.

Other email modules

Although you didn't need them in this script, there are other email-related modules you can make use of if you need more flexibility when dealing with email, or if you need to do something outside what this script can do. The two that I most commonly use, other than the modules in this script, are the mailbox module and getmail.

... SO WE'RE TAKING WEBCAM SHOTS OF THE SCREEN IN ACCOUNTS. RUNNING O.C.R. SOFTWARE OVER IT. ACCOUNTS WILL THEN ADD IT UP MANUALLY. PUT IT INTO A .CSV FILE, WHICH WE'LL THEN DEAL WITH.

The mailbox module contains classes to read several different types of mailbox, including the two most common, mbox and maildir, and provides an easy way to loop over each message in the file. Parsing mbox files is relatively easy, but there are several catches to it, and it's easier to use a library. In addition to writing emails, the email module provides email.parser to read the header lines, body, and attachments out of a flat text file. Together they provide everything you need to be able to handle email.

Getmail is an add-on module written by Charles Cazabon and available from http://pyropus.ca/software/getmail/. It handles POP and IMAP4, including via SSL, and can save messages to mbox or maildir storage as well as passing them to another program. It's also easy to use and only requires one configuration file to work.

Between Python's built-in email modules and getmail, you should be able to deal with almost any email programming problem that comes your way, whether you need to read, download, parse, or analyze email.

A simple script—what could possibly go wrong?

There's a useful question you can ask yourself when completing a project like this: "Am I done?"

Try it now and see what you think the answer is. Are you done? Would you be confident that you could run this script every day and not have to worry about it? Would it ever break? If the CEO or director of your company was relying on the results of your script, would you be able to sleep at night? Even if your script isn't vital, how would you know it was working? Would you have to babysit your script to make sure it worked, perhaps checking the results every few days to make sure nothing had gone wrong?

It's possible to write a program that works at first but needs so much assistance to run that you might as well have not written it in the first place. To keep your sanity, try to analyze your program and find as many potential failure points as you can.

NOTE   This is the toughest part of writing programs—anything and everything might fail in some way, and you have to be ready for the potential consequences. If you've ever wondered why a lot of programmers and system admins seem like cagey pessimists, now you know.

Here's a list of some possible issues that might break your script. Then, in the next section, we'll look at how you can go about fixing them.

No internet

Obviously, if there's no internet connection, the script won't be able to download the stock page or send email, and there will be nothing you can do about it. But what happens exactly? Will your script fail immediately, or will it get halfway through and corrupt your data? If you can't connect for a day, what should appear in the CSV file?

Invalid data

If Yahoo decided to change the design of their site, what would happen to your script? If it's expecting a particular ID within the HTML and that ID is removed, then your script will break. Alternately, there could be a partial outage and you'll see null or zero values. Or if the server is under load, you might see timeout errors or only receive half a page. How does your script handle that? Does it try to parse the error page and fail? Or does it recognize what's happened? In the worst case, it will have data that looks similar to the data you're expecting, you won't notice it's changed, and your data will be silently corrupted.

Data you haven't thought of

There's another failure mode related to invalid data: sometimes you can be given data that's valid, but only within the range you're expecting. It might also be formatted or presented differently if it's within a certain range or currently unknown. These sorts of values are generally known as *edge cases*. They don't happen often, so they can be harder to predict, but they still have a large effect on the stability of your program. The best way to deal with edge cases is to try to consider the entirety of the range of your data and include any cases that are in doubt into your test suite.

Unable to write data

When you're processing, you're assuming you'll be able to write to the CSV file. This is normally the case, but there are some circumstances where you might not be able to: if an administrator on the site has set the wrong permissions, or your computer is out of space. You might want to consider rotating your CSV files every so often: zip the old ones and delete those that have been around the longest (or download and archive them). The exact timeframe will depend on both the amount of free space you have on your server and the requirements of your program.

No mail server

You can also run into problems when trying to send your email. Most of the time, email is pretty foolproof, but it's possible for a mail server to be down. If that's the case, what happens to your script? It might be enough for it to store the row in the CSV file and resend it the next night, or you might need to check that the mail server is up and try an alternative route if it isn't.

You don't have to fix them

These are by no means the only things that can go wrong with your script, but they're the most likely. Depending upon your script, its purpose, and the environment it runs in, these might be more or less of an issue. Or you might not need to worry about them at all. But you still need to consider them.

Let's move on and take a look at ways you might solve, or at least mitigate, some of these issues.

How to deal with breaking scripts

There are a number of strategies for dealing with the weak points you've seen so far in your script. Which one you choose depends on the nature of your script and its purpose. First, let's examine two factors that affect how you program your script as well as how you look at potential failures and how you solve them.

Communication

When you're building software for other people, communication is vital. It's important to know the overall goals of your project, how it impacts on other aspects of the business, what the likely effects of a failure are, and how people in the business will use your final product. Although, strictly speaking, a program that doesn't do what's needed isn't a bug, it might as well not have been written.

It's also important to keep people informed as you build your program, because the problem you're solving can change at any point. There's nothing worse than finishing a program only to find that it's no longer required and that weeks of effort have been wasted.

Tolerance of failure

There are many different ways to deal with a potential error, and they all have varying costs. Which ones you choose will depend on the business's tolerance of failure.

THE EXPENSIVE CASE

For example, if the business were using your script to buy and sell millions of dollars worth of stock, then it would have a low tolerance of any possible failure. You might host the script on a dedicated server or multiple servers in separate locations—an extra several thousand dollars would be a small price compared to the risk of losing millions of dollars worth of trades. You'd also want to pay a few hundred dollars a month to access an API specifically provided for the purpose rather than scraping web pages, and have a full suite of functional and unit tests to catch any errors.

THE CHEAPER CASE

If, instead, you were using your script as a more general business intelligence application, a stock failing here or there or taking a day to propagate through the system might not be so bad. Cost is more of an issue, so you'd run your script on a server with several other applications. This opens you up to the possibility of extra errors, like running out of disk space or having one application use so much CPU that nothing else can get anything done—but the impact of any errors like this is minor compared to the relative cost of separate servers.

Don't break in the first place

It might sound obvious, but the easiest way to avoid bugs in your program is to not write them in the first place. It's easy to throw together a script that looks like it works, but often you'll find there are all sorts of issues lurking in your code, waiting for an opportunity to crash your program.

First, consider all of the possible data, including weird pathological cases, when you write your program. Look for edge cases and things that "can't possibly happen," and make sure they can't. If you're working with numbers, what happens when the number is zero? Or negative? Or enormous? Should the program throw an error? Ignore that particular value? Thinking about this ahead of time is easier than thinking about it when your program crashes and you have to fix it *right now*.

Once you know what data you can and can't handle, you can include it in your tests. Your unit tests and functional tests can verify what happens when you give a program data that's either invalid ("fruit" when you were expecting a number) or likely to be a problem (zero, negative, or very large). If you find input that gives you an error while you're testing or when your program goes live, you can add it to your test suite to ensure that it doesn't happen again.

Fail early and loudly

HMM—WHAT MAKES YOU THINK
THE CHIEF WILL BE ABLE TO
CONFIGURE HIS IPHONE'S EMAIL
FROM THE BAHAMAS?
I THINK A WEB-BASED
INTERFACE MIGHT BE BETTER ...

WUH?
BAHAMAS

BURBLE
BURBLE

If at some point in your program there's an error, normally the best way to deal with it is for your program to stop immediately and start "yelling" (via email or by printing to the screen). This is particularly true during development or if the problem is unexpected. Trying to soldier on in the face of errors is dangerous, because you can overwrite important data with nonsense results.

Wherever possible, check data and any error codes returned from the libraries you're using. If you're trying to load data from the web, you can check the response code: anything other than 200 (success) means there's been an error somewhere and you should stop. If you have trouble parsing the data returned, it's possible you're seeing a different type of page, or the data isn't what you're expecting. In that case, it's also a good idea to log it somewhere and skip processing. Don't forget to include relevant data in the error so you can replicate the problem.

Belt and braces

To mitigate the effects of any errors, it can often help to have multiple fallbacks if things go wrong. For example, you might have two copies of your script running on separate servers. If something goes wrong with one script, such as the network being unavailable, the other script may still be able to access the data.

Another tip is to save intermediate copies of the data whenever possible. In your script, you might want to consider saving the HTML you download from the server before you analyze it. If some of the data looks odd, or you have an error when parsing, you can double-check your results and see what's gone wrong.

Stress and performance testing

A common problem when your program goes live is that it works well on small amounts of data but fails or runs too slowly when used on real data. Make sure your program can handle the workload in the volumes that are expected when it goes live, and use real data when testing wherever possible.

HI MIKE—WHAT'S THE NEWS?

I'VE SET UP A WEB PAGE FOR THE CHIEF TO VIEW HIS ACCOUNTS INFORMATION.

ALREADY? BUT ... BUT ... HOW?

Try again later

If your program fails due to an outside source not being available, you can often try again several times before giving up. Perhaps the site you're trying to load is having some temporary downtime and will be back up in a few minutes. If you take this route, be sure to wait a while between queries, and wait a little longer between them if they're failing. If you want five retries, you might wait 1 minute, then 3, 5, 7, and then finally give up. If you need to send data via email, a queue can simplify your error-handling. Instead of sending emails directly to the server, queue them to a directory on disk instead. A second process reads the files that are saved and tries to send them. If the mail is sent successfully, then you delete the mail file or move it to a separate directory, but if it fails you leave it ready for next time. The following listing shows how you might add that sort of logic to your stock-tracking script.

Listing 5.7   Queuing email to a temporary file

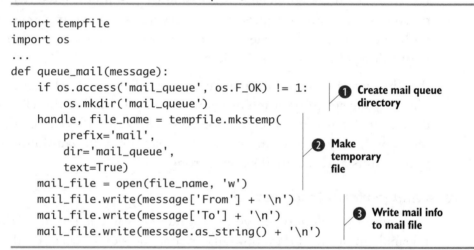

```
import tempfile
import os
...
def queue_mail(message):
    if os.access('mail_queue', os.F_OK) != 1:          ❶ Create mail queue
        os.mkdir('mail_queue')                             directory
    handle, file_name = tempfile.mkstemp(
        prefix='mail',
        dir='mail_queue',                              ❷ Make
        text=True)                                        temporary
    mail_file = open(file_name, 'w')                      file
    mail_file.write(message['From'] + '\n')
    mail_file.write(message['To'] + '\n')              ❸ Write mail info
    mail_file.write(message.as_string() + '\n')           to mail file
```

First, you check that the mail queue directory exists. If it doesn't, then you need to create it ❶.

Next, you use the `tempfile` module to create the mail file ❷. By doing it this way instead of figuring out the filename yourself, you're much less likely to run into a conflict with naming if you're running multiple scripts at once.

Now that you have your file, you can write all the information you need when it's time to send your email: To, From, and the body of the email itself ❸.

Once you have the email queued to disk, you can use a second process to read it and send it out. The next listing shows how the second process might be written.

Listing 5.8   Sending email from a mail queue directory

```
import os
import smtplib
import sys

mailserver = smtplib.SMTP('mail.yourisp.com')
mail_files = os.listdir('mail_queue')

for eachfile in mail_files:
    file_name = 'mail_queue' + os.path.sep + eachfile
    file = open(file_name, 'r')
    me = file.readline()
    them = file.readline()
    mail_body = ''.join(file.readlines())
    file.close()

    mailserver.sendmail(me, them, mail_body)
    os.remove(file_name)

mailserver.quit()
```

❶ Read in mail files

❷ Try to send mail, then delete it

This part of the process is the opposite of the one you just looked at. Given a directory, you want to read in all of the files in it ❶ and, for each of them, read out the To and From lines and then the mail body.

The `smtplib` server will generate an error for anything that means the mail can't be sent, so you try to send the email ❷. If it succeeds, then you know the mail has been sent and you can delete the mail file and continue.

I JUST SET UP A PAGE WITH THE HTML FROM THE INTERNAL REPORTS, AND ADD A BIT TO THE TOTAL EVERY SO OFTEN. BY THE TIME THE CHIEF GETS BACK, WE WON'T NEED IT ANY MORE ...

BUT ... THAT'S CHEATING!

IT WORKED FOR GMAIL, DIDN'T IT?

GAH!

Now you don't have to worry about mail being lost if the mail server is down for maintenance, or if you can't reach it via the network. All mail will be queued in the `mail_queue` directory and will only be deleted after it's been sent.

There are still a few limitations, though. The main one is that the first error your program runs into will abort the entire mail-sending process. For your purposes it works well enough, because if one email fails the others are likely to fail as well. But you'd like your program to be as robust as you can make it. A malformed email address, for example, can cause the SMTP server to reject your connection request, and then that email will be repeated over and over again, blocking all the others queued up behind it.

NOTE   Gracefully handling errors is even more important if your program takes a while to return or is a batch process that runs overnight. If you have to wait six hours to find out whether it ran properly, it can take a week or more to shake out all the errors. Detailed error reports help, but you can also work on smaller data sets until you're confident your program works.

One error shouldn't bring your whole program grinding to a halt, so what you need are exceptions: a feature in Python designed to help you react to errors like this as they occur and recover gracefully.

Exceptions

Whenever Python runs into a problem that it can't handle, it triggers an error called an *exception*. There are a wide variety of exceptions, and you can even define your own to suit particular types of errors if a built-in one doesn't fit your exact error. Exceptions aren't final, though—you can write code to catch them, interpret their results, and take whatever action you need.

Why use exceptions?

Exceptions, when used well, make your program much easier to understand. You don't need as much error-checking and handling, particularly for error codes and return results, because you can generally assume that anything that goes wrong will raise an exception. Not having error-handling code means the part of your program that does things stands out a lot more and is easier to understand because it's not being interrupted by checking return codes.

What it means when your program goes "bang!"

Before we get into how to use exceptions, let's take a look at a few examples and see how they work. When you get an error in your program, you'll see what's called a *traceback*. This will give you the whole function "stack," from the part of your program that triggered the error through intermediate functions to the one that originally started in the core of your program.

Let's start with a traceback from the mail sender you wrote in the previous section. It shows the most recent error last, so you'll be working backward.

Listing 5.9   A traceback when sending mail

```
anthony@anthony:~/Desktop/stocktracker$ python mailsender.py
Traceback (most recent call last):                                    Where's 3
  File "mailsender.py", line 5, in <module>        1 Error           that
    mailserver = smtplib.SMTP('mail.yourisp.com')                     line?
  File "/usr/lib/python2.5/smtplib.py", line 244, in __init__         2
    (code, msg) = self.connect(host, port)          Traceback
  File "/usr/lib/python2.5/smtplib.py", line 296, in connect
    for res in socket.getaddrinfo(host, port, 0,    4 Line that triggered
        socket.SOCK_STREAM):                           exception
socket.gaierror: (-2, 'Name or service not known')    5 Exception
anthony@anthony:~/Desktop/stocktracker$
```

You start at the end of the listing with the name of the exception and a short description of the error that occurred **5**. If you can't figure out what's going wrong with your program, doing a web search for the exception and description can often give you a clue.

The last line that was executed is the one where the exception was raised **4**. Note, though, that the bug may be earlier on in the program, if a variable wasn't set properly or a function is being called with the wrong parameters.

❸ is the file, line number, and function name where the exception in ❹ was raised. Notice that this is within Python's standard library, so you probably haven't found the problem yet. When in doubt, always assume there's a bug in your program, rather than Python's standard library.

The traceback ❷ will continue to the function that called your original one. Notice how the function name you're calling, self.connect, is the same as the function listed in ❸, the last part of the traceback.

Now that you get into the code, the error is obvious. You've forgotten to take out the example ISP mail server and substitute your own ❶. There's no web address at mail.yourisp.com, hence the original error: "name or service not known." Often the root cause of an exception might be several layers deep in the traceback, and it's a case of tracing the function calls back until you find the source of the error.

Python handles exceptions by propagating them *up the stack*: that is, it will first look for an exception handler in the current function. If it can't find one, it will look in the function which called the current one, then that function's parent, and so on, all the way back to the top of your program. If there's still no handler, Python will halt and print out the unhandled exception and the stack trace. Bang!

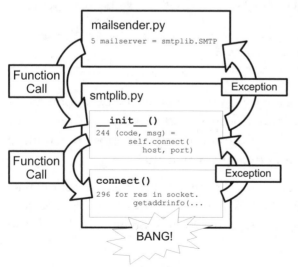

Figure 5.5 shows how the stack trace from listing 5.9 is generated, with the function calls on the left side and the traceback rewinding on the right side.

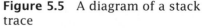

Figure 5.5 A diagram of a stack trace

For a different point of reference, here's another traceback, from parse_stock_html.

Listing 5.10   A traceback when parsing an HTML page

```
Traceback (most recent call last):
  File "./stocktracker.py", line 172, in <module>
    stock_values = parse_stock_html(html, ticker_name)
  File "./stocktracker.py", line 61, in parse_stock_html
    result['ah_change'] = (quote.find(attrs={'id':
'yfs_z08_'+tick}).contents[1])
IndexError: list index out of range
```

❷ Line that triggered it

❶ Exception

The exception that was triggered ❶ is an IndexError, which means you've tried to access an index of an array that doesn't exist. Something like ['foo'][1] will trigger a similar exception, because there's no second element of that array.

If you look at the line above it, you can see what might be causing the problem. You're running a find in Beautiful Soup and are trying to access the second element ❷. There's obviously some data for which the HTML only has one element, and the parsing code doesn't handle it.

The error in this case is due to the up or down arrow image not being shown when the stock price hasn't moved, which is changing the number of elements returned from .contents(). The following figure shows the two versions of the HTML side by side so you can see what I mean.

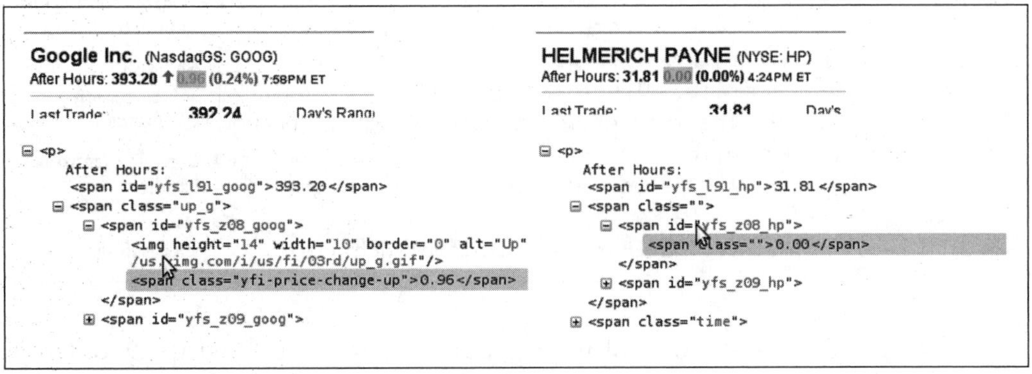

Figure 5.6   The HTML changes if there's no movement in the stock.

This problem is fixed relatively easily by using a negative index, like this: .contents[-1]. Now Python will access the last element of the list: either the second element, if there are two, or the first one if there's only one. You can be pretty sure there won't be more than two elements in that particular span.

Now you should have some pointers in using tracebacks to help you troubleshoot errors. The main thing to bear in mind is to work backward carefully, looking for potential errors or odd results. If that doesn't help, you might need more traditional checks, such as print or assert statements. Once you've tracked down the error, you should add it to your testing suite if possible.

Catching errors

The main reason for having exceptions is to catch them if they are raised and deal with them appropriately. You do this by using a try..except block, commonly known as an *exception handler*. The code within the try part is run, and if an exception is raised, Python looks at the except part to see how to deal with the error. The following listing shows how you how you might catch some common exceptions in your mail-sending program.

Listing 5.11   A mail sender with exception handling

```
try:
    mailserver.sendmail(me, them, mailouttext)          ❶ Normal program
                                                            flow
except smtplib.SMTPAuthenticationError, error:          ❷ Normal exception
    print "Bad username or password:", error                handler
except (smtplib.SMTPConnectError,                       ❸ Multiple
        smtplib.SMTPHeloError), error:                      exception
    print "The server is not responding!", error            handlers
except Exception, error:                                ❹ Generic exception
    print "An unexpected exception: ", error                handler
else:                                                   ❺ If you ran
    os.remove('maildir'+os.path.sep+eachfile)               successfully
```

You start with the part of your program you'd like to wrap ❶, to catch any exceptions. It behaves much like any normal indented block, so you can include if statements, loops, function calls, and whatever else you need to.

❷ is how you handle a single exception, which is how most exception-handling is done. The handler works a little like a function in that you give it the type of exception it needs to handle and a variable to store the error message. When an exception is raised, you can print an error message and the error message you've received.

You can also handle multiple types of exception with one handler by putting the exceptions you're expecting into a tuple, instead of having one by itself ❸.

If you need to catch every exception that's raised, use Exception, which is a generic exception object ❹. It's generally considered poor form to use a generic handler like this, because you may end up masking errors you'd rather have propagate up. If possible, you should handle specific errors, but there are occasions where you don't know what exceptions you'll need to handle.

You can also use else: to include a section of code to execute if the try..except block ran successfully and didn't raise any exception ❺. In this case, you're deleting the mail you've just sent. There's also a finally: option that you can use if you have something that needs to be run all the time, regardless of whether you had any exceptions.

Exception handling like this should handle most of your needs and allow you to write programs that can recover from error conditions, or at least fail gracefully, and you can use it wherever you need to handle errors. Where that is depends on the nature of the program and the errors you're trying to catch. A program that handles user input might have one high-level exception handler that wraps your entire program in a try..except clause. That way, no matter what the user types, you can handle it and return a reasonable error message. You can also use error handlers around subsections of your program, or around specific modules that throw exceptions.

But handling exceptions on servers doesn't give you a lot of information about what went wrong. Especially in the case of critical production systems, it's extremely helpful to know where the error occurred and in what file. You'd like to be able to see tracebacks as if you were running the program locally. Fortunately, there's a Python module that can help you to print out detailed debugging messages and find out what when wrong: the traceback module.

The traceback module

The traceback module gives you a number of functions for handling exceptions as well as formatting and extracting tracebacks and error messages. The two key ones are print_exc() and format_exc(), which print out a traceback and return a traceback as a string, respectively. You can extract this information from the sys module, via sys.exc_type, sys.exc_value, and sys.exc_traceback, but it's much more straightforward to use traceback. Let's extend the error handling in the last section to print out a nice traceback if you get an unknown error, as shown in the following listing.

Listing 5.12   Using the traceback module

```
import traceback
...
    try:
        mailserver.sendmail(me, them, mailouttext)
        ...                              ❶ Shortcut
    except:                                        ❷ Print exception
        traceback.print_exc()
        traceback_string = traceback.format_exc()  ❸ Extract formatted
        print traceback_string                        exception
    else:
        os.remove('maildir'+os.path.sep+eachfile)
```

Let's start with a shortcut: you don't have to specify Exception for a generic handler. If you omit any exception types at all, it behaves in exactly the same way ❶.

The print_exc() function will print a formatted traceback ❷. This is useful if you're running the program interactively or if you use something like cron, which will email you with the output of any programs you run.

If you need to log to a file, then you can use the format_exc() function to return a string with the traceback ❸. Other than that difference, it's exactly the same output.

Now you have everything you need to be able to handle any errors that crop up in your program. You can extend the code in this section to handle most situations you'll run into in practice, and if not, then at least leave enough data behind for you to be able to figure out what's gone wrong.

Where to from here?

The scripts in this chapter are self-contained, so there aren't any specific suggestions as to how you can extend them. Instead, try applying the lessons (and code) from this chapter to automate something you do frequently, either at work or home. Good candidates are anything you find dull and boring, or which requires detailed steps and is difficult to do properly.

If you can't automate all of your process, you can at least cover part of them—for example, download required data so it's all in one place, or send out several emails from a central data store.

Often, a good script can save you several hours of work over the course of a month, so you can use all the new free time you have to write another script. Eventually, you might not have to do any work at all!

Summary

The first half of this chapter covered some of the basic but important libraries in Python that you can use to connect to the outside world and get real work done. We covered a number of technologies:

- Downloading HTML from the web
- Parsing HTML using Beautiful Soup
- Writing data out to a CSV file
- Composing email, including writing HTML email and attaching documents
- Sending email via SMTP

In the second half of the chapter, we took a step back and looked at how you can make your programs more reliable—after all, this is the real world, and other people might have a lot of money riding on your programs.

We first looked at how you can find areas of a program are at risk. Then, we considered whether you should fix them, based on the costs of doing so and the fallout from any potential failures. Finally, we covered some simple strategies to make your programs more reliable, and we also took a look at ways to reduce the damage done if a program fails.

Finally, we covered exceptions and tracebacks, which are Python's way of handling errors when they occur, and how you can catch exceptions, examine them, and deal with the problem if you're able to.

In the next chapter, we'll take a break and write your own adventure game, with monsters, treasure, danger, and excitement!

6

Classes and object-oriented programming

This chapter covers

- *An easier way to think about classes*
- *How to use classes to design your programs*

Until now, we've been skimming over one of the fundamental ways you can organize your program in Python: the class. Classes and object-oriented programming are normally seen as big, scary things that real programmers use to write their programs, and you might think you need a lot of theoretical knowledge in order to use them properly. Nothing could be further from the truth. In Python, it's possible to ease into classes and object-oriented programming.

In this chapter, you'll start with the code you wrote back in chapter 2 to generate caves for Hunt the Wumpus and then see how much easier it is to write it using classes. Then you'll build up from there into a full-fledged adventure game along the lines of Adventure or Zork. While you do that, you'll find out all about Python's classes and how to make the most of them.

What exactly are classes?

If you think all the way back to chapter 2, you might remember that you had a group of functions that dealt with caves for the player and wumpus to live in. There was a function for creating a cave, another for linking two caves together to create a tunnel, one to make sure all the caves were linked, and so on. When you were writing the program, you dealt with the caves entirely through functions. One way to create a class is to identify a group of functions like this and make their relationship official.

Classes contain data

Another way to think about classes is as if a class was a container or a wrapper placed around data you want to use in your program. You can group all the data needed to perform a particular task, and provide functions to deal with it, particularly if the data is complicated, difficult to work with, or needs to be consistent—for example, the program that keeps track of the balance of your account at the bank.

They're a type of their own

Classes are similar to something called an *abstract data type*, which is a set of data and all the operations that can be performed on that data. You don't have to specify all the possible things you can do with the data inside your class, only what's useful for your particular situation. When designing your class, though, it often helps to think of all the possible things you might want to use it for, and add those that make sense.

How do they work?

Think of classes as a big rubber stamp. Once you've created your rubber stamp, you can easily stamp out as many pictures as you like. Classes work the same way. You generally don't work directly with a class: you instead work with *instances* of that class, which you create by using the original class.

Classes in a program have one advantage—if you need a slightly different picture, it's easy to create a copy of the original class, change it a

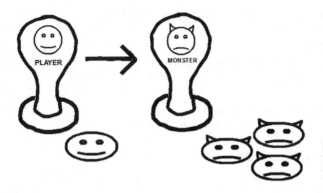

Figure 6.1 Monsters are like the player, except with horns and a frowny face.

bit, and work with that. Figure 6.1 shows you what the classes in this chapter might look like, if they were rubber stamps.

Both the instance and the class itself can have methods for you to call and data to access. For the most part, these will be set when you first create an instance, but Python also allows you to update them on the fly if you need to, even to the point of rebinding methods.

NOTE   Object-oriented programming includes a great deal of terminology — most of it apparently designed to confuse the unwary reader. You'll hear people refer to classes, objects, instances, methods, class methods, getters, setters, and so on. If you're unsure what someone means, try to figure out whether they're talking about the rubber stamp or the mark it's making on your program.

Your first class

The class in the following listing should look familiar, although there are some parts that are quite different. It contains the cave list and methods you wrote in chapter 2, but updated so they're contained within a class.

Listing 6.1   *An object to store caves*

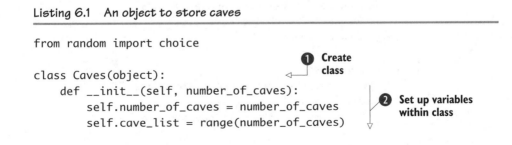

```
from random import choice

class Caves(object):                                    ❶ Create class
    def __init__(self, number_of_caves):
        self.number_of_caves = number_of_caves          ❷ Set up variables
        self.cave_list = range(number_of_caves)            within class
```

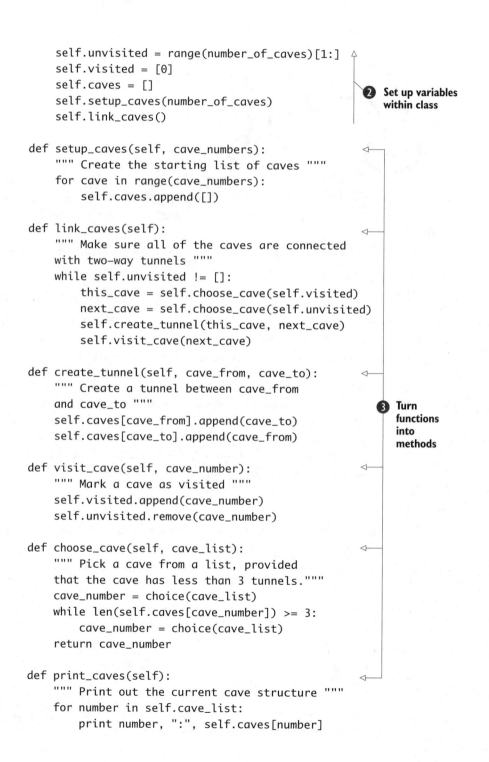

```python
        self.unvisited = range(number_of_caves)[1:]
        self.visited = [0]
        self.caves = []
        self.setup_caves(number_of_caves)
        self.link_caves()

    def setup_caves(self, cave_numbers):
        """ Create the starting list of caves """
        for cave in range(cave_numbers):
            self.caves.append([])

    def link_caves(self):
        """ Make sure all of the caves are connected
        with two-way tunnels """
        while self.unvisited != []:
            this_cave = self.choose_cave(self.visited)
            next_cave = self.choose_cave(self.unvisited)
            self.create_tunnel(this_cave, next_cave)
            self.visit_cave(next_cave)

    def create_tunnel(self, cave_from, cave_to):
        """ Create a tunnel between cave_from
        and cave_to """
        self.caves[cave_from].append(cave_to)
        self.caves[cave_to].append(cave_from)

    def visit_cave(self, cave_number):
        """ Mark a cave as visited """
        self.visited.append(cave_number)
        self.unvisited.remove(cave_number)

    def choose_cave(self, cave_list):
        """ Pick a cave from a list, provided
        that the cave has less than 3 tunnels."""
        cave_number = choice(cave_list)
        while len(self.caves[cave_number]) >= 3:
            cave_number = choice(cave_list)
        return cave_number

    def print_caves(self):
        """ Print out the current cave structure """
        for number in self.cave_list:
            print number, ":", self.caves[number]
```

2 Set up variables within class

3 Turn functions into methods

```
if __name__ == '__main__':
    caves = Caves(20)
    caves.print_caves()
```

④ Test by creating instance

You start with the syntax Python uses to create a class **①**. It's similar to the creation of a function, except that, by convention, a class name starts with a capital letter (classes are important, after all). The object in brackets is the class that this one inherits from—in this case, Python's generic object class, because you're not inheriting anything.

Most Python classes will have the __init__ method, which is responsible for setting up instances of the class when the class is first created **②**. Did you notice that you've gained a self argument in the method? That's so a method can access variables and share state. All the lists you used in chapter 2 are here, but prefixed with self so they refer to the variables in the instance.

The functions you used to set up the caves are here, and they've received the self treatment, too **③**. Other than that, there aren't many changes to them, which is what you're expecting because they're just functions with an explicit self.

Once you've set up your class, you create an instance of it and call its print_caves() method to test it out **④**. Python runs the __init__ method of the class, which in turn calls setup_caves() and link_caves() and creates your cave network, which you can see from the results of caves.print_caves().

HEY GUYS—I'VE JUST WRITTEN AN ADVENTURE GAME!

WOAH! AN ADVENTURE GAME? DIDN'T THEY DIE OUT IN THE 80S?

What have you gained from putting all the functions inside a class? The main benefit is that all the details of the caves are contained within the instance you've created. You could now create extra cave systems at the same time and not have to worry about them conflicting with each other. From here, you can also extend the class—perhaps including the atmospheric cave names and other functions I've excluded—or adding a method to extend the cave system.

NOTE   Classes are another divide-and-conquer mechanism you can use in your programs. Once you've created an instance, you don't need to think about why it works, just about what you can use it for in your code.

There's one problem with your new Caves class, though. Although you've created the class and it works well, it's still not an object-oriented design. You've just taken your existing functional design and pushed it into a class. If, in the future, you wanted to add extra functionality—such as having treasure to pick up within the caves, more monsters, or other features—they'd be hard to add. Much in the same way that adding functions changed the design of your program back in chapter 2, using classes properly will change the emphasis of your design now.

Object-oriented design

One of the reasons many people prefer object-oriented programs is that objects tend to map well onto the things you deal with in the real world and make it easier for you to think about how they interact when you're developing your program. If you were writing a program to manage your finances, you might create classes called Account, Expense, Income, and Transaction. If you were writing a program to control a factory, you could have classes called Component, ConveyorBelt, Assembly (as in, multiple components joined together), and AssemblyLine.

Let's take a step back and think about the adventure game a bit more. What sorts of things will it have? Well, if you take a traditional approach, the player will be an intrepid adventurer, searching for treasure, fame, and glory in an underground dungeon or cave system filled to the ceiling with monsters. The following figure shows a "back of the envelope" sketch of what your game might look like, the sort of drawing you might use to explain it to a friend.

The fundamental feature you should be addressing is the cave, rather than the cave system as a whole. The mechanics of the lists and functions may have tricked you into thinking the cave system was the important part, but you can get a much cleaner design by thinking at the right level: of individual caves and what's inside them. The

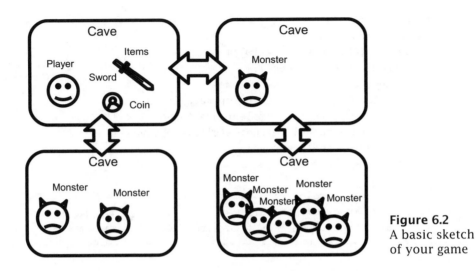

Figure 6.2
A basic sketch
of your game

following listing shows how the caves could be written. You should put it into a file called caves.py; otherwise some of the code later in this chapter won't work.

Listing 6.2   A more object-oriented design

```
from random import choice, shuffle

class Cave(object):
    def __init__(self, name, description):
        self.name = name
        self.description = description
        self.here = []
        self.tunnels = []

    def tunnel_to(self, cave):
        """Create a two-way tunnel"""
        self.tunnels.append(cave)
        cave.tunnels.append(self)

    def __repr__(self):
        return "<Cave " + self.name + ">"

cave_names = [
    "Arched cavern",
    ... ]
```

❶ New Cave object

❷ Each cave "knows" what it's connected to

❸ Add __repr__ method

```
def create_caves():
    shuffle(cave_names)
    caves = [Cave(cave_names[0])]
    for name in cave_names[1:]:
        new_cave = Cave(name, name)
        eligible_caves = [cave for cave in caves
                            if len(cave.tunnels) < 3]
        new_cave.tunnel_to(choice(eligible_caves))
        caves.append(new_cave)
    return caves

if __name__ == '__main__':
    for cave in create_caves():
        print cave.name, "=>", cave.tunnels
```

4 Function to set up caves

5 Print list of caves as a test

You start with the setup for the new Cave object **1**. Rather than set up one list for cave names, another for linking, and a third to tell whether a cave's been visited or not, you store it all within the object itself. When you build lists of caves later, you can easily filter by these attributes. You add a self.here list to store any other objects (such as the player, monsters, and treasure) that might be in the cave, and also a description string, which will describe the cave when the player enters it. You'll ignore these two new values for now.

Because you can easily tell what a cave is linked to **2**, adding a tunnel to another cave is easy: add them into the list of tunnels and add self (self is the current Cave instance) into the list of tunnels. Notice, too, how you're dealing with the caves at the instance level, which makes your program a lot clearer.

WELL, WHAT'S WORLD OF WARCRAFT THEN, EXCEPT AN ADVENTURE GAME WITH PRETTY PICTURES?

I'LL GIVE IT A GO. I USED TO PLAY ADVENTURE BACK BEFORE A.J. WAS BORN.

One last thing you'll do is add a __repr__ method to your class **3**. The one that's built in to the base object is a little unreadable (it will be something like <__main__.Cave object at 0x00B38EF0>), and this makes your program's output look much nicer when you have to print out a cave.

Now all you need to do is to figure out how to link the caves. Borrowing the list of cave names from chapter 2, you can assign each one to a new cave instance, link that instance to an existing cave, and then add it into the caves list ❹. The only even slightly tricky bit is how you find caves to link to. But you can easily figure that out by checking the length of each cave's tunnel list inside a list comprehension. Also, notice that Python doesn't constrain how you solve a problem—you're free to use functions, classes, and bare code wherever you need to.

If you're not convinced that it works, ❺ print out the complete cave list.

The main thing to notice is how much of listing 6.1 is replaced. The original version of Caves had six different methods calling each other; you've replaced that with one class and an external function. As you learned in chapter 2, shorter, simpler code is often a sign that you're on the right track, and an object-oriented design maps well onto your adventure game. Let's move on and tackle the next part of your program: handling input from the player.

Player input

Most adventure games are played by typing instructions at a prompt, things like GO NORTH, GET SWORD, KILL MONSTER, and GET TREASURE. The game then responds with the results of your action, as well as a description of the room you're in and things that are in the room. You'll take the same approach and use some of the properties of objects to make your program easy to extend. Bear in mind that you'll also want to make your code easy to test, so you'll break out your user input into a separate function.

First steps: verbing nouns

You'll start by trying to find a good way to write the "verb noun" interface into your class structure. Normally, because an object will be a noun, and the methods on that object will be verbs, a command like GET SWORD should try to find the sword object in the current room and call its get interface. Designing this way means that, rather than

IN ZAT CASE, PERHAPS FIRST TO COMPLETE ADVENTURE IS NOT HAVINGK TO WORK FRIDAY?

YOU'RE ON!

having one massive `Player` class that knows how to do everything possible in the game, you can instead have more, smaller classes, which are easier to understand (and change and extend).

The following listing has the code for the core of your application: the player object. It's responsible for reading input from the player, as well as finding the right object to call to interpret the command. You put it into a file called player.py.

Listing 6.3   A Player object

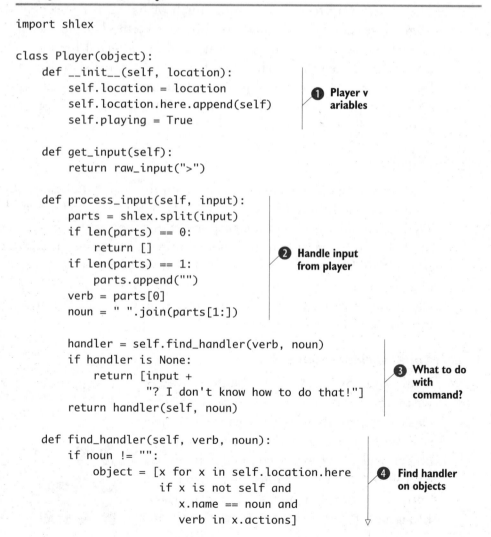

```
import shlex

class Player(object):
    def __init__(self, location):
        self.location = location
        self.location.here.append(self)
        self.playing = True

    def get_input(self):
        return raw_input(">")

    def process_input(self, input):
        parts = shlex.split(input)
        if len(parts) == 0:
            return []
        if len(parts) == 1:
            parts.append("")
        verb = parts[0]
        noun = " ".join(parts[1:])

        handler = self.find_handler(verb, noun)
        if handler is None:
            return [input +
                    "? I don't know how to do that!"]
        return handler(self, noun)

    def find_handler(self, verb, noun):
        if noun != "":
            object = [x for x in self.location.here
                      if x is not self and
                      x.name == noun and
                      verb in x.actions]
```

① Player v ariables

② Handle input from player

③ What to do with command?

④ Find handler on objects

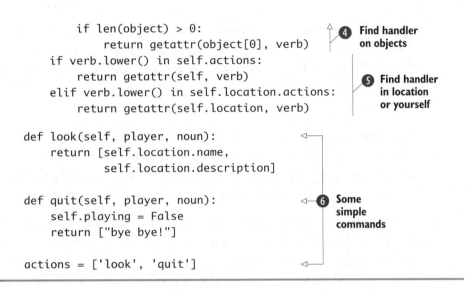

```
        if len(object) > 0:
            return getattr(object[0], verb)
    if verb.lower() in self.actions:
        return getattr(self, verb)
    elif verb.lower() in self.location.actions:
        return getattr(self.location, verb)

def look(self, player, noun):
    return [self.location.name,
            self.location.description]

def quit(self, player, noun):
    self.playing = False
    return ["bye bye!"]

actions = ['look', 'quit']
```

4 Find handler on objects

5 Find handler in location or yourself

6 Some simple commands

The variables you'll initially need within your Player class are pretty straightforward **1**. You add them to a location and tell the game they're playing.

You split up the command here and make sure there's always something in the verb and noun variables **2**. You're using shlex.split() to split your command because it handles quotes much better than the normal split. If, for example, the player types GET "GOLD KEY," then shlex.split() will read GOLD KEY as one part. You join anything after the verb and assume it's part of the noun, so GET GOLD KEY will work, too.

Once you have your command in an easy-to-process format, you try to find a method to call **3**. If the method finder returns None, it means there wasn't a method to handle the command, and you return an error (if you've ever played an adventure game, this will be all too familiar).

When you have your command, you try to find a method to handle it **4**. If you have a noun, you look for an object that matches it—for example, the SWORD in GET SWORD—and see if it can respond. The getattr() function is a good way to do this—it looks for a class attribute or method whose name is set in a variable. If it can't find it, then it passes the command through to either the location or the player (this will help you provide a better interface in the next few sections).

If the player hasn't given you a noun, then it might be a more generic command, like LOOK or QUIT, so you look for it in your current location and the Player object ❺. If neither of those works, then you haven't found one, and you "fall off" the end of the method. This means you return None, which results in an error.

You add two basic commands ❻ to the Player, LOOK and QUIT, so you can get a feel for how they'll work in the finished game. You'll need to add an empty actions list to the Cave class, too; otherwise, this will raise an error if the Player instance can't handle a command.

Now that you have a player, you need to be able to read input from the player and use that input to run the game. A sample framework is shown in the following listing. You make a simple cave, put the player into it, and then loop, reading input until the player is finished playing. Later, you'll probably incorporate this into a Game object, but because Python is flexible, you can leave it as a function while you write and test the other classes.

Listing 6.4   Running your Player class

```
def test():
    import cave
    empty_cave = cave.Cave(
        "Empty Cave",                              ❶ Set up test
        "A desolate, empty cave, "                    environment
        "waiting for someone to fill it.")
    player = Player(empty_cave)

    print player.location.name
    print player.location.description
    while player.playing:                          ❷ Main loop
        input = player.get_input()
        result = player.process_input(input)
        print "\n".join(result)

if __name__ == '__main__':
    test()
```

Your `Player` class needs a location to work properly, so you set up a test cave here and put the player into it ❶. A simple description and name is all you need to get going.

ARE YOU PLAYING GREG'S ADVENTURE GAME TOO?

WELL, I'M A LITTLE WAY INTO IT.

I'M COMPLETELY STUCK—I CAN'T EVEN GET PAST THAT FIRST ORC.

Once you've done that, you get input from the player and pass it to the `process_input()` method, which will run your code and return the results as a list of strings ❷. You then print them one to a line using the `join()` method of the `"\n"` string. When the player has issued the quit command, the `player.playing` variable will be false, and you stop the program.

If you run the adventure program now, you should be able to give it commands such as LOOK and QUIT. It's simple stuff, but you'll see how to extend the interface in the next section.

Treasure!

Let's start adding some more exciting things to the game. First, you'd like to be able to give the player some equipment or treasure early on, to draw them into the game and get them involved. It's not an adventure without treasure or a sword, so let's add those first. Before you do, though, you'll need to think a bit more about your design.

Where should your methods go?

You'll obviously need to interact with your items, which means you'll at least want to be able to do things like GET SWORD, LOOK SWORD, and DROP SWORD. With your current way of doing things, that means there will need to be a method somewhere to handle GET, LOOK, and DROP.

One option is to store it in the `Player` class—after all, it's the player doing the getting and dropping. It's tempting to think along these lines, but when doing any object-oriented programming, you'll want to delegate as much responsibility as possible. For example, later on you'll probably want to add objects that the player can't pick up, like a heavy chest or a statue. That's fine; add a check to see if the object has an immovable flag set. What if the player can pick up the chest if they have the gilded girdle of strength? Hmm, another check. You can see where this is going—by the time you finish the game, you might have 5 or 6 (or 20) conditions in the get() method on your player.

NOTE   Class design can be a tricky thing when you're first starting out. The main thing to remember is that experience counts, so you'll get better with practice. Also, don't forget that you can experiment with different designs and pick the best one.

A better way is to make the objects themselves responsible for judging whether they can be picked up. A chest "knows" it's heavy, and can check to make sure the player has the right items in their inventory before allowing itself to be picked up. It sounds odd, but the Player object shouldn't be responsible for how heavy objects are or how monsters fight, and adding things like that to the Player object will make it too complicated. Let's see how you'd program some objects that can be looked at; then, you'll modify them so they can be picked up.

Listing 6.5   An object that can be looked at

```
class Item(object):
    def __init__(self, name, description, location):
        self.name = name
        self.description = description
        self.location = location
        location.here.append(self)

    actions = ['look']

    def look(self, player, noun):
        return [self.description]
```

The things the Item needs to know are pretty much the same as for the Player and Cave objects: what its name is and where it is. You can feed all those in when you create an Item instance.

Initially, your item responds to one command: LOOK. When the player issues a LOOK ITEM command with the item's name as a noun, this is the method that will be called; all it does is return the item's description.

Finding the treasure

Additionally, you'll want to modify the description of the cave so the player knows what items are in a particular location. While you're at it, you'll follow the lead set so far and move the look() method from the Player class;

delete the method from Player, and add this one into the Cave class.

Listing 6.6   Modifying the look() command

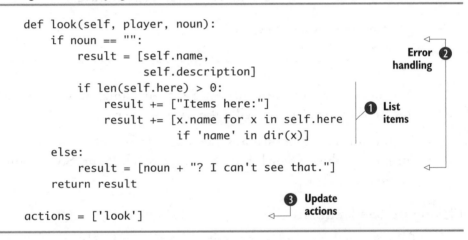

```
def look(self, player, noun):
    if noun == "":
        result = [self.name,
                    self.description]
        if len(self.here) > 0:
            result += ["Items here:"]
            result += [x.name for x in self.here
                        if 'name' in dir(x)]
    else:
        result = [noun + "? I can't see that."]
    return result

actions = ['look']
```

Error handling ❷

List items ❶

Update actions ❸

The main change to this method is to list all the items in the location and place them under the description ❶. Without this, the player won't know there's a sword in the cave, unless they happen to guess there might be.

This function will also be called if the player tries to refer to something that doesn't exist (such as LOOK AARDVARK). If there's no aardvark in the room, you need to return an error ❷.

Don't forget to update the actions the Cave object can handle ❸ and remove 'look' from

the Player class—otherwise, it will continue to try to handle the LOOK command.

Listing 6.7 Updating your setup

```
      ...
      "A desolate, empty cave, "
      "waiting for someone to fill it.")

import item
sword = item.Item("sword",
    "A pointy sword.", empty_cave)
coin = item.Item("coin", "A shiny gold coin. "
    "Your first piece of treasure!", empty_cave)

player = Player(empty_cave)
...
```

Add items into your adventure! Set their name, description, and location, and the Item object will take care of the rest.

If you run the adventure now, you should be able to look at your treasure and a shiny sword, but you can't reach them. So … tantalizingly … close …

Picking up the treasure

All you need now is for the objects to respond to being picked up. You need to make two updates: the first is to the objects, to give them get() and drop() methods, and the second is to update the Player class so it can carry things. The next listing shows how you can add those commands to the game.

Listing 6.8 Items that will let themselves be picked up

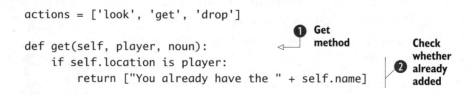

```
actions = ['look', 'get', 'drop']

def get(self, player, noun):                    ❶ Get
    if self.location is player:                     method
        return ["You already have the " + self.name]
```

❶ Get method

❷ Check whether already added

```
        self.location.here.remove(self)
        self.location = player                    ❶ Get method
        player.inventory.append(self)
        return ["You get the " + self.name]

    def drop(self, player, noun):
        if self not in player.inventory:
            return ["You don't have the " + self.name]
        player.inventory.remove(self)             ❸ Drop method
        player.location.here.append(self)
        self.location = player.location
        return ["You drop the " + self.name]
```

The get() method itself is straightforward ❶. The object needs to remove itself from the here array in the current location and put itself into the player's inventory (you'll make that list in a minute) and set its current location. Once you've done that, you return a message to let the player know.

If you run the previous code without this check ❷ it will work fine; but if the player tries to pick up the item again, your program will crash, because it can't remove an item from a list if it isn't there.

The drop() method is pretty much the same as the get() method, only in reverse ❸. Just like the previous get() method, you need to check that the object is in the player's inventory before you move it back to the location you're in.

The next listing updates the Player class so it can hold objects, adds some commands to tell you what you're carrying, and outputs error messages. Let's also look in the inventory when trying to find handlers for commands.

Listing 6.9 Updates to the Player class

```
class Player(object):
    def __init__(self, location):
        self.location = location
```

```
        self.location.here.append(self)
        self.playing = True
        self.inventory = []                    ◁          Player's
                                                        ❶ inventory
    ...

    actions = ['quit', 'inv', 'get', 'drop']

    def get(self, player, noun):
        return [noun + "? I can't see that here."]   ❷ Add error
                                                        handlers
    def drop(self, player, noun):
        return [noun + "? I don't have that!"]

    def inv(self, player, noun):
        result = ["You have:"]
        if self.inventory:
            result += [x.name for x in self.inventory]   ❸ Inventory
        else:                                              command
            result += ["nothing!"]
        return result


    ...


    def find_handler(self, verb, noun):
        # Try and find the object
        if noun != "":                           ❹ Check inventory
            object = [x for x in                    when finding
                self.location.here + self.inventory ◁  handlers
                if x is not self and
                ...
```

say 'xyzzy'

Nice try Sid, but your
spell is too old.
The orc hits you.
You die.

TYPE
TAK

To start with, the player needs to be able to carry things around with an inventory ❶. The easiest option is to add a list to your class. When the player picks up objects, they'll be appended to this list.

These error handlers ❷ are similar to the error handler you wrote for the Cave class. If you try to get something that's not in the current location, then these methods will be called to handle the GET and DROP commands.

Players should be able to remember what they've found so far, so ❸ is a command that will list everything they're carrying.

The final change is to check the items in your inventory when looking for handlers ❹. This way, players can LOOK at or DROP things in their inventory.

Now you can pick up the sword and shiny coin, as well as look at them. You can also put them back down again (although that's much less adventurous). Your trusty sword and first piece of treasure in hand, it's time to venture further into the caves.

Further into the caves

An adventure isn't an adventure without some sort of exploration. In most games, you move around by issuing commands like GO NORTH, or just NORTH or N for short. As you travel, the game will update the descriptions to tell you about the area you've just moved through. You'll set up your movement commands in the

same way you set up the other commands, but you'll add some short-cuts, too, so typing your movement is easier.

First, let's look at how you add the directions themselves into the Cave class. Then, you'll create the commands that let your player move around.

Listing 6.10   Adding movement to the Cave class

```
class Cave(object):
    directions = {
        'north' : 'south',              ❶ List of
        'east'  : 'west',                 directions
        'south' : 'north',
        'west'  : 'east' }

    def __init__(self, name="Cave", description=""):
        ...
        self.tunnels = {}
        for direction in self.directions.keys():    ❷ Add tunnels
            self.tunnels[direction] = None            to cave
```

```
def exits(self):
    return [direction for direction, cave
                in self.tunnels.items()
                if cave is not None]
```
3 List all valid exits

```
def look(self, player, noun):
    if noun == "":

        ...

        if len(self.exits()) > 0:
            result += ['Exits:']
            for direction in self.exits():
                result += [direction + ": " +
                    self.tunnels[direction].name]
        else:
            result += ['Exits:', 'none.']
```
4 Add exits to look command

```
def tunnel_to(self, direction, cave):
    """Create a two-way tunnel"""
    if direction not in self.directions:
        raise ValueError(direction +
            " is not a valid direction!")
    reverse_direction = self.directions[direction]
    if cave.tunnels[reverse_direction] is not None:
        raise ValueError("Cave " + str(cave) +
            " already has a cave to the " +
            reverse_direction + "!")
    self.tunnels[direction] = cave
    cave.tunnels[reverse_direction] = self
```
5 Tunnel from one cave to another

6 Exceptions to handle bad behavior

5 Tunnel from one cave to another

The first part of the changes adds a list of valid directions into the Cave class **1**, so you know all the directions you can travel. You can also use this to find the opposite direction (you'll need that in a minute).

When you're creating each cave, you'll need to set up the basic data structure you'll use to store the caves that can be reached in each direction **2**. For now, they're all None, which means there's no other cave that way.

3 is a convenience method to list the directions of all the exits for a particular cave. It's pretty simple—a list comprehension over self.tunnels—but it makes your code much easier to follow when you can access cave.exits(). Don't let the order the functions are written in fool you—the code for this method was pulled from look when that started to look ugly.

Players will want to know which way they can go from cave to cave, so **4** lists all the valid exits. If there aren't any, then you let them know that, too.

You also need a way to create tunnels between your caves. Linking one way is easy: you put the cave in self.tunnels in the right direction. But you'd like your tunnels to be two-way, so you look up the reverse direction in the list and add a link to yourself from the target cave **5**.

If this method looked a little strange, it's because you added some exceptions to catch error cases when linking tunnels **6**. The raise() command will create errors similar to the ones you've been seeing so far: for example, when you've mistyped something. In this case you're effectively creating your own type of object, much like an integer or a string, so it's much better to behave like one and raise an exception rather than print an error or ignore the bad input. You'll be crashing close to the source of the problem and giving a clear error message, which makes it much easier to troubleshoot your programs.

TIP   When you're designing classes like Cave (which are effectively library classes), it's always a good idea to catch cases like this and raise an exception where possible. That way, when you're using the class later, it's obvious when you've made a mistake.

Now you have a Cave class that can store directions and links to other caves, as well as describe those directions to the player. Let's now add some commands to let the player move between caves, as shown in the following listing.

Listing 6.11   *Commands to move between caves*

```
def go(self, player, noun):
    if noun not in self.directions:
        return [noun + "? "
            "I don't know that direction!"]
    if self.tunnels[noun] is None:
        return ["Can't go " + noun + " from here!"]
```

1 Check player input

```
        self.here.remove(player)
        self.tunnels[noun].here.append(player)
        player.location = self.tunnels[noun]        ❷ Move player
        return (['You go ' + noun] +
                self.tunnels[noun].look(player, ''))

    def north(self, player, noun):
        return self.go(player, 'north')
    n = north
    def east(self, player, noun):
        return self.go(player, 'east')
    e = east                                         ❸ Add some
    def south(self, player, noun):                     shortcuts
        return self.go(player, 'south')
    s = south
    def west(self, player, noun):
        return self.go(player, 'west')
    w = west
    l = look

    actions = ['look', 'l', 'go',                    ❹ Update actions
               'north', 'east', 'south', 'west',       for Cave class
               'n', 'e', 's', 'w']
```

The basic command you're adding is called GO (as in, GO NORTH). First, you need to check the direction the player entered, to make sure it's valid and that there's a cave in that direction ❶.

Once you're sure it's valid, you can go ahead and move the player ❷. The mechanics are straightforward: remove the player from the current cave, add the player to the new one, and update the player's location. You also append the new cave's description onto the results of the command, to make life easier on the player and save wear and tear on their keyboard.

You can also make life easier by providing shortcuts for common commands ❸. Typing GO NORTH over and over again gets tedious, so you allow the player to use NORTH or just N, and similar for each of the other cardinal directions. Behind the scenes, these commands call the original go() method, so there's no difference in how they behave.

The last thing you need to do is update the list of valid actions for the Cave class ❹. You also add a shortcut for the look() command while you're at it.

```
say 'xyzzy'
           |
The orc laughs at your
feeble spell, old timer.
The orc hits you.
You die.
```

There, you're done. Notice how you've split the functionality between the player and the location they're in? This is a normal feature of good object-oriented design, where the objects have well-separated responsibilities. In this case, the cave object is responsible for keeping track of its exits and where they go, and the player object can use that information from inside its go() command. If, later, something else might make use of directions, you don't have to extract the code from the player object, or wherever you've hidden it, to make the new functionality work.

The player still needs somewhere to move to, though, so the next listing extends the previous cave-generating function to help out.

Listing 6.12   Creating a cave network

```
Class Cave(object):
        ...
        def can_tunnel_to(self):
        return [v for v in self.tunnels.values()          ❶ Another convenience
                if v is None] != []                             method

cave_names = [
    "Arched cavern",
    ...
    "Spooky Chasm",
]
                                          ❷ Modify existing
def create_caves():                   ←      function
    shuffle(cave_names)
    caves = [Cave(cave_names[0])]
    for name in cave_names[1:]:
        new_cave = Cave(name)
        print caves
        eligible_caves = [cave for cave in caves
                          if cave.can_tunnel_to()]        ❸ Pick cave
        old_cave = choice(eligible_caves)                     from list
```

```
        directions = [direction for direction, cave
                         in old_cave.tunnels.items()
                         if cave is None]
        direction = choice(directions)
        old_cave.tunnel_to(direction, new_cave)
        caves.append(new_cave)
    return caves
```

4 **Pick direction to link it to**

5 **Link in new cave**

```
player.py:
if __name__ == '__main__':
    import cave
    caves = cave.create_caves()

    cave1 = caves[0]
    import item
    sword = item.Item("sword", "A pointy sword.", cave1)
    coin = item.Item("coin", "A shiny gold coin. "
        "Your first piece of treasure!", cave1)

    player = Player(cave1)
    print '\n'.join(player.location.look(player, ''))
    while player.playing:
        input = player.get_input()
        result = player.process_input(input)
        print "\n".join(result)
```

6 **Update game setup in players.py**

You start with another convenience method **1**. In a minute you'll see how it's used, but it's to tell you whether a cave can be linked to (or not, if all four directions are occupied).

This function **2** is a modification of the previous create_caves() that you wrote all the way back in listing 6.2. The main difference is that this one picks a direction as well as a cave, but other than that, it's the standard connected cave structure.

You pick the next cave to link to by using the can_tunnel_to() convenience method in a list comprehension **3**.

You also need to pick an empty direction to link your cave against ❹. The choice function will fail if you don't have any directions, but you're not too worried about that happening because `can_tunnel_to()` method has already told you that it has at least one.

Once you have your cave with a spare slot, it's easy to link the new cave in ❺. You also add your new cave to the list so other new caves can be linked to it, too.

Finally, update the game setup (in player.py) to use the new cave system ❻. Rather than have only one empty, desolate cave, you now put everything into the first cave in the list, including the player. Other than that, it's pretty much the same.

Now when you run players.py, you should see some exits from your starting position, as well as the normal description and items. You can pick up your sword, move around, drop it in another location, and come back to it.

Congratulations, you've created a world! Feel free to go and explore it. When you come back, you'll add some more parts.

Here there be monsters!

You now have a player, items, and treasure to collect. All that's left to put in your adventure is sudden, painful death, also known as danger and excitement. You'll add to your game some monsters that will move around the map and that might attack the player if they're in the same cave and feeling nasty, or else pick up any treasure lying around. The player can attack the monsters, too, and loot their treasure.

Creating your monsters

Let's think about that for a second. Don't the monsters sound awfully familiar? Let's draw up a chart to help.

Monster	Player
Moves around the map	Moves around the map
Collects treasure	Collects treasure
Attacks the player	Attacks monsters

PITR!!!

The monsters and the player seem to share an awful lot in common. In a function-based program, you'd look at this and recognize that you need to avoid duplication, but how do you do that with an object-oriented program? The answer is to subclass `Player`, commonly referred to as *inheritance*.

Inheritance is a fancy way of saying "make a slightly different copy of my class that does this and this differently." In the case of the monsters in your game, they'll behave much the same way, but instead of the player telling them what to do next, the monsters figure it out for themselves. The monsters will also need to have a name and description so the player can look at them. That means their `__init__` and `get_input` functions need to be different, but you'll keep most of the rest of the `Player` class intact. The next listing is a first draft of the new `Monster` class.

Listing 6.13   Adding monsters to the game

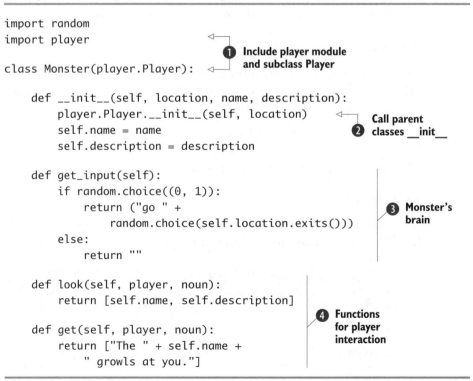

```
import random
import player                                    ❶ Include player module
                                                   and subclass Player
class Monster(player.Player):

    def __init__(self, location, name, description):
        player.Player.__init__(self, location)   ❷ Call parent
        self.name = name                           classes __init__
        self.description = description

    def get_input(self):
        if random.choice((0, 1)):
            return ("go " +                       ❸ Monster's
                random.choice(self.location.exits()))   brain
        else:
            return ""

    def look(self, player, noun):
        return [self.name, self.description]
                                                  ❹ Functions
    def get(self, player, noun):                    for player
        return ["The " + self.name +                interaction
            " growls at you."]
```

The first thing you need to do is to import the `player` module ❶. Once that's done, you can use `player.Player` instead of `object` when you create your class. Now, instead of using the base `object`, Python will look in `player.Player` when it tries to find an attribute or method that isn't defined directly in the `Monster` class.

When you're initializing your `monster` class, you'll also need to initialize the parent class to make sure everything's set up properly ❷. In this case, the main thing that needs to be set is the location of the monster.

Here's where you can see the similarities between the `player` and `monster` classes. Your monster AI is a different version of `get_input` that generates a command rather than asking the player to provide one ❸. To start, you'll keep things simple, returning either a blank string to do nothing or a random direction to move around (making good use of the cave class's `exits()` function).

The player will want to try to interact with the monster, so you need to provide mechanisms for that to occur ❹. `look()` is copied from the `Item` class and returns the monster's description, and `get()` gives an amusing error message.

Now you have a `monster` class that is fully capable of interacting with the world in the same way the player can, and that will see all the same information. This is important for a few reasons. Let's take a closer look at those reasons and how they tie in to object-oriented design.

Some object-oriented design tips

The first reason to use inheritance is that you can rely on having the common functionality of the base class, which reduces the amount of "special casing" that your program needs in order to run. You don't need two separate game loops, one for the player and another for the monsters, or program code that looks like `if player then: ... else if monster then: ...`. Instead, you can treat monsters and players identically.

```
You are at Wall Street.
A capitalist oppressor is here.

\    attack capitalist
You smite the capitalist |
with your hammer.
You smite the capitalist
with your sickle.
The capitalist dies.
```

The second reason to use inheritance is that it makes your program easier to extend; this effectively builds an interface which monsters, players, and whatever else you can think of can interact with the world. If you needed to add a third type of actor to your world, you only need to write the parts specific to that actor.

The final reason is that using inheritance greatly reduces the amount of code you have to write and makes your program much easier to understand, which is always good, whether your program is object-oriented or not.

The other point to note is that this isn't the only way you can design your classes. A different, possibly better, way is to create a third class (called something like Mobile or Actor) with all the common functionality between the player and the monster, and then have both the player and monster classes inherit from that. In object-oriented design, this is normally referred to as an *abstract class*. You're not supposed to create instances of Actor; instead, you inherit from it, add the bits that are missing, and then create an instance from your subclass.

NOTE   Object-oriented terminology can be confusing, but once you've seen a few examples, you'll find it pretty straightforward. Just relate it back to something you know well, like the Cave, Player, and Monster classes in this chapter.

In this case, the advantages of specifying an abstract class aren't immediately clear because you only have two classes. But, it's an option in the future if you find there's functionality that the Player class needs but monsters shouldn't have access to, or vice versa.

Another design point is that, up until now, you've favored composition over inheritance. Inheritance is normally referred to as an "is/a" relationship: a player is an actor, a monster is an actor, too. Composition, on the other hand, is a "has/a" relationship: a cave has a player in it, a player has a number of items. Composition tends to couple your objects less tightly—they have to interact via method calls and inspecting each other's values—unlike inheritance, which automatically inserts the methods of one object into the other. Most of the time, you'll want to use composition; but when used in the right situation, inheritance can

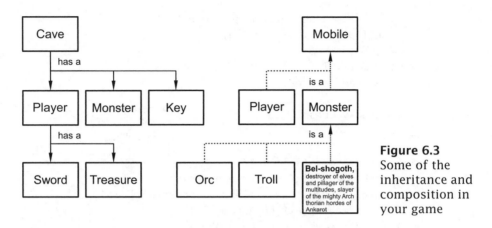

Figure 6.3
Some of the inheritance and composition in your game

make a big difference. Figure 6.3 shows the difference between composition and inheritance in your game so far.

Tying it all together

Now that you have the player and monster classes, you need to make some changes to how the game handles the player when it runs. You no longer want the special case of getting input only for the player; your monsters have equal rights, too! You'd also like all the functions you've been using up until now enclosed within a class, so it's easier for them to interact properly. The following listing features a class that does just that—you can use it to set up a game, build caves, and gather input until the player has finished.

Listing 6.14 A Game class

```
import random
import item, player, monster, cave
import random

class Game(object):
    def __init__(self):                                    ① Move game initialization
        self.caves = self.create_caves()                      to __init__
        cave1 = self.caves[0]
        sword = item.Item("sword", "A pointy sword.", cave1)
        coin = item.Item("coin", "A shiny gold coin. "
            "Your first piece of treasure!", cave1)
        orc = monster.Monster(cave1, 'orc',
```

```
                        'A generic dungeon monster')
        self.player = player.Player(cave1)

cave_names = [
    "Arched cavern",
    ...
    "Spooky Chasm",
]

def create_caves(self):
    random.shuffle(self.cave_names)
    caves = [cave.Cave(self.cave_names[0])]
    for name in self.cave_names[1:]:
        new_cave = cave.Cave(name)
        eligible_caves = [each_cave for each_cave in caves
                          if each_cave.can_tunnel_to()]
        old_cave = random.choice(eligible_caves)
        directions = [direction for direction, each_cave
                      in old_cave.tunnels.items()
                      if each_cave is None]
        direction = random.choice(directions)
        old_cave.tunnel_to(direction, new_cave)
        caves.append(new_cave)
    return caves

def do_input(self):
    get_input_from = [thing for cave in self.caves
        for thing in cave.here
        if 'get_input' in dir(thing)]
    for thing in get_input_from:
        thing.events = []
        thing.input = thing.get_input()

def do_update(self):
    things_to_update = [thing for cave in self.caves
        for thing in cave.here
        if 'update' in dir(thing)]
    for thing in things_to_update:
        thing.update(

def run(self):
    while self.player.playing:
        self.do_input()
        self.do_update()
```

1 Move game initialization to __init__

2 Get input from player and monsters

3 Act on input gathered

4 New game loop

```
if __name__ == '__main__':
    game = Game()
    game.run()
```

⬅ ❺ main() section gets much simpler

This __init__ function contains all the setup code you've been running from the Player class so far, creating items, monsters, and the player. __init__ is a much more sensible place to put it ❶.

Next, you ask each actor in the game what it's going to do next ❷. Note that the dir() function applies equally well to your own classes as it does to Python's built-in objects. Splitting the input away from the processing like this means one actor can't make decisions based on what other actors are about to do, which makes the game easier to understand for both the player and yourself.

Once you've gathered all the input, each actor will act in turn ❸. The mechanism is much the same: build a list of actors and then iterate over them. If you want to be fair, you should probably shuffle this list to determine who acts first, but the monsters don't care about fairness.

Here's your main game loop ❹. It's the same as the one you had previously, except it calls out to do_input and do_update, and the player and monsters store their output in a result list. You've also created a separate events list, to store things that happen during each turn.

The final benefit is that you now have a nice clean __main__ loop ❺. All the tricky code that used to be here has been broken into bits and contained within methods.

The last thing you need to do is to add an update function to the Player class. When the code checks all the objects in the game world, it will see the player, and everything derived from the Player class, as things that need to be updated:

loot corpse of capitalism

You loot the corpse of capitalism.
You have found the means of production, stolen from the workers!

go north

```
Class Player(object):
    ...
    def __init__(self, location):
        self.name = "Player"
        self.description = "The Player"
```

```
...
def update(self):
    self.result = self.process_input(self.input)
```

All this does is call `process_input` with whatever the player's input has been, and store the return value—which will be a list of strings—in `self.result`. You also need to add a name to the `Player` class too, because `Monster` will be calling `process_input` on the player when they're trying to run commands.

If you run your program now, you should see an orc in the room with you. Press the Enter key a few times to simulate waiting a while, and the orc should leave for another room. If you search around, you should be able to find the orc aimlessly wandering the caves. Unless you want your game to resemble a European art house piece exploring the futility of existence, though, you'd better start adding some more interesting game elements.

Danger and excitement

The final part of your game will be to allow the players and monsters to attack each other. Some sort of element of competition is essential in games, whether you're competing on combat, speed, who can build the biggest city, exploring, or building the best house. In this case, you're writing a dungeon adventure, so combat is pretty much essential—anyone who's played Dungeons and Dragons will be expecting to be able to hit orcs. Because combat will be between the player and monsters, you'll start with the `Player` class and add an attack method, as per the following listing.

```
You are in a factory.
There are workers here.

    give means of production
    to workers

You give the means of
production to the workers.
The workers rejoice!
Congratulations!
You have won
the game!
```

Listing 6.15 Attacking other objects

```
class Player(object):

    def __init__(self, location):
```

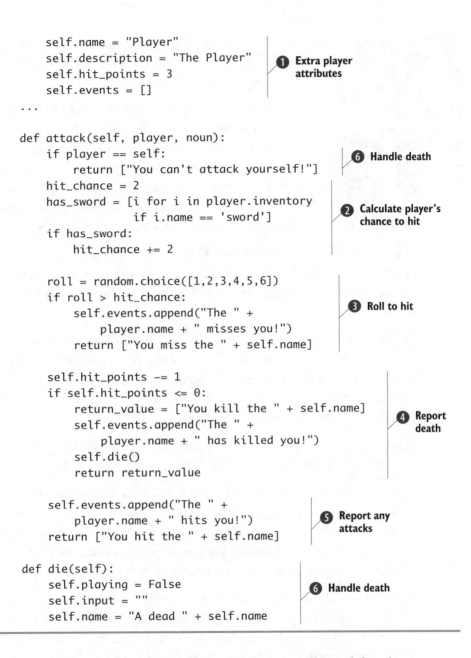

```
            self.name = "Player"
            self.description = "The Player"        ❶ Extra player
            self.hit_points = 3                       attributes
            self.events = []
    ...

    def attack(self, player, noun):
        if player == self:                         ❻ Handle death
            return ["You can't attack yourself!"]
        hit_chance = 2
        has_sword = [i for i in player.inventory
                    if i.name == 'sword']          ❷ Calculate player's
        if has_sword:                                 chance to hit
            hit_chance += 2

        roll = random.choice([1,2,3,4,5,6])
        if roll > hit_chance:                      ❸ Roll to hit
            self.events.append("The " +
                player.name + " misses you!")
            return ["You miss the " + self.name]

        self.hit_points -= 1
        if self.hit_points <= 0:
            return_value = ["You kill the " + self.name]
            self.events.append("The " +           ❹ Report
                player.name + " has killed you!")     death
            self.die()
            return return_value

        self.events.append("The " +
            player.name + " hits you!")            ❺ Report any
        return ["You hit the " + self.name]           attacks

    def die(self):
        self.playing = False
        self.input = ""                            ❻ Handle death
        self.name = "A dead " + self.name
```

You start by adding some extra attributes you'll need for the attack()
method ❶. hit_points is pretty obvious, events is for storing things that
happened to the player (or which they saw) during the turn, and

you've already added a name and description so you can handle combat easily whether the target is a monster or a player.

You'll use a simple combat mechanism: calculate a to-hit number, roll a die, and, if the number rolled is under or equal to the to-hit roll, the player or monster is hit ❷. The to-hit number will normally be 2, but if you have a sword, then it will be 4. Remember that the attack() command will be called on the object that's being attacked, rather than the one doing the attacking.

Next, you roll to see if you hit ❸ — it's a random choice from 1 to 6. If the number rolled is greater than the to-hit number, then you miss. Before you exit, though, you tell both the attacker and the attacked what's happened.

If you're hit, then you lose a hit point. If the hit points are reduced to zero or below, then you die ❹. If it's the player that has died, this will trigger the end of the game. Either way, you report it, but generate the messages before you call out to the die() function, because that may modify it ("You kill the A dead orc!").

If you're not dead yet, then the situation is much the same as a miss: report it to the attacker and the target, and move on ❺.

Because there could potentially be a lot of bookkeeping to be done when a monster dies, you pull that out into its own method ❻. You mark yourself as not playing, cancel any outstanding orders, and change your name to reflect your newly deceased status. You also add a sanity check to make sure you can't attack yourself.

That's all you need to do to enable combat in your game! Because the classes are all nicely encapsulated, there's no need to make any changes to the Cave, Item, and Game classes. Well, not entirely. If you think back to the last chapter or run the code, you'll see an obvious problem: the monsters don't fight back. Worse, after you've killed them, they still run around! Both of these problems are easy to fix with a simple upgrade to the monster's AI, as shown in the next listing.

Listing 6.16   Updating your monster's AI

```
def get_input(self):
    if not self.playing:                    ❶ Monster doesn't
        return ""                              know it's dead
    player_present = [x for x in self.location.here
                      if x.name == "Player"]
                                            ❷ Monster
    if player_present:                         doesn't like
        return "attack " + player_present[0].name    player very
    if random.choice((0, 1)):                  much
        return "go " + random.choice(self.location.exits())
    else:
        return ""
```

Dead monsters tell no tales. If it's dead, then it shouldn't be generating any input at all ❶; without this section, you'd have an undead orc running around your caves after you kill it.

Next, you can let the monster get revenge on the player ❷. If the monster can see the player in the cave, then you issue an attack order, exactly as the player would if they could see the monster. Take that, player! If the monster can't see them, then it goes back to its random wandering around the caves.

Now you have all the elements of an adventure game: a network of rooms to explore, monsters to attack the player, and items and treasure to collect to help players in their quest. Armed with the code in this chapter and your imagination, you should be able to create pretty much any type of adventure game you like.

Where to from here?

The classes and methods that have been introduced in this chapter have only scratched the surface of what you can add to your game. Depending on the type of game you prefer, you can take your development in any direction. Here are some ideas on how you could extend the game you've written so far.

Add more monsters and treasure

Currently, there's only one orc and a couple of different items. You could add more types of monsters and treasure (or more powerful weapons or weapons that affect monsters differently). You'd also want a score that the player can access with a score method on the player, and that should also be printed out when the player quits, or dies.

Extend combat and items

You could extend the Item class or Player.attack() method, to add other items that might be useful, such as armor or rope, and something to use them on. If you're adding lots of weapons or armor with different to-hit modifiers, you might want to think about ways to simplify how to find the amount you add or subtract from the to-hit roll or damage done.

Add more adventure

Some adventure games are more about exploring atmospheric locations than killing monsters. You could add proper descriptions during the setup phase, or have a pre-generated cave system instead of a randomly generated one, and add specific methods to handle particular events—such as a boat that sets sail, or a castle drawbridge that you can raise or lower.

Experiment with verbs and nouns

You might want to play around with adding different methods to the Item class, to see what you can do when you override built-in methods. For example, you could add the movement methods go(), north(), and so on to an item, and make a door that's impassable until the player has the right key. That's also possible with a static monster that needs the right magic sword or a secret password in order to pass. There's also scope for allowing other items to handle particular commands if the game can't find the original object.

Investigate some more advanced features of classes

It's important to note that you haven't dealt with all the functionality of classes, just the common parts you'll deal with in 95% of your programs. There are other advanced class features, such as missing method and attribute handling, properties, and mix-in classes, that we'll introduce in later chapters as they become relevant. If you're already familiar with classes from other languages, though, you might want to have a look through Python's class documentation to see what else you can do with them.

Summary

We've covered a number of object-oriented topics and design issues in this chapter and looked at how classes can help make your programs clearer and easier to understand. In particular, we addressed the following:

- How classes can encapsulate data and functions and initialize them to make instances, which you can reason about and understand much more easily than separate data and functions
- How classes can interact, calling each other's methods and looking at data to make decisions about what to do
- That classes can be combined using composition (where instances can contain other instances) and inheritance (where classes can be declared to be particular subtypes of another class)

We haven't covered all the features of Python's class system yet—far from it—but you now have a firm grasp of the fundamentals of how classes are used and, more important, how to use them to solve problems in your programs. In future chapters, you'll be making more use of classes and their more advanced features. In the next chapter, though, we'll be taking a look at another Python feature that is closely related to the function: the generator.

7

Sufficiently advanced technology...

This chapter covers

- *More advanced features of classes*
- *Generators*
- *Functional programming*

In this chapter, we're going to be looking at some of the more advanced tasks Python can do. In chapter 1, you learned that Python is known as a multi-paradigm language, which means it doesn't confine you to just one way of doing things. There are three main styles of programming: imperative, object-oriented, and functional. Python lets you work with all three, and even mix and match them where necessary.

We've already covered imperative and most of object-oriented programming in the chapters so far, so this chapter will focus mostly on functional programming and the more advanced parts of object-oriented programming in Python.

Object orientation

Let's start by taking a second look at how object-oriented classes should be organized, using two separate methods: mixin classes and the super() method.

Mixin classes

Sometimes you don't need an entire class to be able to do something. Perhaps you only need to add logging, or the ability to save the state of your class to disk. In these cases, you could add the functionality to a base class, or to each class that needs it, but that can get pretty repetitive. There's an easier way, called a *mixin class*.

The idea is that a mixin class contains only a small, self-contained piece of functionality, usually a few methods or variables, which are unlikely to conflict with anything in the child class. Take a look at this listing, which creates a Loggable class.

Listing 7.1   A logging mixin

```
class Loggable(object):
    """Mixin class to add logging."""
    log_file_name = 'log.txt'
    def log(self, log_line):
        file(self.log_file_name).write(log_line)

class MyClass(Loggable):
    """A class that you've written."""
    log_file_name = "myclass_log.txt"
    def do_something(self):
        self.log("I did something!')
```

The mixin class is defined in exactly the same way as a regular class. Here, you add a class variable for the file name and a method to write a line to that file. If you want to use the mixin class, all you need to do is inherit from it.

Once you're in the child class, all of the mixin's methods and variables become available, and you can override them if you need to.

Using simple file logging like this works well, but the following listing features a slightly more involved version that uses Python's built-in logging module. The advantage of this version is that, as your program grows, you can take advantage of some of the different logging methods—you can send it to your system's logs, or automatically roll over to a new file if the old one gets too big.

Listing 7.2   Using Python's logging module

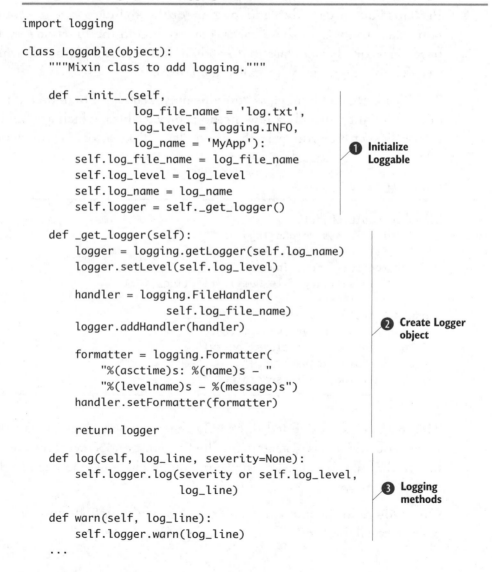

```
import logging

class Loggable(object):
    """Mixin class to add logging."""

    def __init__(self,
                 log_file_name = 'log.txt',
                 log_level = logging.INFO,
                 log_name = 'MyApp'):
        self.log_file_name = log_file_name
        self.log_level = log_level
        self.log_name = log_name
        self.logger = self._get_logger()

    def _get_logger(self):
        logger = logging.getLogger(self.log_name)
        logger.setLevel(self.log_level)

        handler = logging.FileHandler(
                     self.log_file_name)
        logger.addHandler(handler)

        formatter = logging.Formatter(
            "%(asctime)s: %(name)s - "
            "%(levelname)s - %(message)s")
        handler.setFormatter(formatter)

        return logger

    def log(self, log_line, severity=None):
        self.logger.log(severity or self.log_level,
                        log_line)

    def warn(self, log_line):
        self.logger.warn(log_line)
    ...
```

➊ **Initialize Loggable**

➋ **Create Logger object**

➌ **Logging methods**

```
class MyClass(Loggable):
    """A class that you've written."""

    def __init__(self):
        Loggable.__init__(self,
                         log_file_name = 'log2.txt')
        #super(MyClass, self).__init__(
        #                  log_file_name = 'log2.txt')

    def do_something(self):
        print "Doing something!"
        self.log("I did something!")
        self.log("Some debugging info", logging.DEBUG)
        self.warn("Something bad happened!")

test = MyClass()
test.do_something()
```

4 **How do you call Loggable.__init__()?**

5 **Create class and logging methods**

Rather than rely on class methods, it's better to instantiate them properly from an __init__ method **1**. This way, you can take care of any extra initialization you need to do, or require that variables be specified on creation.

2 is all the setup you need to do when creating a logger from Python's logging module. First, you create a logger instance. Then, you can add a handler to it, to specify what happens to log entries, and a formatter to that handler, to tell it how to write out log lines.

GREG, PITR—WE'VE DECIDED THAT YOU PROGRAMMERS NEED A NEW, BIGGER OFFICE. ONE WITH A DOOR!

Your mixin class also needs methods so you can log **3**. One option is to use a generic log method that you give a severity when you call it, but a cleaner way is to use the logger's methods like debug, info, warn, error, and critical.

Now that you're using __init__ in Loggable, you'll need to find a way to call it **4**. There are two ways. The first is to call each parent class explicitly by using its name and method directly, but passing in self. The second is to use Python's super() method, which finds the method in the next parent class. In this case, they do much the same thing, but super() properly handles the case where you have a common grandparent class. See the next section for potential problems when using this method, and the sample code in super_test.py in the code tarball for this book.

Once all that's done, you can use the logging class exactly the same way you did in the previous version ❺. Note that you've also exposed the logger object itself, so if you need to, you can call its methods directly.

super() and friends

Using the super() method with *diamond inheritance* (see figure 7.1) can be fraught with peril—the main reason being that, when you use it with common methods such as __init__, you're not guaranteed which class's __init__ method you'll be calling. Each will be called, but they could be in any order. To cover for these cases, it helps to remember the following things when using super():

- Use **kwargs, avoid using plain arguments, and always pass all the arguments you receive to any parent methods. Other parent methods might not have the same number or type of arguments as the subclass, particularly when calling __init__.

- If one of your classes uses super(), then they all should. Being inconsistent means an __init__ method might not be called or might be called twice.

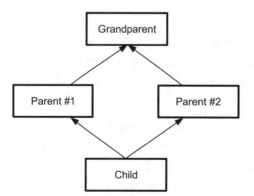

Figure 7.1
A diamond inheritance structure

- You don't necessarily *need* to use super() if you can design your programs to avoid diamond inheritance—that is, without parent classes sharing a grandparent.

Now that you have a better sense of how classes should be organized and what to watch out for when using multiple inheritance, let's take a look at some of the other things you can do with classes.

Customizing classes

Python gives you a great deal of power when it comes to defining how the methods in your class work and which methods are called. Not only do you have access to all of Python's introspection power, but you can also decide to use different methods at runtime—even methods that don't exist.

When Python looks up an attribute or method on a class (for example, self.log_file_name or test.do_something() in listing 7.2), it will look up that value in a dictionary called __dict__. __dict__ stores all the user-defined values for a class and is used for most lookups, but it's possible to override it at several points.

Python provides a number of possible ways to customize attribute access by overriding some built-in methods. You do so in the same way you've been using __init__ to initialize classes.

__getattr__

__getattr__ is used to provide methods or attributes when they're not found in the class or a parent class. You can use this to catch missing methods or write wrappers around other classes or programs. The following listing shows how you can use the __getattr__ method to override the way Python looks up missing attributes.

Listing 7.3   Using __getattr__

```python
class TestGetAttr(object):

    def __getattr__(self, name):
        print "Attribute '%s' not found!" % name
        return 42
```

```
test_class = TestGetAttr()
print test_class.something

test_class.something = 43
print test_class.some-
thing
```

The __getattr__ method takes one argument, the attribute name, and returns what the value should be. In this case, you print the name and then return a default value, but you could do anything—log to a file, call an API, or hand over the responsibility to another class or function.

Now when you try to access a value that doesn't exist in the class, __getattr__ will step in and return your default value.

Because __getattr__ is only called when the attribute isn't found, setting an attribute first means that __getattr__ won't be run.

Now that you can get your attributes, let's also learn how to set them.

__setattr__

__setattr__ is used to change the way that Python alters attributes or methods. You can intercept calls to your class, log them, or do whatever you need to. The following listing shows a simple way to catch attribute access and redirect it to a different dictionary instead of inserting it into the default __dict__.

Listing 7.4   Using __setattr__

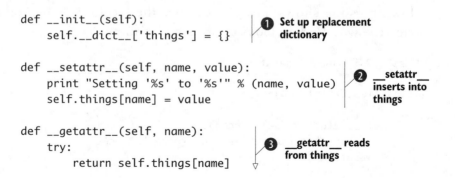

```
class TestSetAttr(object):

    def __init__(self):                              ❶ Set up replacement
        self.__dict__['things'] = {}                    dictionary

    def __setattr__(self, name, value):              ❷ __setattr__
        print "Setting '%s' to '%s'" % (name, value)    inserts into
        self.things[name] = value                       things

    def __getattr__(self, name):                     ❸ __getattr__ reads
        try:                                            from things
            return self.things[name]
```

```
        except KeyError:
            raise AttributeError(
                "'%s' object has no attribute '%s'" %
                    (self.__class__.__name__, name))

test_class2 = TestSetAttr()
test_class2.something = 42
print test_class2.something
print test_class2.things
print test_class2.something_else
```

4 Use class

❶ is where you set things, which will store all the attributes you'll set. One catch when using __setattr__ is that you can't directly set something in the class, because that will result in __setattr__ calling itself and looping until Python runs out of recursion room. You'll need to set the value in the class's __dict__ attribute directly, as you do here.

ME? A PROGRAMMER?
GIFT OF PEOPLEWARE LAST XMAS IS ALREADY PAYINK DIVIDENDS!

Once things is set in __dict__, though, you can read from it normally, because __getattr__ won't be called when you access self.things. __setattr__ takes a name and a value, and in this case you're inserting the value into the things dictionary ❷ instead of into the class.

This version of __getattr__ looks in the self.things dictionary for your value ❸. If it's not there, you raise an AttributeError to mimic Python's normal handling.

The class you've written behaves exactly like a normal class, except you have close to complete control over how its methods and attributes are read ❹. If you want to override everything, though, you'll need to use __getattribute__.

__getattribute__

Another approach is to override all method access entirely. If __getattribute__ exists in your class, it will be called for all method and attribute access, right?

Well, that's sort of true. Strictly speaking, even __getattribute__ doesn't override everything. There are still a number of methods, such as __len__ and __init__, which are accessed directly by Python and won't be overridden. But everything else, even __dict__, goes through __getattribute__. This works, but in practice it means you'll have a hard time getting to any of your attributes. If you try something like self.thing, then you'll end up in an infinite __getattribute__ loop.

How do you fix this? __getattribute__ won't be much use if you can't access the real variables. The answer is to use a different version of __getattribute__: the one you would normally be using if you hadn't just overridden it. The easiest way to get to a fresh __getattribute__ is via the base object class, and feed in self as the instance. The following listing shows you how.

Listing 7.5   Using __getattribute__

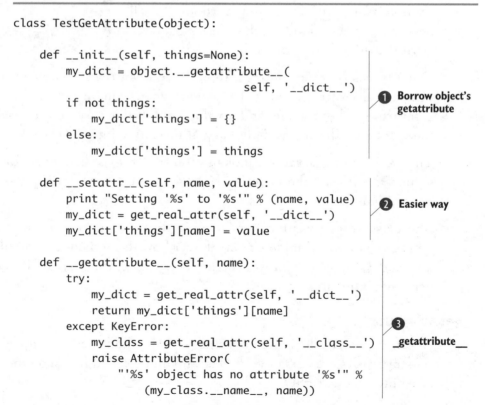

```
class TestGetAttribute(object):

    def __init__(self, things=None):
        my_dict = object.__getattribute__(
                                self, '__dict__')          ❶ Borrow object's
        if not things:                                         getattribute
            my_dict['things'] = {}
        else:
            my_dict['things'] = things

    def __setattr__(self, name, value):
        print "Setting '%s' to '%s'" % (name, value)
        my_dict = get_real_attr(self, '__dict__')          ❷ Easier way
        my_dict['things'][name] = value

    def __getattribute__(self, name):
        try:
            my_dict = get_real_attr(self, '__dict__')
            return my_dict['things'][name]
        except KeyError:
            my_class = get_real_attr(self, '__class__')    ❸
            raise AttributeError(                              __getattribute__
                "'%s' object has no attribute '%s'" %
                    (my_class.__name__, name))
```

```
def get_real_attr(instance, name):
    return object.__getattribute__(instance, name)
```
❷ **Easier way**

```
test_class3 = TestGetAttribute({'foo': 'bar'})
print object.__getattribute__(test_class3, '__dict__')
test_class3.something = 43
print object.__getattribute__(test_class3, '__dict__')
print test_class3.foo
```
❹ **Use class**

Python methods are functions, so it's relatively easy to call back to object. The only thing you need to do is to pass it self as the instance, and the name of the attribute you want ❶. I've also updated __init__ so you can pass in values to set up the internal things dictionary.

To tidy up the calls to object, you can define a helper function to make the call for you. ❷ is a version of __setattr__ that uses it.

Other than the fact that you need to use object to get the dictionary you're editing, the call to __getattribute__ ❸ is much like the one to __getattr__; it receives a name and returns a value, converting KeyError to AttributeError along the way.

After you've been through all that, your class is ready to be used ❹. It follows the same usage pattern, but you can now hide the things dictionary from casual inspection (it's still visible if you use the old object.__getattribute__, though).

If using __getattribute__ seems like a lot of work, don't worry. Most of the time, you won't need to use it. But many third-party libraries make use of it in addition to __getattr__ and __setattr__. If you need to use them, they can save a lot of work and make your class interfaces a lot more Pythonic and easy to use.

YOU'LL NEED TO CLEAR IT OUT, THOUGH—IT'S WHERE THE BOSS STORES HIS OLD EMAILS.

Properties

A more specific method for customizing your attributes is to use Python's property function. Whereas __getattr__ and __getattribute__ work across the entire class, property allows you to specify functions, commonly known as *getters* and *setters*, that are responsible for controlling access to an attribute or method.

Properties solve a common programming problem: how to customize attribute access without altering your class's external interface. Without properties, it's standard practice to use getters and setters for every attribute, even if you don't need them, due to the difficulty in switching from attribute access to using a function. Python allows you to do this without having to change everything that uses your class. The next listing shows how you might create an integer attribute that can only be set to an integer from 0 to 31.

Listing 7.6   Using properties

```
class TestProperty(object):

    def __init__(self, x):          ❶ Class setup
        self.x = x

    def get_x(self):                ❷ x is really _x
        return self._x

    def set_x(self, value):
        if not (type(value) == int and 0 <= value < 32):
            raise ValueError("TestProperty.x "          ❸ Set _x
                "must be an integer from 0 to 31")
        self._x = value
                                    ❹ Define
    x = property(get_x, set_x)          property

test = TestProperty(10)
print test.x
test.x = 11                         ❺ Interface
test.x += 1
assert test.x == 12
print test.x

try:
    test2 = TestProperty(42)
except ValueError:                  ❻ Bounds
    # ValueError: TestProperty.x must be      checking
    # an integer between 0 and 32
    print "test2 not set to 42"
```

The initial setup ❶ looks similar to any class's __init__ function. Some introductions set the hidden variable directly; but I prefer it this way, because it means you can't have x set to something out of bounds.

❷ is your getter, which returns the value of _x—although you could convert it to whatever you liked, or even return None.

❸ is your setter, which first checks to make sure the value is an integer from 0 to 31. If it isn't, then you raise a ValueError.

Finally, you set x on the class to be a property ❹ and pass it the getter and setter functions, get_x and set_x. Note that you can also define a read-only property if you only pass a getter. If you then try to set x, you'll get AttributeError: can't set attribute.

If you didn't know it was a property, you wouldn't be able to tell by using the class. The interface ❺ for your defined x is exactly the same as if it were a regular attribute.

The only exception to the interface is the one you've included. If you try to set the value of test2.x to something out of bounds, you'll get an exception ❻.

In practice, you'll want to use the methods that are most suited for your use case. Some situations, such as logging, wrapping a library, and security checking, call for __getattribute__ or __getattr__, but if all you need to do is customize a few specific methods, then properties are normally the best way to do it.

Emulating other types

One other common practice is to write classes to emulate certain types, such as lists or dictionaries. If you have a class that is supposed to behave similarly to a list or a number, it helps when the class behaves in exactly the same way, supporting the same methods and raising the same exceptions when you misuse it.

There are a number of methods you can define that Python will use when you use your class in certain ways. For example, if you need two instances of your class to compare as equal, you can define an `__eq__` method that takes two objects and returns `True` if they should be treated as equal.

The next listing provides an example: here, two methods are added to the previous class so you can compare them to each other. I've renamed the class `LittleNumber`, to make its purpose clearer (you'll also want to rename the class name in the exception).

Listing 7.7   Extending properties

```
class LittleNumber(object):
    ...

    def __eq__(self, other):
        return self.x == other.x                    ❶ __eq__

    def __lt__(self, other):
        return self.x < other.x                     ❷ __lt__

    def __add__(self, other):
        try:
            if type(other) == int:
                return LittleNumber(self.x + other)
            elif type(other) == LittleNumber:
                return LittleNumber(self.x + other.x)
            else:
                return NotImplemented
        except ValueError:                          ❸ Add values
            raise ValueError(
                "Sum of %d and %d is out of bounds "
                "for LittleNumber!" % (self.x, other.x))

    def __str__(self):
        return "<LittleNumber: %d>" % self.x

one = LittleNumber(1)
two = LittleNumber(2)                               ❹ Use class
print one == one
print not one == two
```

```
print one != two
print one < two
print two > one
print not one > two
print two >= one
print two >= two

onetoo = LittleNumber(1)
print onetoo == one
print not onetoo == two

print onetoo + one
print one
print onetoo + one == two
```

❹ **Use class**

This method ❶ checks the value against the other one you're given. Whenever Python encounters a == b, it will call a.__eq__(b) to figure out what the real value should be.

In the same way as __eq__, __lt__ ❷ will compare two values and return True if the current instance is less than the one passed in.

__add__ is also useful and should return the result of adding something to the class ❸. This case is somewhat more complex—you return a new LittleNumber if you're passed an integer or another LittleNumber, but you need to catch two cases: where the value goes out of bounds and where someone passes you a different type, such as a string. If you can't (or won't) handle a particular case, you can return NotImplemented, and Python will raise a TypeError. Again, a more understandable error message here will save you a lot of debugging further down the track.

Believe it or not, that's all you need to get your class to behave something like an integer ❹. Note that you don't necessarily need to implement all of the mirror functions like __gt__ and __ne__, because Python will try their opposites if they're not defined. All of the expressions here should return True.

Here's a table of some of the most common methods you'll want to override if you're providing a class similar to some of the built-in types.

Table 7.1   Common methods you may want to override

Type	Methods	Description

Most types	`__eq__(self, other)`
	`__ne__(self, other)`
	`__gt__(self, other)`
	`__lt__(self, other)`
	`__le__(self, other)`
	`__ge__(self, other)`
		Tests for equality and relative value, ==, !=, >, <, <=, and >=.

	`__str__(self)` `__repr__(self)`	Returns a printable version of the class and a printable representation of the class.

Dictionary, list, or other container	`__getitem__(self, key)`
	`__setitem__(self, key, value)`
	`__delitem__(self, key)`
		Gets, sets, and deletes an entry.

	`keys(self)`	Returns a list of keys (dictionaries only).
	`__len__(self)`	Returns the number of entries.
	`__iter__(self) and` `iterkeys(self)`	If your object is large, you might want to consider using these methods to return an iterator (see the next section for details).
	`__contains__(self, value)`	The value of an entry (of a list or set), or a key (of a dictionary).

Numbers	`__add__(self, other)`
	`__sub__(self, other)`
	`__mul__(self, other)`
	`__floordiv__(self, other)`
	`__pow__(self, other)`
		Returns the result of adding, multiplying, dividing, and raising to a power.

	`__int__(self)` `__float__(self)`	Converts an instance of a class into an integer or float.

These are by no means the only methods you can set, but they're by far the most common, unless you're doing something exotic. Let's look at a practical example of how these methods are used in practice, by examining Python's generators and iterators.

Generators and iterators

Generators are one of Python's best-kept secrets after list comprehensions, and they're worth looking into in more detail. They're intended to solve the problem of storing state in between function calls, but they're also useful for cases where you need to deal with large amounts of data, perhaps too large to fit easily in memory.

First we'll look at iterators, Python's method for dealing with looping objects. Then we'll look at how you can make use of generators to quickly deal with large amounts of data in log files.

Iterators

You've been using iterators throughout the book, right from chapter 2, because every time you use a for loop or a list comprehension, iterators have been acting behind the scenes. You don't need to know how iterators work in order to make use of them, but they're useful for understanding how generators operate.

NOTE   Iterators are a common solution to a frequent programming task: you have a bunch of things—now how do you do something to each one of them? The trick is that most Python collections, be they lists, files, or sets, can be used as iterators.

The interface of an iterator is straightforward. It has a .next() method, which you call over and over again to get each value in the sequence. Once all the values are gone, the iterator raises a StopIteration exception, which tells Python to stop looping. In practice, using an iterator looks something like figure 7.2.

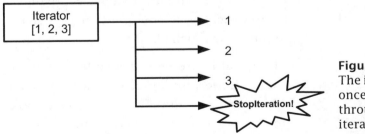

Figure 7.2
The iterator protocol: once you run through three iterations, it stops.

When you ask Python to iterate over an object such as a list, the first thing it does is call `iter(object)`, which calls that object's `__iter__` method and expects to get an iterator object. You don't need to use the `__iter__` call directly unless you're creating your own custom iterator. In that case, you'll need to implement both the `__iter__` and the `next()` methods yourself. This listing shows how to use the `iter` function to create an iterator from any iterable Python object.

Listing 7.8   Using an iterator the hard way

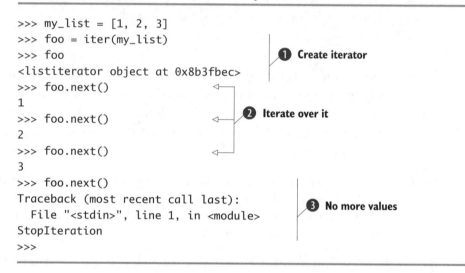

```
>>> my_list = [1, 2, 3]
>>> foo = iter(my_list)
>>> foo                                        ❶ Create iterator
<listiterator object at 0x8b3fbec>
>>> foo.next()
1
>>> foo.next()                                 ❷ Iterate over it
2
>>> foo.next()
3
>>> foo.next()
Traceback (most recent call last):
  File "<stdin>", line 1, in <module>          ❸ No more values
StopIteration
>>>
```

You use the `iter()` function to create an iterator object for `my_list` ❶. If you print it, you can see that's it's a new type of object—a `listiterator`—not a list. When you call the `next()` method of your iterator ❷, it returns the values from the list: 1, 2, and 3.

HERE YOU GO. REARRANGE THE OFFICE HOWEVER YOU LIKE—JUST DON'T LOSE ANY OF THE BOSS'S EMAILS.

Once you've run out of values ❸, the iterator will raise a `StopIteration` exception to signal that the iterator has finished.

The iterator protocol is simple, but it's a fundamental underpinning of the looping and iteration mechanisms in Python. Let's have a look at how generators use this protocol to make your programming life easier.

Generators

Generators are similar to iterators. They use exactly the same .next() method, but they're easier to create and to understand. Generators are defined exactly like functions, except they use a yield statement instead of a return. Here's a simple example of a generator, which counts down to zero from a specified value:

```
def counter(value):
    print "Starting at", value
    while value > 0:
        yield value
        value -= 1
```

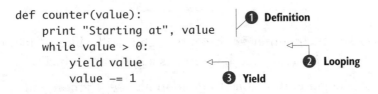

1 Definition

2 Looping

3 Yield

Let's look at this one step at a time.

Generators start out like functions, including the way you give them arguments **1**. We're also including a debugging string here, so you can follow how the generator is called.

Generators need some way to return values repeatedly, so usually you'll see a loop **2** within the body.

The yield statement **3** will stop your function and return the value you give it.

Finally, after each call, Python will return into the generator via the next() method. You subtract 1 from the value each time, until it's no longer greater than zero, and then the generator will finish with a StopIteration exception.

That's only half of the puzzle, though—you still need to be able to call your generator. The following listing shows how you can do that, by creating a counter and then using it in a for loop. You can also call it directly with a line like for x in counter(5).

Listing 7.9   Using your counter generator

```
>>> foo = counter(5)
>>> foo
<generator object at 0x896054c>
>>> for x in foo:
...     print x
```

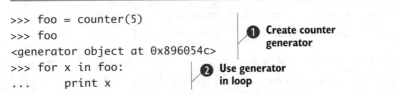

1 Create counter generator

2 Use generator in loop

```
...
counting down from 5
5
4
3
2
1
>>>
```

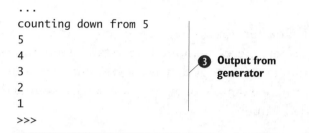

❸ **Output from generator**

First, you create the counter ❶. Even though it looks like a function, it doesn't start right away; instead, it returns a generator object.

You can use the generator object in a loop like ❷. Python will call the generator repeatedly until it runs out of values or the generator exits normally.

❸ is what the loop prints out. The first line is the initial debug from the generator, and the other lines are the results it returns.

There's one last mechanism you should know, which can save you a lot of time setting up generator functions.

Generator expressions

Generator expressions are a lot like list comprehensions, except that, behind the scenes, they use generators rather than building a whole list. Try running the following expressions in a Python prompt:

```
foo = [x**2 for x in range(100000000)]
bar = (x**2 for x in range(100000000))
```

Depending on your computer, the list comprehension will either take a long time to return or else raise a MemoryError. That's because it's creating a hundred million results and inserting them into a list.

This generator, on the other hand, will return immediately. It hasn't created any results at all—it will only do that if you try to iterate over bar. If you break out of that loop after 10 results, then the other 99,999,990 values won't need to be calculated.

If generators and iterators are so great, why would you ever use lists or list comprehensions? They're still useful if you want to do anything else with your data other than loop over it. If you want to access your values in a random order—say the fourth value, then the second, then the eighteenth—then your generators won't help because they access values linearly from the first through to the one millionth. Similarly, if you need to add extra values to your list or modify them in some way, then generators won't help—you'll need a list.

Now that you know how generators work, let's look at where they can be useful when you write your programs.

Using generators

As you learned at the start of the chapter, you can use generators in cases where reading in a large amount of data would slow your program down or make it run out of memory and crash.

NOTE   In case you haven't realized it yet, Python is an intensely pragmatic language. Every feature has gone through a rigorous community-based vetting process known as a Python Enhancement Proposal (PEP), so there will be strong use cases for each feature. You can read more about PEPs at www.python.org/dev/peps/pep-0001/.

A common problem that involves a large amount of data is the processing of files. If you have a few hundred log files and need to find out which ones have a certain string in them, or collate data across several website directories, then it can be hard to make sense of what's happening within a reasonable amount of time. Let's take a look at a few simple generators that can make your life easier if you run into this sort of problem.

Reading files

One of the areas where Python makes use of generators is in the file-processing sections of the os module. os.walk is a good example—it allows you to iterate recursively through directories, building lists of the files and subdirectories within them, but because it builds the list as it goes, it's nice and fast. You've

I'LL GO GET THE SNOW SHOVEL.

NO, GREGORY. I AM HAVINK BETTER IDEA ...

already encountered os.walk in chapter 3, when you were building a program to compare files. A typical use is shown in the following listing, which is a program to read a directory and return the files that are of a certain type—in this case, .log files.

Listing 7.10   **os.walk revisited**

```
import os

dir_name = '/var/log'        ❶ Directory and
file_type = '.log'              file type
                                                            ❷ Iterate using
                                                               os.walk
for path, dirs, files in os.walk(dir_name):   ◄─┘
    print path
    print dirs                                            ❸ Log files
    print [f for f in files if f.endswith(file_type)]  ◄─┘
    print '-' * 42
```

First, you specify your directory and the file type you want to search for ❶. os.walk returns a generator you can use to iterate over the directory ❷. It will give you the path of the directory, as well as any subdirectories and files within it.

You assume that anything that ends in .log is a log file ❸. Depending on your specific situation, an assumption like this may or may not be warranted, but because you will, in practice, have control of the web server, you can add the .log part if you need to.

When you run the program in listing 7.10, it will output something like the following. Each section contains the directory you're iterating over and then its subdirectories and the log files within the current directory.

Listing 7.11   **The output from os.walk**

```
/var/log
['landscape', 'lighttpd', 'dist-upgrade', 'apparmor', ... ]
['wpa_supplicant.log', 'lpr.log', 'user.log', ... ]
-------------------------------------------
/var/log/landscape
[]
['sysinfo.log']
```

```
-----------------------------------------
/var/log/dist-upgrade
[]
['main.log', 'apt-term.log', 'xorg_fix_intrepid.log', ... ]
-----------------------------------------

...
```

You can use some generators to make your code a little easier to work with. As an example, let's say you're monitoring your web server for errors, so you want to find out which of your log files have the word *error* in them. You'd also like to print out the line itself so you can track down what's going on if there are any errors. Here are three generators that will help you do that.

Listing 7.12   Generators to work through a directory

```python
import os

def log_files(dir_name, file_type):
    if not os.path.exists(dir_name):
        raise ValueError(dir_name + " not found!")
    if not os.path.isdir(dir_name):
        raise ValueError(dir_name + " is not a directory!")    ❶ Wrap
    for path, dirs, files in os.walk(dir_name):                    os.walk in
        log_files = [f for f in files                              generator
                    if f.endswith(file_type)]
        for each_file in log_files:
            yield os.path.join(path, each_file)


def log_lines(dir_name, file_type):
    for each_file in log_files(dir_name, file_type):            ❷ Generator for
        for each_line in file(each_file).readlines():             each line
            yield (each_file, each_line.strip())                  of files


def list_errors(dir_name, file_type):
    return (each_file + ': ' + each_line.strip()
            for each_file, each_line in                         ❸ Filter out
                log_lines(dir_name, file_type)                    non-error
            if 'error' in each_line.lower())                      lines


if __name__ == '__main__':
```

```
dir_name = '/var/log'
file_type = '.log'
for each_file in log_files(dir_name, file_type):
    print each_file
print
for each_error in list_errors(dir_name, file_type):
    print each_error
```

④ Create generators

MORE DUCT TAPE,
GREGORY. THE
SCANNER WILL NOT
HOLD ITSELF ...

THERE! THAT OUGHT
TO DO IT.

This is the same code you saw in listing 7.10, but wrapped in a generator function ❶. One issue with os.walk is that it won't raise an exception if you give it a nonexistent directory or something that's not a directory, so you catch both of those cases before you start.

Now that you have log_files as a generator, you can use it to build further generators. log_lines reads each file in turn and yields successive lines of each log file, along with the name of the file ❷.

This generator builds on the log_lines generator to return only those lines that have the word *error* in them ❸. Notice also that you're returning a generator comprehension instead of using yield. This is an alternative way of doing things, one that can make sense for small generators, or where the values you're returning fit the generator comprehension style well.

Once you've done all the hard work of creating the generators ❹, calling them is easy—give them the directory and file type, and do what you need to with each result.

Now you can find all the error lines in all the log files in a certain directory. Returning the lines with *error* in them isn't particularly useful, though. What if you had an error that didn't contain the word *error?* Instead, it could contain something like *Process #3456 out of memory!* There are all sorts of conditions you'd like to check in your log files, so you'll need something a little more powerful.

Getting to grips with your log lines

You'd like to have a lot more control over the data in your log files, including being able to filter by any field or combination of fields. In practice, this means you'll need to break the data from each line in your log file up and interpret the bits. The following listing shows some examples from an old Apache access log I had lying around.

Listing 7.13   Apache log lines

```
124.150.110.226 - - [26/Jun/2008:06:48:29 +0000] "GET / HTTP/1.1" 200 99
"-" "Mozilla/5.0 (X11; U; Linux i686; en-US; rv:1.8.1.14) Gecko/20080419
    Ubuntu/8.04 (hardy) Firefox/2.0.0.14"

66.249.70.40 - - [26/Jun/2008:08:41:18 +0000] "GET /robots.txt HTTP/1.1"
404 148 "-" "Mozilla/5.0 (compatible; Googlebot/2.1;
            +http://www.google.com/bot.html)"

65.55.211.90 - - [27/Jun/2008:23:33:52 +0000] "GET /robots.txt HTTP/1.1"
404 148 "-" "msnbot/1.1 (+http://search.msn.com/msnbot.htm)"
```

These lines are in Apache's Combined Log Format. Most of the fields are self explanatory—IP address is the computer making the request, referer is the URL of the page (if any) that was used to reach the page, HTTP request contains the path the user was requesting, size is the number of bytes transferred as a result of the request, and so on.

In listing 7.13, you should be able to see three separate requests: one from Firefox running under Linux, one from Google's search spider,

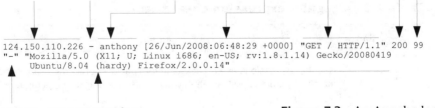

IP address remote host id remote user id date and time HTTP request status size

```
124.150.110.226 - anthony [26/Jun/2008:06:48:29 +0000] "GET / HTTP/1.1" 200 99
"-" "Mozilla/5.0 (X11; U; Linux i686; en-US; rv:1.8.1.14) Gecko/20080419
    Ubuntu/8.04 (hardy) Firefox/2.0.0.14"
```

referer   user agent string   **Figure 7.3** An Apache log line and one from Microsoft's MSN. As you learned in chapter 5, the user agent string is supplied by the client and so can't be trusted, but in most cases it's accurate. The HTTP request part is the full command sent to the web server, so it includes the type of request (usually GET or POST) and the HTTP version as well as the path requested.

Pulling out the bits

That explains what the separate fields mean, but how are you going to get them? You could split on quotes or spaces, but it's possible they'll appear in odd places and throw the split function off track. For example, there are spaces in both the user-agent and the date-time string. It's also possible to have quotes within the user agent string and the URL, although they're supposed to be URL encoded.

TIP   My rule of thumb is to use Python's string methods, like endswith() and .split(), when looking for simple things—but I find they can get unwieldy when you're trying to match against more complicated patterns, like the Apache log line.

In cases like this, it's usually easier to break out the big guns right at the start, rather than experiment with splitting the fields on various characters and trying to make sure it will work for everything. In this case, the fastest solution is probably to use a parsing tool called a *regular expression*, which is useful for reading single lines like this and breaking them down into chunks.

Regular expressions work by using special matching characters to designate particular types of character, such as spaces, digits, the letters *a* to *z*, *A* to *Z*, and so on. A full description of the gory details of regular expressions is out of the scope of this book, but the handy quick reference in table 7.2 will get you started.

Table 7.2   A regular expression cheat sheet

Expression	Definition
\	Regular expressions use a backslash for special characters. If you need to match an actual backslash, then you can use two backslashes together, \\.
\w	A "word" character: *a–z*, *A–Z*, *0–9*, and a few others, such as underscore.

Table 7.2   A regular expression cheat sheet *(continued)*

Expression	Definition
\W	A non-word character—the opposite of \w.
\s	A whitespace character, such as space or tab.
\S	A non-whitespace character.
\d	A digit character, 0–9.
.	Any character at all.
+	Extends a special character to match one or more times. \w+ will match at least one word character, but could match 20.
*	Like +, but matches zero or more instead of one or more.
?	You can use this after a * or + wildcard search to make them less "greedy." .*? will match the minimum it can, rather than as much as possible.
()	You can put brackets around a set of characters and pull them out later using the .groups() method of the match object.
[]	You can put characters between square brackets to match just those. [aeiou], for example, matches vowels.
r''	A string preceded with r is a *raw* string, and Python won't escape any backslashes within it. For example, "line 1\nline 2" will normally be split over multiple lines, because Python will interpret \n as a return, but r"line 1\nline 2" won't.
match vs. search	Two main methods are used on the regular expression object. match will try to match from the start of a line, but search will look at the whole string. Normally, you'll want to use search, unless you know you want to match at the start.

The regular-expression string you're going to use to match the Apache log lines looks like this:

```
log_format = (r'(\S+) (\S+) (\S+) \[(.*?)\] '
              r'"(\S+) (\S+) (\S+)" (\S+) (\S+) '
              r'"(.+)" "(.+)"')
```

It looks complicated, but it's not so hard if you break it down and look at the individual parts:

- Most of the fields are groups of alphanumeric characters separated by spaces, so you can use (\S+) to match them. They're surrounded by brackets so you can access the fields after they've been matched. Each part corresponds to one field in the Apache log line.

- The date-and-time field is the only one with square brackets around it, so you can also match that easily and pull out everything, including spaces, with a wildcard match. Notice that you escape the [and] by putting a backslash in front of them so the regular expression treats them as normal characters.

- The referer and the user agent are also matched using wildcards, because they might have quotes or spaces in them.

IS WORKINK! TIME TO GO HOME!

SCHLOOORP! VRMMMM! ZZZZAARRTT!

- The whole string is wrapped in brackets so you can break it over multiple strings but still have Python consider them as a single string.

Now that you have a rough idea of how you can use regular expressions to match the fields in a log line, let's look at how you write the Python functions and generators to make sense of the overall scope of your log files. The following listing extends listing 7.7 to add new Apache-related functions and generators.

Listing 7.14   Parsing Apache log lines

```
import re
...

apache_log_headers = ['host', 'client_id', 'user_id',
    'datetime', 'method', 'request', 'http_proto',
    'status', 'size', 'referrer', 'user_agent']           ❶ Set up
log_format = (r'(\S+) (\S+) (\S+) \[(.*?)\] '
             r'"(\S+) (\S+) (\S+)" (\S+) (\S+) '
             r'"(.+)" "(.+)"')
log_regexp = re.compile(log_format)
```

```
def parse_apache(line):
    log_split = log_regexp.match(line)
    if not log_split:
        print "Line didn't match!", line      ❷ Parse apache
        return {}                                 line
    log_split = log_split.groups()

    result = dict(zip(apache_log_headers, log_split))
    result['status'] = int(result['status'])
    if result['size'].isdigit():                   ❸ Convert parsed
        result['size'] = int(result['size'])          line into
    else:                                             dictionary
        result['size'] = 0
    return result

def apache_lines(dir_name, file_type):          ❹ Generator
    return (parse_apache(line)                      for line
            for line in log_lines(dir_name, file_type))  parser

...
if __name__ == '__main__':
    for each_line in log_lines('/var/log/apache2', '.log'):
        print each_line
        print parse_apache(each_line)

    print sum((each_line['size']
        for each_line in                           ❺ Use new
            apache_lines('/var/log/apache2', '.log')  generator
        if line.get('status', 0) == 200))
```

Before we get into the functions proper, it's a good idea to set up some of the variables that you'll need for your regular expressions ❶. apache_log_headers is a list of names for all of the fields you'll see in your log file, and log_format is the regular expression string we looked at earlier. You also compile log_format into log_regexp so your matching is faster when you're parsing the log line.

First, you set up a function that is responsible for parsing a single line ❷. Here's where you use the compiled regular expression object against the line you've been passed, using the match method. If it matches, log_split will be a match object, and you can call the

.groups() method to extract the parts you matched with brackets. If there's no match, log_split will be None, which means you have a line that is probably illegal. There's not much you can do in this case, so you'll return an empty dictionary.

If your function is going to be widely useful, you'll need to easily access different parts of the log line. The easiest way to do that is to put all of the fields into a dictionary ❸, so you can type line['user_agent'] to access the user-agent string. A fast way to do that is by using Python's built-in zip function, which joins the fields together with the list of headers. It creates a sequence of tuples (identical to the results of an .items() call on a dictionary), and then you can cast that to a dictionary with the dict() function. Finally, you turn some of the results into integers to make them easier to deal with later.

Now that you have your line-parsing function, you can add a generator to call it for each line of the log file ❹.

If you have more information about what's in the line, you can search for more detail in your logs ❺. Here you're adding up the total size of the requests, but only where the request is successful (a status code of 200). You could also do things like exclude the Google, MSN, and Yahoo spiders to get "real" web traffic, see what volume of traffic is referred to you by Google, or add up individual IP addresses to get an idea of how many unique visitors you have.

When you run the program in listing 7.14, you should see a list of lines and their parsed representation, with a number at the end. That's the number of bytes that were transferred in successful transactions. Your program is complete, and you can start adding to it if there are particular features you'd like to add.

Functional programming

As you become more familiar with programming, you'll start to find that certain features are more or less error-prone than others. For example, if your program makes use of a lot of shared state or global variables, then you might find that a lot of your errors tend to be around managing that state and tracking down which *!$%@%* function is replacing all your values with None.

It makes sense to try to find ways to design your program that don't involve error-prone features, and which are clearer and easier to understand. In turn, you'll be able to write larger programs with more features, and write them faster than you could before.

One of those strategies is called *functional programming*. Its main criterion is that it uses functions that have no side effects—their output is entirely determined by their input, and they don't modify anything outside the function. If a function is written like this, it makes it much easier to reason about and test, because you only need to consider the function by itself, not anything else.

Another feature of functional programming is that functions are objects in their own right — you can pass them as arguments to other functions and store them in variables. This might not seem particularly important, but it enables a lot of functionality that would otherwise be quite difficult to implement.

NEXT MORNING ...

BY NOW, EMAILS SHOULD BE ALL SHREDDED AND IN BAGS.

Side effects

Side effects refer to anything a function does that is outside its sphere of control or that doesn't relate to the value it returns. Modifying a global variable or one that's been passed in, writing to a file, and posting values to a URL are all examples of side effects. Functions should also only rely on values that are passed in, not on anything outside the function.

Map and filter

Once you know that functions are safe to run and aren't going to do anything weird, you can use them much more frequently—and for situations where you might not normally use functions.

Two common examples are map and filter. map takes a function and an iterable object, like a list or generator, and returns a list with the result of that function applied to each item in the iterable. `filter`, on the other hand, takes an iterable function and returns only those items for which the function returns `True`.

In the case of your log files, you might have code like this:

```
errors = map(extract_error, filter(is_error, log_file.readlines()))
```

Note that `extract_error` pulls the error text from a log line, and `is_error` tells you whether the line is an error line. The result will be a new list of the error messages from your log file, and the original list will be untouched.

But, in practice, `map` and `filter` tend to make your programs less readable than using something like a list comprehension:

```
errors = [extract_error(line) for line in log_file.readlines()
          if is_error(line)]
```

A better use of functional programming is to use functions to change the behavior of other functions and classes. A good example is the use of decorators to change how functions and methods behave.

Passing and returning functions

Decorators are essentially wrappers around other functions. They take a function as an argument, potentially with other arguments, and return another function to call in its place. To use a decorator, you place its name above the function you're decorating, preceded by an @ symbol and any arguments you need afterward, like a function.

A real-world example is Django's `user_passes_test` function, shown next, which is used to create decorators like `login_required`. `login_required` checks to see whether the user is logged in, and then either returns the regular web page if they are (Django calls them *views*) or redirects them to the site's login page if they aren't. It's fairly complex, but it uses most of the functional programming techniques described so far, plus a few others. I think you're ready to handle it, and we'll take it step by step.

Listing 7.15   Django's `user_passes_test` decorator

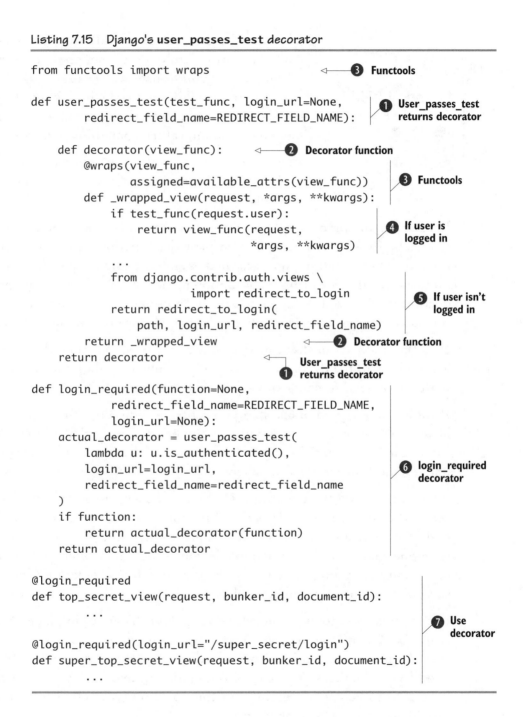

```python
from functools import wraps                         ◁—— ❸ Functools

def user_passes_test(test_func, login_url=None,                    ❶ User_passes_test
        redirect_field_name=REDIRECT_FIELD_NAME):                     returns decorator

    def decorator(view_func):          ◁——❷ Decorator function
        @wraps(view_func,
                assigned=available_attrs(view_func))      ❸ Functools
        def _wrapped_view(request, *args, **kwargs):
            if test_func(request.user):
                return view_func(request,                 ❹ If user is
                                *args, **kwargs)             logged in

            ...
            from django.contrib.auth.views \
                        import redirect_to_login
            return redirect_to_login(                     ❺ If user isn't
                path, login_url, redirect_field_name)        logged in
        return _wrapped_view          ◁——❷ Decorator function
    return decorator                                 ❶ User_passes_test
                                                        returns decorator
def login_required(function=None,
            redirect_field_name=REDIRECT_FIELD_NAME,
            login_url=None):
    actual_decorator = user_passes_test(
        lambda u: u.is_authenticated(),
        login_url=login_url,                          ❻ login_required
        redirect_field_name=redirect_field_name          decorator
    )
    if function:
        return actual_decorator(function)
    return actual_decorator


@login_required
def top_secret_view(request, bunker_id, document_id):
        ...                                           ❼ Use
                                                         decorator
@login_required(login_url="/super_secret/login")
def super_top_secret_view(request, bunker_id, document_id):
        ...
```

HMM. VACUUM BAG MUST BE JAMMED ...

I'LL GO GET THE SNOW SHOVEL.

The first thing to notice is that user_passes_test isn't a decorator itself: it's a function that returns a function for you to use as a decorator ❶. This is a common trick if you need a few similar functions—pass in the bits that are different, and have the function return something you can use.

❷ is the decorator itself. Remember, all it has to do is return another function to use in place of view_func.

If you're planning on writing a few decorators, it's worth looking into functools ❸, a Python module that provides functional programming–related classes and functions. wrap makes sure the original meta information, such as the docstring and function name, are preserved in the final decorator. Notice also that you're using *args and **kwargs in your function, so the request's arguments can be passed through to the real view.

❹ is the first part of the test. If test_func returns True, then the user is logged in, and the decorator returns the results of calling the real view with the same arguments and keyword arguments.

If they're not logged in ❺, then you return a redirect to the login page instead. Note that I've snipped out some extra code that figures out path based on some Django internals—but that's not necessary to understand how the decorator works.

Next, you define the decorator ❻. You call user_passes_test with the relevant arguments and get back a function you can use in place of the real view. You also use lambda, which is a Python keyword you can use to define small, one-line functions. If your function is much more complex than this, though, it's usually better to define a separate function so you can name it and make it clearer.

Python will use the function returned by login_required in place of the real view ❼, so your top_secret_view function will first check to make sure the user is logged in before it returns any secret documents from one of your bunkers. You can also include arguments if you want the decorator to behave differently: in this case, by redirecting to a separate login system at /super_secret/login.

The emphasis in most programming is on objects and how they interact, but there's still a place for well-written, functional programs. Anywhere you need some extra configuration, have common functionality that can be extracted, or need to wrap something (without the overhead of a whole class), you can use functional programming.

Where to from here?

From here, you can extend your log-parsing script to capture different sorts of traffic. You could categorize log entries by type (visitor, logged-in user, search engine, bot), which section of your site they use, or what time of day they arrive. It's also possible to track individuals by IP address as they use your site, to work out how people make use of your site or to determine what they're looking for.

You can use Python's generators in other types of programs, too. If you were reading information from web pages rather than log files, you could still use the same strategies to help you reduce the amount of complexity in your code or the number of downloads you needed. Any program that needs to reduce the amount of data it has to read in, or that needs to call something repeatedly but still maintain state, can benefit from using generators.

You should also keep an eye out for areas in your programs might benefit from using some of the advanced functionality we looked at in this chapter. The secret is that, when you use it, it should make your programs simpler to understand by hiding the difficult or repetitive parts in a module or function. When you're writing an application in Django, you only need to include @login_required above each view you want protected—you don't need to explicitly check the request's user or redirect to a login page yourself.

Summary

In this chapter, you learned about the more advanced Python features, like generators and decorators, and you saw how you can modify classes' behavior and bend them to your will.

You saw how to alter the way a class's methods are looked up, catch a missing method, and even swap out the normal method lookups and use your own criteria. You saw how to transparently swap out attributes for functions by using properties, and make your class behave like an integer, list, or dictionary by defining special methods.

We also looked at how to use generators to help you organize the data in your programs, and how they can reduce the memory required in your program by only loading data as it's needed, rather than ahead of time in one big chunk. We covered how to link generators together to help write more complicated programs, using an example where you parsed information from an Apache log file. We also explored using the regular expression module when you need a good way to match or extract information from some text.

Finally, we discussed functional programming, and you saw how Python supports it with `map` and `filter`, in addition to having functions that can be assigned to a variable. Then we looked at decorators and how they work in practice by defining and returning different functions.

We've covered most of Python's features, so from here on, we're going to take a slightly different tack and look at some common libraries that are used with Python. In the next chapter, we'll examine Django, the main web framework used with Python.

8

Django!

This chapter covers

- *Writing web applications in Django*
- *Designing a web application*
- *Some common web practices, such as only editing via POST*

In chapter 3, we looked at building a simple todo list to help you track what you were working on. Now we're going to look at expanding the application and making it available through a web browser, so you can see what you need to do next regardless of where you are (as long as you have an internet connection, obviously). To make your life easier, you're going to use a web framework called Django.

What's a web framework, you ask? When you're developing for the web, you need to keep track of a lot of details. In addition to displaying the HTML and handling form input, there are lots of extra bits and pieces:

- Handling cookies, sessions, and logins
- Detecting errors and displaying them
- Storing data in a database

❖ Separating your page design from the rest of the application (so your web designers can design the pages without having to bother you)

And so on. With a framework like Django, you can use code to handle all these things and get your web application built more quickly.

Writing web-based applications with Django

Django is the main Python web framework, and has a large developer following. It's not the only Python framework by a long stretch, but it's the most commonly used and best documented one. It mostly follows the Model-View-Controller (MVC) style of programming, but it sometimes bends that structure a little. In Django, there's a lot of built-in functionality to make your life much easier when developing web applications.

Table 8.1   Django-ese to MVC-ese

Django	MVC	Purpose
Model	Model	Stores data
Template	View	Presents a user interface
View	Controller	Does "stuff"

Model-View-Controller

Model-View-Controller (MVC) is a method of design that separates out your data from how it's presented. The Model stores your data and has functions for manipulating it. The View presents your data and a user interface to the end user. Finally, the Controller does everything in between.

MVC is often used as a catch-all term, but different people, applications, and web frameworks interpret and use it in different ways; it's hard to give a definition that will work in every situation. See table 8.1 for the differences between Django's terminology and "classic" Model-View-Controller. The most important thing to take away is that it separates your data, the presentation of that data, and the business logic "glue" that exists in between.

Installing Django

Django is straightforward to install, because you already have Python. Download the latest release from www.django project.com/download/, decompress it, and run `python setup.py install` from within the install directory. On Linux and

a long time ago, in a meeting room far, far away, Greg and Pitr battle the Dark Lord of Sleep...

Mac OS X, you'll need to prefix it with `sudo`, and on Windows you'll need to run it from a command shell with administrator privileges. Once the install process has finished, type `import django` from within Python to make sure it's working. You shouldn't see any errors.

If you run into any issues, or if you think you might need to install a more complicated setup (if you want to run a PostgreSQL or MySQL database server, or use a separate web server such as Apache or Nginx), more detailed installation instructions are available at http:// docs.djangoproject.com/en/dev/topics/install/.

Setting up Django

Now that you've installed Django, you can start work on your project. Django sets most things up for you; all you need to do is to plug your code into the right places and change a few settings. Pick a directory on your computer where you'd like to store and run your project, and type the code in listing 8.1 into the command line. This should work as-is under Linux, but for Windows you'll need to do two extra things:

- Add C:\Python26\Scripts to your PATH environment variable, as you did in chapter 1, and then restart your terminal for `django-admin` to work.
- Include your project path in a second environment variable called `PYTHONPATH`. This variable lets you add extra paths for Python to check when importing modules. Django's settings are imported as a Python module, so Python needs to know where to find them. The following figure shows how I edited them on my PC.

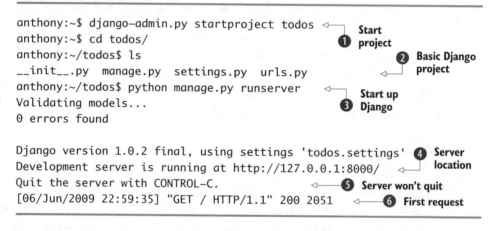

Figure 8.1 Setting system paths for Django

Once you've made the necessary adjustments, you're ready to go!

Listing 8.1 Django first run

```
anthony:~$ django-admin.py startproject todos    ◁────┐  Start
anthony:~$ cd todos/                                   ❶  project
anthony:~/todos$ ls                                              ❷  Basic Django
__init__.py  manage.py  settings.py  urls.py    ◁──────────         project
anthony:~/todos$ python manage.py runserver    ◁────┐  Start up
Validating models...                                 ❸  Django
0 errors found


Django version 1.0.2 final, using settings 'todos.settings'  ❹  Server
Development server is running at http://127.0.0.1:8000/   ◁──┘  location
Quit the server with CONTROL-C.    ◁────────❺  Server won't quit
[06/Jun/2009 22:59:35] "GET / HTTP/1.1" 200 2051   ◁────❻  First request
```

BLA BLA WEB 2.0
BLA BLA SHINY
SHINY BLA BLA

Most of the setup and later interaction with your server is done through `django-admin` ❶, which is a script that comes included with Django.

Once you've created your project, you can take a look around and see what Django has created ❷. There's not much to see right now, but you'll be building on it as you write the application.

While you're at it, start up Django and see what happens. From within the todos folder, type `python manage.py runserver` ❸.

When the server starts, it will tell you what IP address and port number it's running on ❹. If you'd like to run on a different IP address or port, specify it when you run manage.py. For example, python manage.py runserver 0.0.0.0:80 will connect to every interface on your PC on port 80, so you can impress your friends by allowing them to connect to the fancy new web server running on your computer.

Django will keep running until you stop it manually ❺. runserver is the development server, which will automatically detect changes to your files and restart if necessary, so in most cases you don't even need to restart to refresh your application.

As requests come in, Django will print log lines out so you can see what it's doing ❻; this can be useful for debugging.

If you go to the URL listed in the previous output, http://127.0.0.1:8000/, you should see something like figure 8.2.

If you look carefully, you'll see that Django even tells you what steps to take next; but you'll ignore the database part for now and install an application. In Django's terminology, an application is a module that does a specific thing, such as managing todos or user registration. A

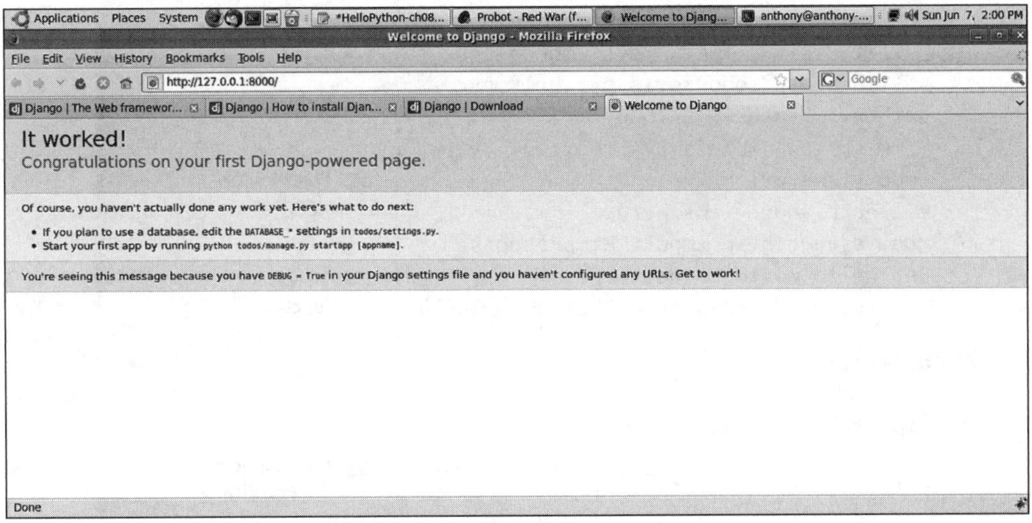

Figure 8.2   Django's starting screen

project might have several applications included, and Django will set up and coordinate between them. You can leave the development server running—it will automatically detect and reimport most changes you make.

NOTE   The Django developers encourage you to reuse code, and one of the ways they do that is to split projects into applications. Ideally, you'll have a number of applications within any one project, which all contribute their own part. You might have one application for storing your todos, another for email handling, a third for Paypal sign-ups, and so on. The next time you create a site with Django, you'll be able to reuse some of these applications to help you build it.

Now you can add an application and create your first simple page. This will help you confirm that everything's working and give you your first taste of creating a Django application. You need to edit two files: urls.py and todo/view.py. The next listing shows how I set up my todo application and what I put into my settings.py and url.py files.

Listing 8.2   First steps

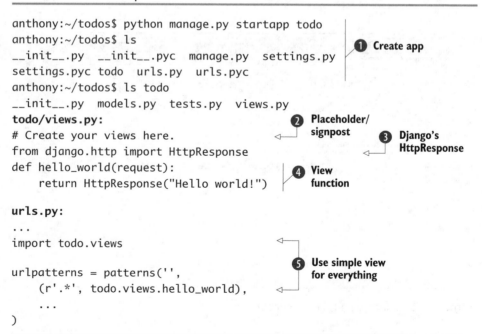

```
anthony:~/todos$ python manage.py startapp todo
anthony:~/todos$ ls                                               ❶ Create app
__init__.py  __init__.pyc  manage.py  settings.py
settings.pyc todo  urls.py  urls.pyc
anthony:~/todos$ ls todo
__init__.py  models.py  tests.py  views.py
todo/views.py:                                      ❷ Placeholder/
# Create your views here.                             signpost        ❸ Django's
from django.http import HttpResponse                                    HttpResponse
def hello_world(request):                           ❹ View
    return HttpResponse("Hello world!")               function

urls.py:
...
import todo.views

urlpatterns = patterns('',                          ❺ Use simple view
    (r'.*', todo.views.hello_world),                  for everything
    ...
)
```

The first step is to create your application with `manage.py` ❶. Django will create a `todo` folder to store all of your application-specific code.

Next you create your view. Django helpfully puts a comment in so you know you're in the right place ❷.

When you create a page to send back to the requester, there's a lot of detail involved: setting MIME types, status codes, and so on. Django's `HttpResponse` takes care of all that ❸ and stores all the possible variables in one place if you need to alter them.

❹ is a function that Django can call to display a web page. It takes a `Request` object, which represents the request for a web page, and returns a `Response` object. You're not doing anything fancy for now—just returning a response of "Hello world!"

`urls.py` is where you tie everything together ❺; you could think of it as Django's traffic controller, making sure each request goes to the right place. The `patterns` function takes a number of tuples containing regular expressions and functions. If a regular expression matches, Django will call the corresponding function and display whatever it returns. For now, you'll use `.*`, which will match everything.

TIP   Save time by keeping a directory somewhere with everything you need to set up a new project—in this case, the Django installer, your initial "Hello world!" setup, and anything you find useful as you go. It makes setting up your next project much faster.

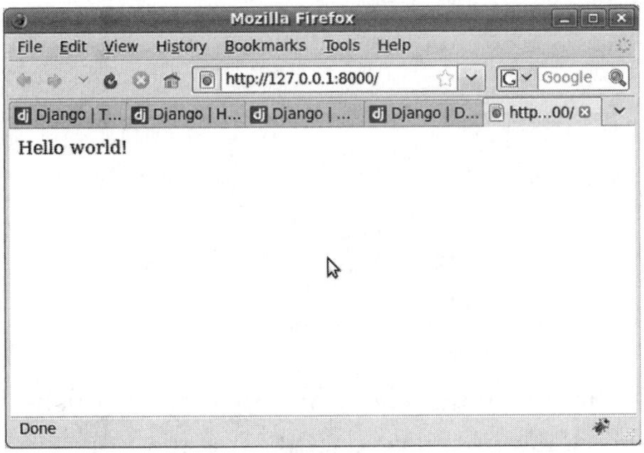

If you refresh your page now, you should see the not-quite-so-helpful "Hello world!" message, something like figure 8.3.

Figure 8.3 "Hello world!"

It's not much, but it's *your* "Hello world!" Now that you know a bit more about Django and how it works, let's start working on your todo list!

Writing your application

Because you have a pretty good idea of what your todo application should look like, you'll start with the front view and add back-end functionality as you need it, or else create a simple stand-in. As the need arises, you'll gradually introduce more and more of Django's functionality.

NOTE   This development strategy is only one way of building a program with Django. You can use other methods, such as creating the models you'll be working with first, or the business logic you'll need to control everything. It all depends on your application, where the technical risks lie, and what makes the most sense.

The simplest possible todo list

Here's your new todo list! It's simple, but you can already use it to keep track of your todos. You need to return the HTML for your todo page from your view, instead of the simple "Hello world!"

Listing 8.3   A simple todo list

```
def hello_world(request):
    return HttpResponse("""<html>
<head>
<title>My Todo list!</title>
</head>
<body>
<h1>Todos:</h1>
<p>Mow the lawn</p>
<p>Backup your PC</p>
<p>Buy some Milk</p>
</body>
</html>""")
```

If you need a new todo, add it into your view. When you've finished something, delete it. Perhaps that's not very useful, and it's annoying having to enter all the HTML by hand, but bear in mind that this is what Django does with any web page you ask it for. You need a better way of generating your HTML markup.

I'VE HEARD *GOOD* THINGS ABOUT THIS "RUBY ON TOP OF RAILS" THING, TOO. YOU SHOULD DEFINITELY LOOK INTO THAT.

Using a template

Django and most other web frameworks solve this problem by using a template. Rather than typing all the HTML up front, you can use a simple programming language to generate it from variables and lists that you have access to. The following listing gives a simple example.

Listing 8.4   Using a template

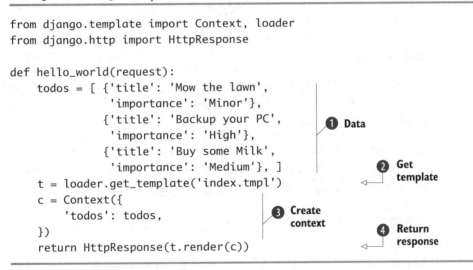

```
from django.template import Context, loader
from django.http import HttpResponse

def hello_world(request):
    todos = [ {'title': 'Mow the lawn',
               'importance': 'Minor'},
              {'title': 'Backup your PC',
               'importance': 'High'},
              {'title': 'Buy some Milk',
               'importance': 'Medium'}, ]
    t = loader.get_template('index.tmpl')
    c = Context({
        'todos': todos,
    })
    return HttpResponse(t.render(c))
```

❶ Data
❷ Get template
❸ Create context
❹ Return response

Here's your todo list. Nothing fancy for the moment: just remembering to mow the lawn, back up your PC, and buy some milk ❶.

The template handles the display of the page ❷, including all the fiddly HTML bits. You'll see what a template looks like and how to create it in a minute.

A context is a way of passing in variables to a template ❸. In this case, you're only interested in your list of todos, so that's all the template needs to know about.

TemplateDoesNotExist at /

todos/index.tmpl

Request Method:	GET
Request URL:	http://127.0.0.1:8000/
Exception Type:	TemplateDoesNotExist
Exception Value:	todos/index.tmpl
Exception Location:	/var/lib/python-support/python2.6/django/template/loader.py in find_templa
Python Executable:	/usr/bin/python
Python Version:	2.6.2
Python Path:	['/home/anthony/todos', '/usr/lib/python2.6', '/usr/lib/python2.6/plat-linux2', '/usr/lib/python2.6/dist-packages', '/usr/lib/python2.6/dist-packages/PIL', '/us /python2.6/dist-packages/gtk-2.0', '/var/lib/python-support/python2.6/gtk-2.0
Server time:	Sun, 7 Jun 2009 23:32:53 -0500

Template-loader postmortem

Django tried loading these templates, in this order:
- Using loader django.template.loaders.filesystem.load_template_source:
- Using loader django.template.loaders.app_directories.load_template_source:

Figure 8.4
Where's my
template?

❹ is where all the work gets done. You call the template's .render()
method with a particular context, create an HttpResponse object with it,
and send it back.

If you run this code as is, though, you'll get a TemplateNotFound error (as
shown in figure 8.4), because you haven't told Django about the
index.tmpl template.

You'll need to create the index.tmpl template, either within your todos
application or within a separate template directory. My version of the
template is shown in the following listing.

Listing 8.5   A simple template

```
<html>
<head>                                      ❶ HTML template
<title>My Todo List</title>
<style type="text/css">
    body { font-family: Arial, Helvetica, sans-serif;
           color: black;
           background: #ffffff; }
</style>
</head>
<body>
{% if todos %}                          ❷ if … else
<table border="1">
<tr><td>Todo</td><td>Importance</td></tr>
```

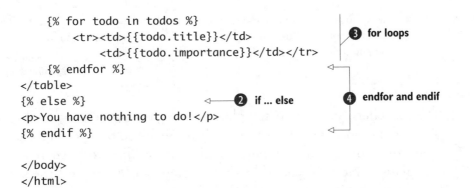

```
    {% for todo in todos %}
        <tr><td>{{todo.title}}</td>                    3 for loops
            <td>{{todo.importance}}</td></tr>
    {% endfor %}                                        4 endfor and endif
</table>
{% else %}                          2 if ... else
<p>You have nothing to do!</p>
{% endif %}

</body>
</html>
```

Your Django template is just an HTML page **1**, but with a few special commands to create some extra HTML on the fly. If you're familiar with HTML, templates won't be too much of a stretch.

Your first bit of template code is an `if` statement **2**. Python within the templates is wrapped within either `{% %}` brackets for program code, or `{{ }}` brackets for variables. The variables are sourced from the context the template is passed when it's rendered by your application.

You can also use `for` loops in your templates, to loop over a list or iterator **3**.

Normal Python programs rely on indentation to tell where a `for` loop or `if` statement begins and ends, but that's impossible when embedding code in a HTML template. To get around this problem, you need to include explicit end tags when closing your `if` statements or `for` loops **4**.

Last of all, you need to edit the settings.py file within your todos project so Django knows where to find the templates for your todo application.

Listing 8.6   Editing settings.py

```
...
TEMPLATE_DIRS = (
    # Put strings here, like "/home/html/django_templates"
    # or "C:/www/django/templates".
```

```
# Always use forward slashes, even on Windows.
# Don't forget to use absolute paths, not relative paths.
'/home/anthony/todos/todo',
)
```

Template directory ❶

Here's where your todo templates are stored ❶. Django will search subfolders, so if you find the application directory getting cluttered, you can store your templates within a subdirectory such as todo/templates/. Now if you refresh the page within your browser, you should see a nicely formatted table listing the tasks you have to do. If you think of another task, then add another item to the todos dictionary, and the template will take care of the rest.

But you still have a similar problem: you've gone from editing your HTML directly to editing a dictionary directly. Separating the presentation and data is an improvement, though, since now you're able to store your tasks in a database.

Using a model

But before you do that, you need to start a database, tell Django where it is, and populate it with your initial data. That's quite a lot of work—but Django will do most of it for you. You're using the built-in SQLite database, which is fine for your needs, but if you're writing a larger application, you might want a more industrial strength database, like MySQL or PostgreSQL.

Setting up the database

First of all, you need to edit your settings.py file to tell Django what database file to use. Open it up in your favorite editor, and change the database lines to look like this:

```
DATABASE_ENGINE = 'sqlite3'
DATABASE_NAME = 'todo.db'
```

The rest of the database lines you can leave as they are. There are some other settings to do with admin emails and time zones—which you can edit if you want to—but they're not immediately necessary. The one exception is that your time zone needs to be set to the same one as your system if you're running under Windows. See the documentation at http://docs.djangoproject.com/en/dev/ref/settings/#time-zone for more details, including a link to a list of valid time zone settings.

Now, type

```
python manage.py syncdb
```

and Django will set up your database. During the process, it will also ask you to create an admin user (a good idea). If you don't set up an admin user at this point, you can do so later on by running `python manage.py createsuperuser`.

Creating a model

Now you're ready to create model to store your data. Because you've already done a todo application back in chapter 4, you'll build on that data structure. You'll need to open up the models.py file within the todo directory and type something similar to what's in the following listing.

Listing 8.7   A todo model

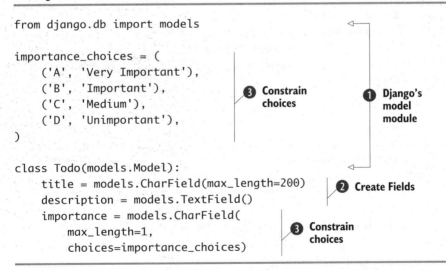

```
from django.db import models

importance_choices = (
    ('A', 'Very Important'),
    ('B', 'Important'),
    ('C', 'Medium'),
    ('D', 'Unimportant'),
)

class Todo(models.Model):
    title = models.CharField(max_length=200)
    description = models.TextField()
    importance = models.CharField(
        max_length=1,
        choices=importance_choices)
```

❸ Constrain choices

❶ Django's model module

❷ Create Fields

❸ Constrain choices

All the database interaction code is stored within Django's db module ❶. To declare your todos in a format Django can understand, you create a Todo class as a subclass of models.Model.

Fields in the database ❷ are similar to variables in Python—they store the values you need. Django has a number of different field types, and you can even create your own.

One of the important parts of using a database is that you can restrict the values that get entered into it ❸. This way, you can't enter nonsense information into your application—Django will catch it and refuse to add or edit your todo. You've placed importance_choices outside the model so you can access it in other contexts.

Once you've created your model, you need to let Django know it exists. You'll update your settings.py to tell Django about the todo application, and then sync your database, which tells Django to look for new models or fields and create them. The next listing shows how I did it.

Listing 8.8   Adding the todo application to your project

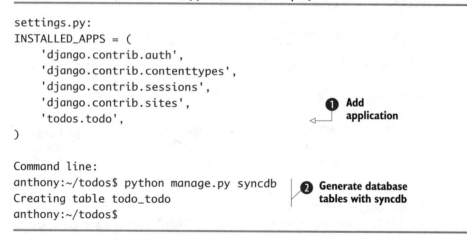

```
settings.py:
INSTALLED_APPS = (
    'django.contrib.auth',
    'django.contrib.contenttypes',
    'django.contrib.sessions',
    'django.contrib.sites',
    'todos.todo',                            ❶ Add
)                                               application


Command line:
anthony:~/todos$ python manage.py syncdb      ❷ Generate database
Creating table todo_todo                         tables with syncdb
anthony:~/todos$
```

❶ is the line you need to add. These lines will be converted to import lines by Django, so to be safe, you'll generally want to include the project name and the application.

Once you've done that, you can use manage.py to create your tables ❷.

If you have some database experience and want to look at what Django's doing behind the scenes, the next listing shows you how to use manage.py's sql command to inspect the todo model.

Listing 8.9   Showing your model's SQL

```
anthony:~/todos$ python manage.py sql todo
BEGIN;
CREATE TABLE "todo_todo" (
    "id" integer NOT NULL PRIMARY KEY,
    "title" varchar(200) NOT NULL,
    "description" text NOT NULL,
    "importance" varchar(1) NOT NULL
)
;
COMMIT;
```

Now that you have a database, all you need to do is add in some data so you can test the application. Django has an easy way to do that, too.

NOTE   When picking a framework like Django, one of the things to look out for is how many time-saving libraries it offers. Most web frameworks offer features like Model-View-Controller and routing URLs to views, so it's the extra features like the admin module that will make your life easier.

Django's admin module

One of Django's strengths is its built-in admin system, which will let you view and edit your data without having to write a lot of data handling and checking yourself. You only need to make a few changes to settings.py and urls.py, and sync your database, and you'll be ready to define an admin interface. Let's start by switching it on

Listing 8.10   Activating Django's admin system

```
settings.py:
INSTALLED_APPS = (
    ...
    'django.contrib.sites',
    'django.contrib.admin',
```
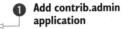 **1** Add contrib.admin application

```
        'todos.todo',
)

urls.py:
from django.contrib import admin          ❷ Autodiscover admin
admin.autodiscover()                          interfaces

urlpatterns = patterns('',
    (r'^admin/(.*)', admin.site.root),    ◁─┐  Pick URL for the
    (r'.*', todo.views.hello_world),      ❸    admin app
...
)
```

IS TELLINK
BOSS IS WRITTEN
IN WEB 2.1!
HE WILL BE WERY
HAPPY.

BUT ...

All the admin functionality is stored in the admin application, and it needs to create some database tables, so you include `django.contrib.admin` as an application ❶.

The `autodiscover` function looks through the admin interfaces you've written and automatically generates the configuration Django needs ❷. You'll also find that the admin functionality is already added to your urls.py—you only need to remove the comment characters from the start of the relevant lines.

The convention is for ^admin/(.*), but you can add whatever path you'd like if you'd prefer to keep things secret ❸. Anything that matches the path gets sent off to the admin module's root function.

Now all you need to do is to sync your db again, using `python manage.py syncdb`, and Django will create the admin tables and indexes it needs to function. Then visit http://127.0.0.1:8000/admin/, and you should see the login page for your server. Use the admin username and password you entered earlier and you should be able to get access to the admin page.

You're in, and there are some website-looking things, but where do you edit your todos? First you need to register your model with the Django admin interface, so it will know to include the model, which fields to display, and so on.

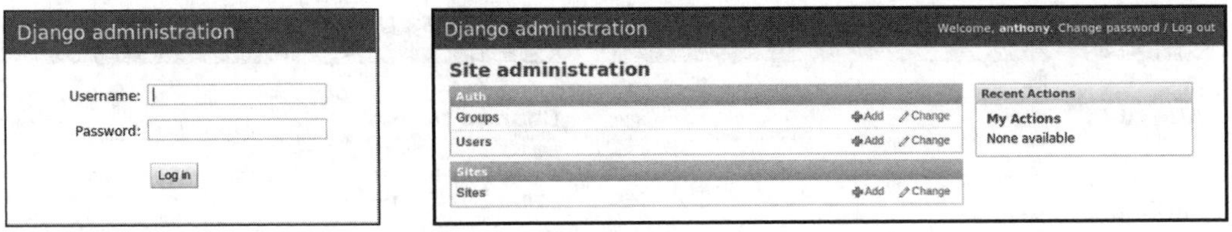

Figure 8.5 Logging into Django's admin system

Adding an admin interface

Django gives you a lot of flexibility in how your admin interfaces are designed, but for now, we're going to keep things simple. The following listing gives you the bare minimum you need to be able to see your todos in the admin interface. All the admin code is stored in todo/admin.py. There's not a lot—import your Todo model and admin, and register the Todo class as something that should be in the admin interface. Django will take care of the rest.

Listing 8.11   Registering your model: admin.py

```
todo/admin.py:
from todos.todo.models import Todo
from django.contrib import admin
admin.site.register(Todo)

todo/models.py:
class Todo(object):
    ...
    def __unicode__(self):
        return self.title
```

The only change you'll need to make to your model is to add a __unicode__ method. Without this, Django won't know how to refer to any particular todo, and you'll get the model name: Todo. You'll need to restart the server for the admin.autodiscover function to pick up your admin changes, but once you do, you should see a Todos link appear in the interface. If you click Todos and then Add Todo, you'll see something like figure 8.6. Also, notice that if you don't enter a value, or enter

---

Django administration

Home › Todo › Todos › Add todo

Add todo

Title:	Test Todo

Description: blah blah blah

Importance: `--------`

Very Important
Important
Medium
Unimportant

Django administration

Home › Todo › Todos › Test Todo

Change todo

⊖ Please correct the errors below.

Title:	Test Todo

⚠ This field is required.

Description:

⚠ This field is required.

Importance: `--------`

✖ Delete

Figure 8.6   Editing a todo in the Django admin interface

something that doesn't fit in your model, Django will notice and give you an error.

You can go ahead now and enter some todo items for yourself, then go back and have a look at the Todos page. You'll see that Django's admin page gives you a table of all the todos, and you can click through and edit any you need to.

The admin interface is also easy to customize if you need to show or hide some of the fields, or sort by a certain field. Let's add a column to show the importance of each todo:

```
class TodoAdmin(admin.ModelAdmin):
    list_display = ['title', 'importance']
    search_fields = ['title', 'description']
admin.site.register(Todo, TodoAdmin)
```

Normally, the Django admin will create this class for you automatically, based on some simple defaults. To create your own custom version, you subclass ModelAdmin and override the parts you'd like to change, such as which items to display in the list view.

YOU ARE WORRYING TOO MUCH, COMRADE GREGORY. THEY ARE NOT KNOWING RUBY FROM BADGERS!*

IF YOU SAY SO ...

* TODO: REPLACE "BADGERS" WITH SOMETHING FUNNY.

There are many other attributes that can affect the admin display. For example, you can include searching of title and description by adding this one line.

Now, when you register your class, you include the custom admin class instead of letting Django pick its own one.

If you restart your server and look at the todo list now, you'll see a second column. When you created your list of priorities earlier, you might remember that it used the values A, B, C, and D. The secret reason is that you can sort your todos according to priority by clicking at the top of the column.

All right, I think your admin interface is done. You don't normally want to give everyone access to the admin interface, so we'll take a look at how to provide a front end suitable for general consumption in the next section.

Making use of your data

Now that you have data to work with, you should provide an interface so other people can see what you're up to. It's often a good idea to have tangible output from your programs as soon as possible; that way, you can see what needs to be done, and people can give you feedback and ideas as early as possible.

Using the model

Let's first find out how you can get at the data in your database and make use of it. You'll update your previous view so it makes use of the database instead of your dictionary.

Listing 8.12   Altering your view

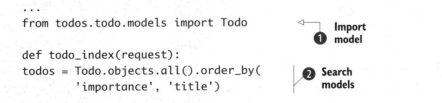

```
...
from todos.todo.models import Todo              Import
                                             ❶ model

def todo_index(request):
todos = Todo.objects.all().order_by(        ❷ Search
        'importance', 'title')                  models
```

```
t = loader.get_template('index.tmpl')
c = Context({
    'todos': todos,
})
return HttpResponse(t.render(c))
```

❸ Nothing else changes

Your model class is the main interface between the view and the database, so you need to import it ❶.

❷ looks for all your todos—nothing too fancy yet. `Todo.objects.all()` will return a QuerySet object that contains all your Todos, that you can then order with the `.order_by` method. There are other QuerySet methods that will help you to search through your model—a short list is in table 8.2.

Other than that, you don't need to make any changes to your view ❸— Django's templates are smart enough to adjust when you feed it a set of objects instead of a list of dictionaries.

Table 8.2   Some common Django `QuerySet` methods

Method	Description
`.all()[0]`	A QuerySet object won't trigger a query until it absolutely has to, so you can use slices like these to filter only the first few results in a query.
`.filter(criteria)` `.exclude(criteria)` `.get(criteria)`	`.filter()`, `.exclude()`, and `.get()` will return results according to criteria you specify as keyword arguments.
`.get(id__exact=14)` `.filter(importance__lte='B')` `.exclude(` `title__contains=` `'[blocked]')`	The keywords are specified as follows: `<field>__<type of match>` Django will convert them to the relevant SQL. You can also chain QuerySets together to further restrict the results you return.

There's one thing you need to change about your display, though. Your priorities are shown using the underlying letter, rather than the human-readable one. Fortunately, that's a simple change to the model and template, so let's do it now.

Listing 8.13   Readable priorities

```
models.py:
class Todo(models.Model):
    ...
    def text_importance(self):
        choices = dict(importance_choices)    ❶ Convenience
        return choices[self.importance]          function
```

```
index.tmpl:
...
    {% for todo in todos %}
        <tr>
            <td>{{todo.title}}</td>
            <td>{{todo.text_importance}}</td>    ❷ Update
        </tr>                                        template
    {% endfor %}
    ...
```

The first step is to update your model so it can provide you with the human-readable version of the priority without having to jump through too many hoops. The easy way to do that is to convert the `importance_choices` tuple to a dictionary ❶ and then use `self.importance` to access the right one.

Now, use the `text_importance` method within the template to display the importance of your todo ❷. Notice that Django's templates are once again smart enough to do the right thing regardless of what you feed them.

That's the basic functionality you need to display your todo items. You can extend your template to make the page look prettier, perhaps color-code the items according to how important they are, and so on. The `for` and `if` elements and the methods of your models should be enough to create most of the application.

GREG, WE'VE JUST SIGNED A MAJOR COSMETICS COMPANY.

WHICH ONE?

Table 8.3 shows some other template syntax elements that might be useful—but you're normally better off trying to include the functionality within the model or controller rather than the template if you need anything more complicated.

Table 8.3   Django template syntax cheat sheet

Syntax	Usage

```{% for variable in iterable %}```
   ```<tr class="{% cycle 'row1' 'row2' %}"```
   ```{{ variable }}```
```{% endfor %}```
	You've already seen the for loop in action. One handy extra, though, is cycle—it will swap between the values you give it on each pass through the loop.

```{% comment %}```
   ```...```
```{% endcomment %}```
	If you need to add comments to your template, this is the way to do it. Neither the comment tags nor the code between them will appear in the final output. Adding comments can be useful, but generally your templates should be simple enough that you don't need them.

```{% filter force_escape|lower %}```
   ```HTML-escaped lower case text.```
```{% endfilter %}```
```{{ variable|urlencode}}```
	You can apply various filters to the output of the template by either wrapping filter tags around what you need to escape or using the pipe character | and filter names. There are many different filters, such as upper, lower, and urlencode, that you can use—you can even write your own!

Now you have a way of getting data from the database out to the end user—but you need to be able to get data back again. To do that, you'll need to be able to submit forms.

Setting up your URLs

First, you need to think a little about how your application will be laid out. One good way that is easily supported by Django is called Representational State Transfer, or REST for short. In a nutshell, it's a style you can use to represent resources on the web, and the actions that can be performed on them.

REST works well for typical data-based applications, such as your todo application. In this case, you have a number of todos, and you'd like to be able to view, add, edit, and delete each individual todo. A typical REST design might look like the following listing.

Listing 8.14   A RESTful URL design

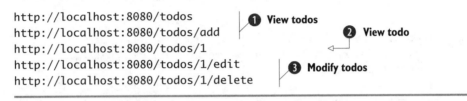

```
http://localhost:8080/todos
http://localhost:8080/todos/add
http://localhost:8080/todos/1
http://localhost:8080/todos/1/edit
http://localhost:8080/todos/1/delete
```

❶ View todos

❷ View todo

❸ Modify todos

If you think of the list of todos as a resource, this is the root level of your application **❶**. Adding a todo won't be linked to a todo, so it's best to make *add* a method of your root resource.

Once you've created a todo, viewing it means appending its ID onto the end of the URL **❷**.

Generally, the default method for any resource is to view it, but when you need to edit or delete a todo, you'll sometimes want to append the method **❸**. In this application, though, you'll just use the same URL for viewing and editing.

NOTE   One of the advantages of using a RESTful interface is that it encourages you to do one piece at a time. It's not normally a big deal if you haven't got deletion working yet—you can still test the other parts, because they're independent.

Now that you've mapped out how the application should work, how do you put it into practice? All your URL handling is stored within urls.py. It's there that you can specify which URLs will work and which views should handle them, and also extract the IDs. To help encapsulate your todo application a little better, though, you're going to create your own urls.py within todo and then include it from the standard urls.py.

Listing 8.15   Setting URLs and views

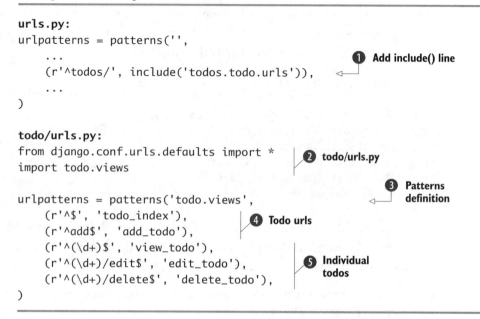

```
urls.py:
urlpatterns = patterns('',
    ...
    (r'^todos/', include('todos.todo.urls')),      ❶ Add include() line
    ...
)


todo/urls.py:
from django.conf.urls.defaults import *            ❷ todo/urls.py
import todo.views

                                                   ❸ Patterns
urlpatterns = patterns('todo.views',                   definition
    (r'^$', 'todo_index'),
    (r'^add$', 'add_todo'),                        ❹ Todo urls
    (r'^(\d+)$', 'view_todo'),
    (r'^(\d+)/edit$', 'edit_todo'),                ❺ Individual
    (r'^(\d+)/delete$', 'delete_todo'),                todos
)
```

I CAN'T TELL YOU JUST YET. BUT I'LL NEED YOU TO MAKE THE CUSTOMER ENTER THEIR EYE AND HAIR COLOR WHEN THEY SIGN UP TO OUR TODO LIST SITE.

UH ...

First, you include a separate urls.py file from within the root urls.py ❶. Note that the path is relative to the root of the project. You can also remove import todo.views.

Next, create urls.py within todo and add these two lines to it ❷. The first includes the default Django URL-handling functions, and the second imports the views.

Your pattern definition ❸ is exactly the same function definition you've been using in the root urls.py. One time saver here is that you can include the starting part of the function, rather than call todo.views.some_function several times.

Next, you define the URLs for viewing your todo list ❹ and adding a todo. Note that I've renamed the hello_world view to todo_index, which is a bit more sensible. The include function will also snip the previous todos/ part off the front, so you're matching a blank URL.

Finally, ❺ is the URLs for individual todos. There's one for viewing, one for editing, and another for deleting. Note that the URL regular expression has a group defined with brackets. The number that it matches will be fed in as an extra argument to the view—you'll see how to make use of it when we look at how to handle individual todo items.

WELL, IF YOU GUYS CAN'T DO IT, WE'LL HAVE TO HIRE SOMEONE WHO CAN ...
SHOULD NOT BE PROBLEM.
GREAT. GREAT.

Note that in the todo/urls.py file, you're not specifying the absolute path to any of your views, or anything outside your area of responsibility. This will help you later, particularly if you're trying to combine several different applications or you need to use your application somewhere else.

That's all you need to do to your URLs for now. Let's move on and write some views that can handle input from the user.

Submitting forms

The first thing you'll do is create the form and view necessary to handle adding a new todo. There's not much point in writing a todo-editing form if there aren't any todos to start with. You'll add it to the root page—it makes the most sense to include it there. When it's submitted, it will go to http://localhost:8080/todos/add, which will take care of the rest. The next listing shows how you can add a form to your template.

Listing 8.16　A submission form

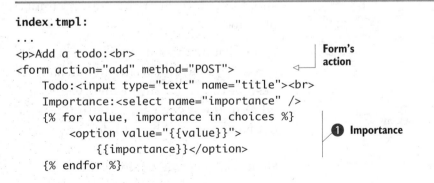

```
index.tmpl:
...
<p>Add a todo:<br>
<form action="add" method="POST">        ◁─── Form's action
    Todo:<input type="text" name="title"><br>
    Importance:<select name="importance" />
    {% for value, importance in choices %}
        <option value="{{value}}">        ❶ Importance
            {{importance}}</option>
    {% endfor %}
```

```
        </select><br>
        <textarea name="description"></textarea>
        <input type="submit" value="Add">
    </form>
    </p>
    ...
```

views.py:
```
from todos.todo.models import Todo, importance_choices

def todo_index(request):
    todos = Todo.objects.all().order_by(
                'importance', 'title')
    t = loader.get_template('index.tmpl')
    c = Context({
        'todos': todos,
        'choices': importance_choices,
    })
    return HttpResponse(t.render(c))
```

Feed choices ❷ into template

Don't forget that you'd like your todo application to be portable. It's tempting to use a hard-coded path like /todos/add, but that would mean you'd need to edit your template whenever you reused the application.

So that you don't have to repeatedly add separate instances of importance_choices —which could get out of sync —you include the version from your model ❶. The choices will need to be passed through to the template from the model ❷.

Todo	Importance
Test Important Todo	Very Important
Test Todo	Medium
Not very important	Unimportant

Add a todo:

Todo: asdf
Importance: Medium ⌄
Testing!

[Add]

Now, if you refresh the /todos/ page, you should see a form at the bottom, under the list of todos.

But if you try to submit the form, you'll get an error. You haven't written your handler yet, so despite the fact that, in theory, Django knows what to do, it can't find the function. The next listing shows you how to do that.

Figure 8.7   A form to add a todo

Listing 8.17 A view to handle adding a todo

```
...
from django.http import HttpResponseRedirect
from django.core.urlresolvers import reverse
...
def add_todo(request):
    t = Todo(
        title = request.POST['title'],
        description = request.POST['description'],
        importance = request.POST['importance'])
    t.save()
    return HttpResponseRedirect(
                reverse(todo_index))

def view_todo(request, todo_id):
    pass
def edit_todo(request, todo_id):
    pass
def delete_todo(request, todo_id):
    pass
```

❶ Addition view

❷ Create new todo

❸ Don't forget to save new todo!

❹ Redirect todo_ index view

❺ Stubs for other views

Handling post requests is no different than any other view. Define a function that takes a request parameter ❶.

Next, you create a new Todo instance, based on the values fed in via HTTP POST ❷. There aren't any restrictions on what you can enter, so you feed the parameters straight in.

Once you've created the todo, its .save() method writes it out to the database ❸.

GREG—GREAT NEWS! WE'VE JUST SIGNED A DEAL WITH A MAJOR PET FOOD DISTRIBUTOR! SO WE'LL NEED TO KNOW WHAT SORTS OF PETS OUR CUSTOMERS HAVE ...

You're finished, so you return to the index page with HttpResponse-Redirect ❹. So you're not hard-coding the URL with something like /todos/, you use the reverse() function, which takes either a view or the name of a view and returns its URL.

The reverse() function doesn't like having unimplemented views, so you'll add some now. Because they're all related to a particular todo, you make sure the ID for the todo is included ❺.

That should be all you need to do. If you enter a todo in the form and submit it, you should see it appear in the list. Congratulations! You now have a functioning web application. You can display data to the user from a database and accept input back, which your application can use to make additions to that data.

SECURITY IN DJANGO   If you've had some previous experience in web development, you're probably gritting your teeth over the previous code. Normally, blindly accepting input from the people using your site is a major security hole, leading to SQL injection and XSS (cross-site scripting) attacks, but Django's database layer and templating layer will automatically escape any input and data being displayed unless you tell it otherwise.

Almost any web framework, or even a CGI application, will let you do show data and accept requests. The nice thing about Django is that you can do it with only a small amount of simple, straightforward code, and build more advanced things on it easily.

You still need to take care of the individual todos, though — editing and deleting are just as important as being able to create new ones. We'll also look at some other ways you can make your development even easier, using some of Django's more advanced functionality.

Handling individual todos

One of the main advantages in using a web framework is that a lot of the simple, boilerplate stuff is already written for you. In Django's case, two of the most useful parts are generic views and model forms:

- Generic views are implementations of common types of views, for example, displaying a list of items from a particular model in the database, and all of the editing, updating, and deleting associated with it.

- Model forms are forms that are built directly from your model. Because they know the structure and type of your data, they can take care of the parsing and sanitizing of form data automatically, making it easy to get information back from the user of your application.

You'll mainly be using generic views for your application, but we'll touch on some of the model forms. Because your models and views are already written, you'll start with the URLs for your application and move on to templates in a minute.

Listing 8.18   Updating urls.py

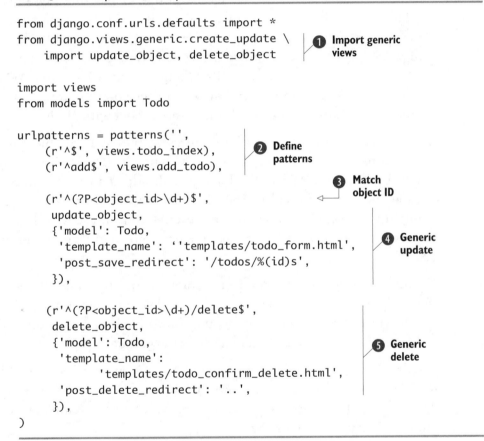

```
from django.conf.urls.defaults import *
from django.views.generic.create_update \          ❶ Import generic
    import update_object, delete_object               views

import views
from models import Todo

urlpatterns = patterns('',
    (r'^$', views.todo_index),                      ❷ Define
    (r'^add$', views.add_todo),                        patterns

                                                    ❸ Match
                                                       object ID
    (r'^(?P<object_id>\d+)$',
     update_object,
     {'model': Todo,
      'template_name': ''templates/todo_form.html',   ❹ Generic
      'post_save_redirect': '/todos/%(id)s',             update
     }),

    (r'^(?P<object_id>\d+)/delete$',
     delete_object,
     {'model': Todo,
      'template_name':                               ❺ Generic
            'templates/todo_confirm_delete.html',       delete
      'post_delete_redirect': '..',
     }),
)
```

`django.views.generic.create_update` contains the two views you need to use ❶. There are other views within `create_update`, but these are the only two you need.

Now that you're using generic views, the sources of your views differ and you can't use the `'todo.views'` shortcut. Instead, you'll feed in the functions directly ❷.

GREG! THE TAILOR'S ON BOARD NOW. SO CAN YOU ADD "INSIDE LEG MEASUREMENT" TO THE SIGN-UP FORM TOO?

❹ is a more advanced way of linking to a view, broken into multiple lines to make it easier to follow. The first line is the URL regular expression as usual, and the second is the view function. The third line onward is a dictionary of arguments to the view, which you also put one per line. The only mandatory one is model, but you're overriding template_name too (the default is todo/todo_form.html). The final parameter, post_save_redirect, tells Django where to go next. %(id)s is interpreted in the context of whatever object you're editing, so it will evaluate to /todos/1 if you're editing a Todo model with ID 1.

If you read ❹ and wondered how the view knew which object to edit, the ?P<object_id> part here is how it's done ❸. If you have a named match like this in your URL, Django will add it to the dictionary of arguments that is passed to the view, so you don't need to specify it explicitly. I normally name all the parameters in my URLs, because if you don't, they'll be fed in as arguments, and might be in the wrong order.

Finally, ❺ is the generic delete function. It's pretty much the same as the update one, except that once you've deleted your todo, you won't be able to redirect back to it; so you jump back one directory to the index page with the post_delete_redirect argument.

That's all you need to do within your URLs. Now you need to add two templates: one for updating and the other for confirming deletion. These have the same HTML as the previous index template, so I've omitted everything that's the same.

Listing 8.19   A todo editing template

```
...
<title>Edit Todo #{{object.id}}</title>                    ❶ Todo is called
...                                                             object
<form action="" method="POST">                            ❷ Form
    <table>                                                     action
    <tr><td valign="top">
```

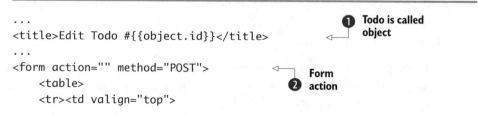

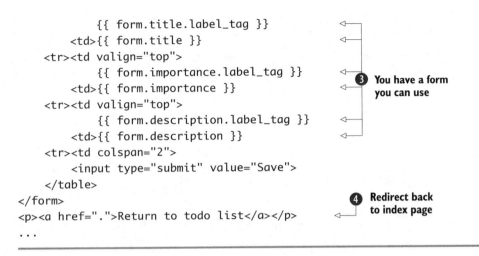

```
            {{ form.title.label_tag }}
        <td>{{ form.title }}
    <tr><td valign="top">
            {{ form.importance.label_tag }}
        <td>{{ form.importance }}
    <tr><td valign="top">
            {{ form.description.label_tag }}
        <td>{{ form.description }}
    <tr><td colspan="2">
        <input type="submit" value="Save">
    </table>
</form>
<p><a href=".">Return to todo list</a></p>
...
```

❸ You have a form you can use

❹ Redirect back to index page

The generic edit template is fed two variables automatically. The first one is object ❶, which is the object you're editing—in this case, your todo.

The view handles both the display and editing, so you don't need to do anything with the form's action attribute ❷; your input will be passed to the current URL.

The second variable you're given is form, which is one of Django's ModelForm objects that we touched on at the start of this section ❸. It has fields that match the ones defined in your model, along with a label_tag attribute, so you don't have to repeat the field names in your template. The ModelForm field will automatically output the right input element for the fields: text for the title, a dropdown for the importance, and a textarea element for the description.

If you don't want to edit a todo, or you've finished editing, you can use this link to go back to the main index page ❹. The 1 in todos/1 doesn't count as a directory, so you want to go to your current directory, which is ".".

Let's see what the edit form looks like. For now, you'll need to type the URL to your todo manually. http://localhost:8080/todos/1 should look like figure 8.8.

Title	Test Todo
Importance	Medium ⌄
Description	blah blah blah

Save

Return to todo list

Figure 8.8 Your edit view

If you enter new values for the todo and click Save, they should be saved to the database. You might want to have a separate window open with the index page, and refresh when you save, to double check.

Last but not least, you'll need to be able to delete a todo once you're done with it. The following form will let you do that.

Listing 8.20   A deletion template

```
...
<form action="" method="POST">
        <p>Are you sure you want to delete
           todo #{{object.id}}:
           "{{object.title}}"?<br>
        <input type="submit" value="Delete!"><br>
        <a href="..">Back...</a>
</form>
...
```

❶ POST vs. GET

❷ Return to index page

It's a good idea to force destructive behavior, such as editing or deleting a todo, to be done with a POST rather than a GET request ❶; this way, if someone accidentally browses to that page, or Google tries to index your site, nothing is damaged. Django follows this behavior — typing `http://localhost:8000/todos/1/delete` into the address bar of your browser is a GET request, so Django will prompt you to confirm your action via a POST.

You might not want to delete the todo (perhaps you clicked the wrong thing or mistyped), so you include a way to go back to the index page ❷. /todos/1/delete is one level deeper than /todos/1 because the /1/ is counted as a directory, so this back link goes one directory up.

Now if you go to http://localhost:8000/todos/1/delete, you should be prompted to delete todo #1. If you click Delete, your todo should be deleted from the system.

Final polishing

You're almost done with adding, editing, and deleting—the last thing you need to do is tie it all together and make it easy to click through to edit and delete an entry. You'll improve a few other things in the interface while you're at it.

Listing 8.21   Editing the index page

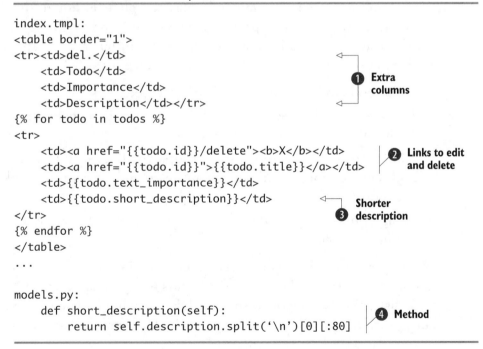

```
index.tmpl:
<table border="1">
<tr><td>del.</td>
    <td>Todo</td>
    <td>Importance</td>
    <td>Description</td></tr>
{% for todo in todos %}
<tr>
    <td><a href="{{todo.id}}/delete"><b>X</b></a></td>
    <td><a href="{{todo.id}}">{{todo.title}}</a></td>
    <td>{{todo.text_importance}}</td>
    <td>{{todo.short_description}}</td>
</tr>
{% endfor %}
</table>
...

models.py:
    def short_description(self):
        return self.description.split('\n')[0][:80]
```

❶ Extra columns

❷ Links to edit and delete

❸ Shorter description

❹ Method

You've added two extra columns to your listing ❶. The first is for a link to delete the todo, and the second is a snippet of the description.

OK GUYS—WE NEED TO FIND OUT WHY NOBODY'S SIGNING UP FOR OUR TODO LIST APPLICATION!

You also added links to the edit and delete functionality you've just written ❷.

A description might be several lines long and mess up your beautiful page, so you include `todo.short_ description` ❸ instead. This is a convenience method ❹ that returns, at most, 80 characters from the first line of the description.

Now you can add, edit, and delete todos by clicking through from the index page. Polish isn't so important while you're developing your application, but once you start to use it, you'll appreciate the extra effort you put in to make your application more usable.

Where to from here?

Your application is pretty much feature complete, although the design of the front page is bare "programmer HTML" and might need a little work. You can also add more functionality, to make your application easier to use or more featureful. Here are some ideas:

- Color-code todos based on their importance.
- Include some JavaScript to sort the columns by clicking the header of the table.
- Allow todos to be assigned to a group. You'll need to be able to add and remove groups, and you'll want to create a foreign-key link from the todo model to a particular group.
- Assign optional due dates to the todos, and sort by those instead of the importance.

We're not done with Django yet. In chapter 11, you'll extend the todo application further, allowing your friends to log in and create their own todo lists. We'll also look at some of Django's more advanced functionality, such as built-in unit testing, and look at some advanced database manipulation.

Summary

Now you can create your own web applications in Python using Django. We've covered all the basics in this chapter, including designing the URLs for your site and setting up views, models, and templates.

We also touched on several design issues when writing web applications, such as separating the design and data models from each other, limiting destructive edits to POST requests, and some simple design strategies. These suggestions are based on common practices and experience; working "with the grain" like this can save you lots of time and energy fighting with your development environment.

We'll return to the todo application in chapter 11, but for now take a break and try your hand at writing a desktop application. In this case, you'll be using a graphics library called Pyglet to create your own arcade game.

9

Gaming with Pyglet

This chapter covers

- *Display images and text on the screen*
- *Using event loops and timers*
- *Game design, and making your game fun*

In this chapter, you'll be writing your own arcade game using a library called Pyglet. Pyglet bills itself as a "cross-platform windowing and multimedia library for Python," but you'll be using it for its *real* purpose—writing games!

If you're familiar with various arcade games, yours will be sort of a cross between Spacewar!, Asteroids, and Space Invaders—it will have a spaceship, evil aliens to shoot, and a planet to run into. To make the game more interesting, you'll give the planet some gravity, so it draws in the ship gradually.

But first, you'll need to get Pyglet installed and working on your computer.

Installing Pyglet

The first thing you'll need to do is to download and install Pyglet. A Windows installer and source code are available from www.pyglet.org/download.html, and Pyglet is available as a package for several Linux distributions. Pyglet installation is straightforward under Windows: download the installer program, and run it. Mac users can download a .dmg image with an installer on it, and there are packages for most Linux distributions. The next figure shows the Windows installer doing its thing.

NOTE   Pyglet uses OpenGL under the hood, so you'll need an OpenGL-capable graphics card. This normally isn't a problem, unless you're running an old computer—most cards released in the past five years or so support OpenGL automatically.

If none of those options work for you, you can always download the source package and run `python setup.py install`, though you'll also need to install AVbin separately if you take this route.

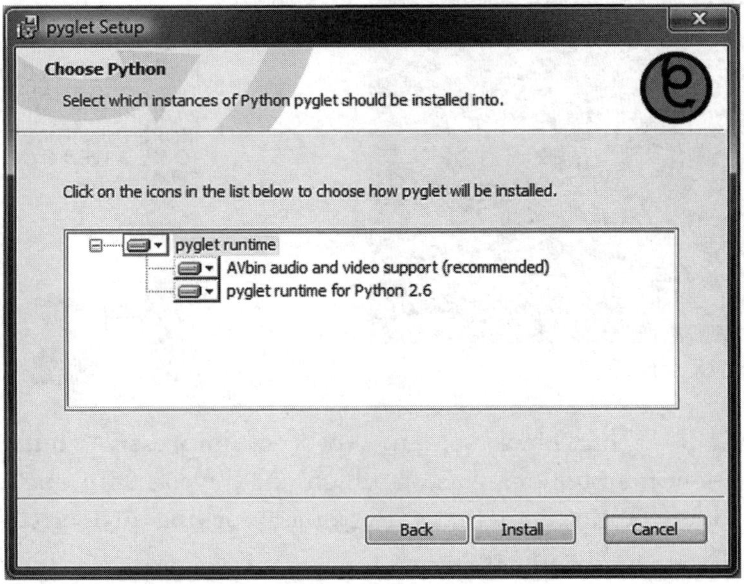

Figure 9.1   Installing Pyglet

Let's start with a simple Pyglet program, breaking it down line by line:

```
import pyglet
window = pyglet.window.Window(fullscreen=True)
pyglet.app.run()
```

All the submodules of Pyglet are stored within the pyglet module. You can access the window module, for example, with pyglet.window. This saves you importing several modules at the top of your program, and makes your code easier to read.

Pyglet's Window object handles all the screen initialization and rendering. You'll generally need one in every Pyglet application you write. You're passing in fullscreen=True as an argument so the window takes up the whole screen.

Pyglet is a framework, so after you've set everything up, you need to call its main application loop.

If you type this program in and run it, you should see a screen similar to figure 9.2.

I MANAGED TO CONVINCE THE BOSS THAT OUR WORKPLACE NEEDS A BIT MORE FUN IF WE'RE GOING TO BE A WEB 2.0 COMPANY ...

OH?

Figure 9.2   A black screen

That's right—a big black screen. Not very impressive, but it's *your* black screen: the blank canvas on which you'll write your masterpiece. As an added bonus, you know Pyglet is working properly. To exit Pyglet, press the Escape key.

Next, we'll figure out how to make that black screen more impressive.

First steps

Let's get started! The first thing you'd like to do is display an image on the screen. Because you're writing a space game, let's make it a nice big planet. I've used an image of Mars that I downloaded from NASA's website at www.nasa.gov/multimedia/imagegallery/, but feel free to create your own if you're feeling artistic. The next listing will display your planet image on the screen.

Listing 9.1   Drawing on the screen

```
import pyglet

window = pyglet.window.Window(fullscreen=True)
pyglet.resource.path.append('./images')          ❶ Image resource
pyglet.resource.reindex()                            folder

def center_anchor(img):
    img.anchor_x = img.width // 2
    img.anchor_y = img.height // 2                 ❷ Load planet
                                                      image
planet_image = pyglet.resource.image('mars.png')
center_anchor(planet_image)

class Planet(pyglet.sprite.Sprite):
    def __init__(self, image, x=0, y=0, batch=None):
        super(Planet, self).__init__(
            image, x, y, batch=batch)
        self.x = x                                 ❸ Create
        self.y = y                                   Sprite
                                                      class
center_x = int(window.width/2)
center_y = int(window.height/2)
planet = Planet(planet_image, center_x, center_y, None)

@window.event
def on_draw():                           ❹ Handle image
    window.clear()                          drawing
    planet.draw()

pyglet.app.run()
```

SO HE AGREED TO INSTALL AN ARCADE TABLE.

WHAT? REALLY?

Before you display images, you need to tell Pyglet where to find them. To do that, you append the path to an images folder onto Pyglet's resource path ❶ and ask it to reindex its resources. You'll also need to create the folder manually and save your planet image in it.

Once you have your image source, all you need to do is call the `pyglet.resource.image` function, which will read the image from your resource directory ❷. By default, an image has an anchor at the lower-left corner; you'd prefer it in the center. I've created a function that will do that for you. Because you want the x and y coordinates to be integers, Python's integer division operator (//) makes sure the result is an integer.

Pyglet is capable of drawing images directly to the screen, but a faster and cleaner way is to use a `Sprite` class ❸. Sprites track their position and image and have their own optimized drawing routines, which make your program run faster. You'll create one instance of your planet and stick it right in the middle of the screen. One thing to note is that you're calling `super(Planet, self)` to get the parent class of your sprite—so you don't have to worry about manually updating it.

TIP   Games are an area where a class-based design often makes a lot of sense, because there are usually a number of entities that behave similarly.

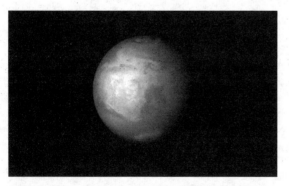

Figure 9.3 Your planet. Ideal for running into with your spaceship! (Image courtesy of NASA/JPL/Malin Space Science Systems)

Once you've created the sprite, you need to tell Pyglet to draw it every frame. To do this, you create an `on_draw` event handler ❹ for the window (we'll cover event handlers in more detail in the next section). You'll do more later, but for now you clear the screen and draw the planet.

You should see a nice big planet in the middle of your screen.

The planet will be a hazard for your space-ship, but first you need a spaceship. Let's do that part next. In the process, we'll introduce some important concepts when writing games or any event-based program.

ALL THE COOL STARTUPS ARE HAVINK THEM. I PERSONALLY WAS SPACE INVADER CHAMPION AT EVIL TECHNICAL COLLEGE IN MOSCOW.

Starship piloting 101

Your ship follows much of the same process as the planet, with one main exception: it will move around the screen in response to the player pressing keys. If you've ever played Asteroids, you'll be familiar with the control method you'll use. The up arrow will fire your engines, and left and right will turn your ship. If you want to slow down or go backward, you need to turn your ship around completely and fire your engines in the opposite direction.

The following listing shows the start of your Ship class. You'll be adding features to it through the rest of this section. I've included this class in the same file as the planet, but feel free to create a new file and import it.

Listing 9.2   **Ship class**

```
ship_image = pyglet.resource.image('ship.png')        ❶ Load ship
center_anchor(ship_image)                                image
...
class Ship(pyglet.sprite.Sprite):
    def __init__(self, image, x=0, y=0,
                dx=0, dy=0, rotv=0, batch=None):
        super(Ship, self).__init__(
            image, x, y, batch=batch)
        self.x = x
        self.y = y                                    ❷ Sprite
        self.dx = dx                                     class
        self.dy = dy
        self.rotation = rotv
        self.thrust = 200.0
        self.rot_spd = 100.0

...
```

```
ship = Ship(ship_image,                              ❸ Create Ship
            x=center_x + 300, y=center_y,              instance
            dx=0, dy=150, rotv=-90)                     #...
@window.event
def on_draw():                    ❹ Don't forget to
    window.clear()                   draw the ship!
    planet.draw()
    ship.draw()
```

First, you load the image for your ship ❶, in the same way you did for the planet. Your `Ship` class looks similar to `Planet`, but you have some extra information ❷: `.dx` and `.dy` are the ship's speed in the x and y directions, and `.rotation` is how far left or right you've turned. You also put in `.thrust` and `.rot_spd` to determine how fast the ship should accelerate and turn. The higher these numbers are, the faster the ship will go.

Now you can create an instance of your ship ❸. You feed in the ship's speed here as `dx` and `dy`, but it won't have any effect until you start updating the ship's position in the next section.

Once you have your ship, you can add `ship.draw()` to the on_draw event handler, and your ship will appear on the screen ❹.

Now you can see where your ship will start, and what it looks like.

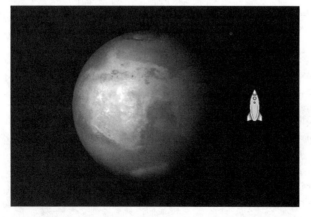

Figure 9.4 Your spaceship

WELL, WE'LL SEE. I'LL GIVE YOU A FEW DAYS TO PRACTICE BEFORE I KICK YOU TOO HARD ...

So far it's no different than the planet you're drawing, but now that you've set up your sprite, you can start making it do things.

Making things happen

In most games, you have control over some aspect—such as the main character—and can give input to tell them what to do next. Push the left arrow and move left; push the right arrow and move right. In this section, you'll see how games accomplish this.

Pyglet uses an *event-based* programming model, and it's how most interactive programs like games and graphical user interfaces are written. Rather than checking or waiting for input at certain sections of your program, you instead register functions to be called when something interesting happens. Pyglet refers to these functions as *event handlers*. If you're used to a standard imperative design ("do this, then this..."), an event-based structure can seem odd, but it's a much cleaner way of writing some sorts of programs. The next listing introduces two event handlers—one for when keys are pressed, and another for when they're released.

Listing 9.3   Handling events

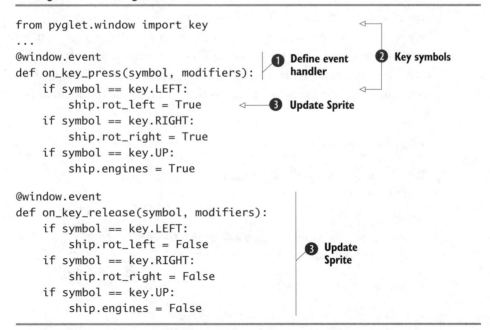

```
from pyglet.window import key
...
@window.event                          ❶ Define event    ❷ Key symbols
def on_key_press(symbol, modifiers):      handler
    if symbol == key.LEFT:
        ship.rot_left = True           ◀── ❸ Update Sprite
    if symbol == key.RIGHT:
        ship.rot_right = True
    if symbol == key.UP:
        ship.engines = True

@window.event
def on_key_release(symbol, modifiers):
    if symbol == key.LEFT:
        ship.rot_left = False
    if symbol == key.RIGHT:             ❸ Update
        ship.rot_right = False             Sprite
    if symbol == key.UP:
        ship.engines = False
```

WOW, SID REALLY WENT ALL OUT.

DA! EVEN HAS GENUINE FAKE WOOD PANELLING FROM EARLY 80S!

To respond to keys, Pyglet defines two event handlers, on_key_press and on_key_release ❶. They're defined in much the same way the on_draw function is, but they have two arguments: the key that is pressed, and any extra keys that are held down, such as Shift or Ctrl.

The symbol argument is an integer, but Pyglet defines a large number of keys you can use ❷ without having to worry about how to represent non-printable keys, like left arrow or the Esc key. To use them, import key from pyglet.window.

If arrow keys are pressed, you need to make some change to the game's state. In this case, they correspond directly to the ship, so you'll make a change to the ship's state, and let the ship handle the changes during its update method ❸.

TIP　Events are a powerful technique that make your programs simpler and easier to write. The alternative is to write one big loop that checks everything in your game. It has to run as quickly as possible, or your game will be slow and unplayable.

Once you've done that, pressing the arrow keys will trigger an on_key_press event and update your ship's status—but you won't see anything happen on the screen. That's because you haven't told the ship how to respond to changes in its status. For that, you'll need to write an update method to change the rotation of the ship according to its status.

Listing 9.4 Updating the ship

```
class Ship(pyglet.sprite.Sprite):
    def __init__(...):
        ...
        self.rot_left = False
        self.rot_right = False          ❶ Set initial state
        self.engines = False

    def update(self, dt):               ❷ Ship's update
                                          function
```

```
        if self.rot_left:
            self.rotation -= self.rot_spd * dt
        if self.rot_right:
            self.rotation += self.rot_spd * dt
...
def update(dt):
    ship.update(dt)

pyglet.clock.schedule_interval(update, 1/60.0)
```

❸ **Rotating ship**

❹ **Main update function**

❺ **Call update function**

When the ship is first created, it won't be turning left or right, or firing its engines. You set the ship's state here ❶ so your update function won't throw an exception later.

By convention, most Pyglet classes will have an update method that gets called on each "tick" of the game engine ❷. This is where your sprites change their position, create new objects in the game, and update their internal state. An update method takes one argument, dt, which tells you how much time has passed since the last time update was called.

You're starting out simply, so you're rotating the ship left and right for now ❸. If you're turning, then you update the .rotation attribute (a Pyglet built-in that rotates the sprite) by multiplying your rotation speed by dt.

Later, you'll have other objects with update methods, so it's a good idea to collect all of the method calls in one place ❹.

Figure 9.5 Turning the ship

Finally, you set Pyglet's built-in scheduler to call your main update method 60 times per second ❺. This is the maximum speed at which Pyglet will run your game. If it's slower, then you'll get different values for dt, but your game will still run.

Now your feedback loop is finished, and you can see the results of all your hard work. If you run the program, you should be able to rotate your ship left and right by pushing the left and right arrow keys.

The next step is to make your ship move. To do that properly, though, you'll need to learn a bit about how to specify directions and distances.

Back to school: Newton's first law (and vectors)

In order to make your ship move consistently, you'll need to apply a little bit of theory. You may remember some of this from school, from math or physics courses. If not, don't worry—we'll be taking things one step at a time. The first thing to know is that x represents values that go left to right, and y represents values that go up and down, as illustrated here.

NEWTON'S FIRST LAW

If you think back to your physics classes, you might remember Newton's first law. Briefly, it states, "A body in motion will continue that motion unless acted on by an external force." What this means is that your ship should move in a straight line unless you fire the engines. You already have a velocity—that's the .dx and .dy attributes of your Ship class.

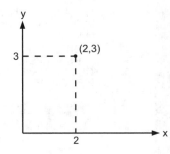

Figure 9.6   x and y coordinates. x represents values that go left to right, and y represents values that go up and down.

VECTORS

The second thing you need is a way to convert the angle of the ship and its acceleration into values you can add to the ship's x and y velocities. Whenever your ship's engines are firing, you'll need

to break up its angle like this to work out the effect on your velocity in the x and y directions. The direction in the next figure means that when the ship's engines fire, you'll need to add 2 to your x velocity and 3 to your y velocity.

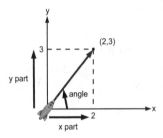

Figure 9.7
The ship's angle can have x and y parts.

You'll need a few math modules to do this in Python, but the principle isn't any different from figure 9.7: figure out the x and y parts of the acceleration, and add those to your x and y velocities. During each update, add your velocity to your position.

Listing 9.5   Moving the ship

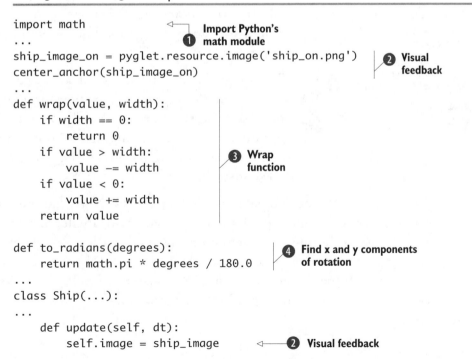

```python
import math                                    ①  Import Python's
...                                               math module
ship_image_on = pyglet.resource.image('ship_on.png')    ②  Visual
center_anchor(ship_image_on)                               feedback
...
def wrap(value, width):
    if width == 0:
        return 0
    if value > width:
        value -= width                         ③  Wrap
    if value < 0:                                 function
        value += width
    return value


def to_radians(degrees):                       ④  Find x and y components
    return math.pi * degrees / 180.0              of rotation
...
class Ship(...):
...
    def update(self, dt):
        self.image = ship_image                ②  Visual feedback
```

```
    if self.rot_left:
        self.rotation -= self.rot_spd * dt
    if self.rot_right:
        self.rotation += self.rot_spd * dt
    self.rotation = wrap(self.rotation, 360.)    ◄────❸ Wrap function

    if self.engines:
        self.image = ship_image_on    ◄────❷ Visual feedback
        rotation_x = math.cos(
            to_radians(self.rotation))
        rotation_y = math.sin(                    ❹ Find x and y
            to_radians(-self.rotation))              components
                                                     of rotation
        self.dx += self.thrust * rotation_x * dt    ❺ Alter
        self.dy += self.thrust * rotation_y * dt       velocity

    self.x += self.dx * dt        ❻ Update
    self.y += self.dy * dt           position

    self.x = wrap(self.x, window.width)     ❸ Wrap
    self.y = wrap(self.y, window.height)       function
```

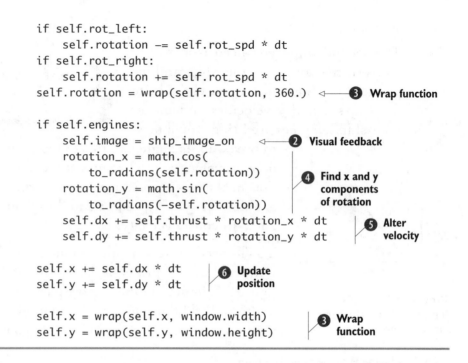

A FEW HOURS LATER ...

57,030! A NEW HIGH SCORE!

WE WILL BE SEEINK ABOUT THAT ...

All the trigonometric functions you need are stored in Python's math module, so you start by importing it ❶.

Thinking ahead a little, you'll also want to be able to handle the case where the ship moves off the edge of the screen. You'll take the easy option and wrap the game up and down and left to right ❸. wrap is a function that does that—given the value and the amount you'd like it to be constrained to.

Next, you break your angle into x and y parts ❹. Note that these might be negative if the angle points left or down. Also, Pyglet and the .math module use different representations of angles (degrees versus radians), so you need a function to convert from Pyglet's version into something the math module can use. You also need to flip your rotation around to get the right values in the y direction.

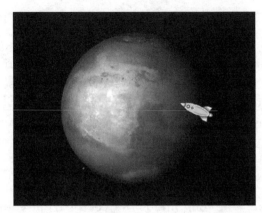

Figure 9.8
Now you can drive your spaceship around. Brrm! Brrm!

Once you have your two components, the rest is relatively straightforward. You multiply each part by the ship's acceleration and how long it's been since your last update, and add each 1 to your velocity ❺.

The last step is to update your position on the screen ❻. You also check to make sure you can't go over the edge of the screen by wrapping your x and y positions based on the height and width of the window.

Finally, it looks a bit odd for your ship to be flying around without any visual feedback, so I created an extra image with some flames shooting out of the back. You swap it over whenever the ship's engines are on ❷.

Now you can drive your ship around the screen, accelerate, and turn around to decelerate. Wheee! It's fun for a while, but ultimately there's not much to do, and the mechanics are easy to understand. What you'd like is to have something more complex, so you have more opportunities for different sorts of interaction with the game.

Gravity

You'll add to the game by making the planet have gravity, so it pulls on the ship. If the ship collides with the planet, then BOOM! No more ship! Fending off aliens while trying to keep clear of the planet should add enough difficulty to keep the player occupied and entertained.

Calculating gravity

How exactly do you go about adding that functionality? Well, the obvious place to put it is within the Planet class. It makes sense because it's the planet that's affecting the ship, and if you want anything else to be pulled by the planet's gravity, it won't be too hard to add. Essentially, you're adding another force to the ship, just as you did when firing its engines.

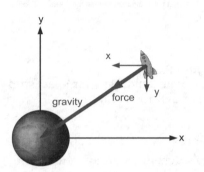

Figure 9.9 shows you what the problem looks like. The long line is the vector from your ship to the planet. You'd like to find that, convert it into a force vector, and then split that vector into an x and y so you can easily add it to your ship's velocity. Let's deal with the easy bit first: splitting the force vector.

Figure 9.9 Gravity applies a force to your ship.

Listing 9.6   Planet updates

```
class Planet(pyglet.sprite.Sprite):
    def __init__(self, image, x=0, y=0, batch=None):
        super(Planet, self).__init__(
                    image, x, y, batch=batch)
        self.x = x
        self.y = y

    def update(self, dt):
        force, angle = self.force_on(ship)
        force_x = force * math.cos(angle) * dt
        force_y = force * math.sin(angle) * dt
        ship.dx += force_x
        ship.dy += force_y
...
def update(dt):
    planet.update(dt)
    ship.update(dt)
```

❶ Apply force to ship

❷ Update planet

First you need to find out how much gravitational force the planet will put on the ship. We'll gloss over this part for now; all you need to know is that, in a minute, you'll create a method that will tell you the magnitude and direction of the force ❶. Other than this, it's the same as when you updated the ship when its engines were firing.

Don't forget to include the update method ❷ in the main update function.

72,490! YOU WILL NOT BE BEATING THAT ONE FOR SOME TIME, COMRADE GREG!

Now you have a nice, well-defined problem to solve: find the distance and angle to the ship. This is the opposite problem to the one you solved earlier. Back then, you had an angle and distance and wanted the x and y parts; now you have the x and y parts and want to know the angle and distance.

Listing 9.7   Figuring out gravity

```
class Planet(...):          ◁─┐   Planet has
                            ❶  mass
    def __init__(self, image, x=0, y=0, batch=None):
        super(Planet, self).__init__(image, x, y, batch=batch)
        self.x = x
        self.y = y
        self.mass = 5000000  # experiment!


                                        ❷  Which way is
                                           the ship?
    def dist_vec_to(self, target):   ◁─┘
        dx = target.x - self.x       ❸  Calculate
        dy = target.y - self.y          x and y
        sqr_distance = dx**2 + dy**2    ❹  Find distance
        distance = math.sqrt(sqr_distance)

        angle = math.acos(float(dx) / distance)
        if dy < 0:                               ❺  Find angle
            angle = 2*math.pi - angle
        return (distance, angle)     ◁─┐
                                     ❻  Return vector
    def force_on(self, target):
        G = 1  # experiment!                        ❼  Calculate
        distance, angle = self.dist_vec_to(target)     force
        return ((-G * self.mass) / (distance ** 2), angle)
```

First, set your planet's mass ❶. The heavier your planet is, the more it will pull on your ship. This is one of the elements of your game you can tweak to make it easier or harder.

The core of your method is to find out how far away the ship is, and in which direction ❷. Based on that, you can calculate everything else you need.

Next, you find out the distance to the target (the ship) in the x and y directions ❸. The distances might end up being negative if the ship is to the left or below — that's normal.

Now you can find the first part of what you need, which is the distance to the ship ❹. This is determined using the Pythagorean theorem: square the two smaller sides, and take the square root.

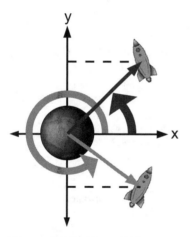

Figure 9.10 Two different angles, same x position and distance

The angle is a little trickier ❺. With a horizontal and vertical distance, you can use `math.acos` or `math.asin` to find the angle, but you need to take the complete 360-degree range into account. `math.acos` is only valid for the first half of the circle, so you need to reflect the angle by subtracting it from `2*math.pi` if it's in the wrong half. Figure 9.10 shows this in a little more detail: the two angles are different, even though the x distance and the direct distance are the same.

Once you have the distance and angle, you can return those vectors ❻. I've chosen (distance, angle) as the way a vector is represented, to avoid accidental confusion later.

NOTE If all this math seems a little complicated, don't worry too much. You have easy-to-use methods for calculating vectors and forces that you can reuse in your next game.

Now that you know the distance and direction to the ship, calculating the force due to gravity is easy ❼. It's proportional to the mass of the

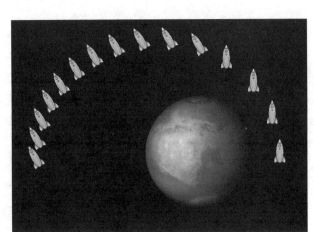

Figure 9.11
Your ship in orbit
around the planet

planet and diminishes with the square of the distance. The closer the ship, the more force you apply to it. Figure 9.11 shows a time lapse of the ship moving.

When you run the program, you should see the ship being affected by gravity! Rather than moving in a straight line, it will have a force applied to it by the planet and will move in a graceful curve. If you're careful, you can even put your ship into an orbit around the planet.

Watch out for that planet!

For collision detection, we're sticking with circles around the ship, planet, and alien. Circles like those in figure 9.12 make the code simpler and more straightforward; but in trading accuracy for simplicity,

you might notice a few collisions that should have been near misses. It's possible to get pixel-perfect accuracy with Pyglet by comparing the overlap of the images themselves, but that's outside the scope of this chapter.

In practice, though, you don't need to draw circles—you can compare the distance between the ship and the planet, and then compare that to the radius of the planet and the ship.

Figure 9.12 The planet's and ship's collision circles

Listing 9.8   Crashing into the planet

```
class Planet(...):
    def __init__(...):
        ...
        self.radius = (self.image.height +           ❶ Add attributes
                        self.image.width) / 4            objects
    ...
    def update(self, dt):
        distance, angle = self.dist_vec_to(ship)     ❷ How far away
        if distance <= ship.radius + self.radius:        is the ship?
            ship.reset()
            ship.alive = False      ❸ Crash!
            return
        ...


class Ship(...):
    def __init__(...):
        ...
        self.alive = True                            ❶ Add attributes
        self.radius = self.image.width / 2              objects

    def reset(self):
        self.life_timer = 2.0  # seconds until respawn
        self.x = center_x + 300;
        self.y = center_y                            ❹ Reset
        self.dx = 0; self.dy = 150                       ship
        self.rotation = -90


    def update(self, dt):
        ...
        if not self.alive:
            print ("Dead! Respawn in %s" %
                    self.life_timer)
            self.life_timer -= dt
            if self.life_timer > 0:                  ❺ Handle player's
                return                                  death; respawn
            else:
                self.reset()
                self.alive = True
...
ship = Ship(ship_image)         ❹ Reset
ship.reset()                       ship
```

```
...
@window.event
def on_draw():
    window.clear()
    planet.draw()
    if ship.alive:
        ship.draw()
```

6 **Dead players aren't drawn**

You'll need a few attributes on your objects **1**. One is to tell the game whether the ship is alive or not, and the others are the radius of the planet and the ship. To make life easier, you'll calculate the radius of the ship and the planet from the size of their images. If you change the image later, you won't need to update the object's radius.

SID, YOU'VE BEEN PLAYING FOR AN HOUR. AND YOUR SCORE'S ONLY 30,000?

PEWPEWPEWPEW
FANFARE
PEWPEWPEPWPEWP
EWPEWPEWPEWPEW
PEWPEW ...

With circles to detect collisions, all you need to do is compare the distance between the ship and the planet, and the sum of their radiuses **2**. If the distance is shorter, then the circles intersect, and you have a collision.

Once your spaceship has crashed **3**, you mark the ship as dead and reset the player's position.

The ship's .reset() method puts the ship back at the start **4** and sets its velocity to something reasonable. You're also setting a "life timer" that determines the time until the ship restarts, giving the player a few seconds to think about what went wrong. You can use this to set the ship's position at the start so you don't need to feed in a position when you create your class.

To delay the ship's return, you check the life_timer attribute you set in the .reset() method **5**. If you're dead and the timer is greater than zero, then you still have some time left. If it's less than 0, then you can mark the ship as alive and reset its position once more (because gravity still affects it), and you're back to normal.

The last thing you need to do is make sure the ship isn't drawn when it's dead **6**. A simple if statement takes care of that.

Now that your game is starting to take shape, you can see the general form a game takes. It has a certain state, effectively a simulation of a number of things like planets and ships, and you can have an effect on that simulation in certain ways. With some thought, a bit of luck, and some experimentation, your simulation will have aspects that are fun.

Next up, let's add some excitement to your game.

Guns, guns, guns!

What's a space game without aliens to shoot? Even space trading games have guns of some sort, so if you don't have any, you'll look a bit odd. They're easy to add, given the work you've already done on angles and timers: set the bullet travelling at high speed at the same angle as the ship, and update it in a similar way. You'll also want to keep track of whether the bullet has run into anything, and after a certain amount of time, remove it from the game.

Listing 9.9   Shooting

```
bullet_image = pyglet.resource.image('bullet.png')
center_anchor(bullet_image)
...
class Ship(pyglet.sprite.Sprite,
          key.KeyStateHandler):
    def __init__(...):
        self.shot_timer = 0.1
        self.reload_timer = self.shot_timer
        self.bullets = []

    def update(self, dt):
        if self[key.LEFT]:  ...
        if self[key.RIGHT]: ...

        rotation_x = math.cos(to_radians(self.rotation))
        rotation_y = math.sin(to_radians(-self.rotation))
        if self[key.UP]:     ...
        ...
        if self.reload_timer > 0:
            self.reload_timer -= dt
```

❷ **Limit number of shots**

❸ **Delete bullets**

❶ **Use KeyStateHandler**

❹ **FIRE!**

❷ **Limit number of shots**

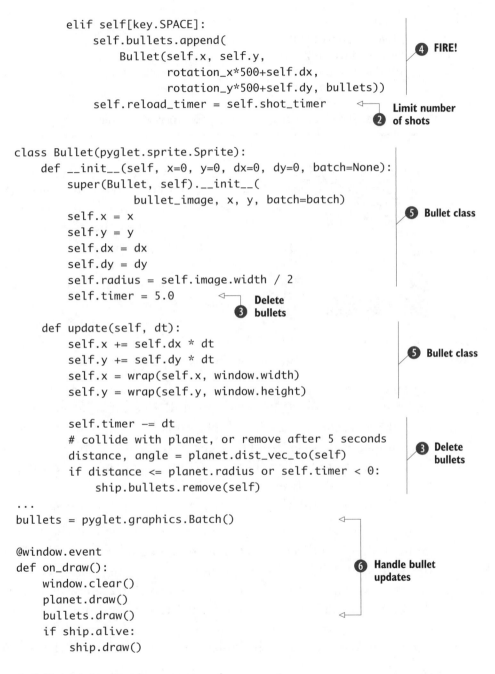

```
        elif self[key.SPACE]:
            self.bullets.append(
                Bullet(self.x, self.y,
                       rotation_x*500+self.dx,
                       rotation_y*500+self.dy, bullets))
            self.reload_timer = self.shot_timer
```

4 **FIRE!**

2 **Limit number of shots**

```
class Bullet(pyglet.sprite.Sprite):
    def __init__(self, x=0, y=0, dx=0, dy=0, batch=None):
        super(Bullet, self).__init__(
                bullet_image, x, y, batch=batch)
        self.x = x
        self.y = y
        self.dx = dx
        self.dy = dy
        self.radius = self.image.width / 2
        self.timer = 5.0
```

5 **Bullet class**

3 **Delete bullets**

```
    def update(self, dt):
        self.x += self.dx * dt
        self.y += self.dy * dt
        self.x = wrap(self.x, window.width)
        self.y = wrap(self.y, window.height)

        self.timer -= dt
        # collide with planet, or remove after 5 seconds
        distance, angle = planet.dist_vec_to(self)
        if distance <= planet.radius or self.timer < 0:
            ship.bullets.remove(self)
...
bullets = pyglet.graphics.Batch()

@window.event
def on_draw():
    window.clear()
    planet.draw()
    bullets.draw()
    if ship.alive:
        ship.draw()

# Call update 60 times a second
```

5 **Bullet class**

3 **Delete bullets**

6 **Handle bullet updates**

```
def update(dt):
    planet.update(dt)
    ship.update(dt)
    for bullet in ship.bullets:          ❻ Handle bullet
        bullet.update(dt)                    updates
...
window.push_handlers(ship)          ◁────❶ Use KeyStateHandler
```

THIS BEHAVES EXACTLY LIKE THE OLD ARCADE MACHINES, REMEMBER? ONCE YOU GET TO 999,999, IT'LL WRAP AND START AGAIN FROM ZERO.

WRAP?!

TWICE.

An easier way to manage key presses is to use Pyglet's KeyStateHandler class ❶. This class keeps track of which keys have been pressed and makes them available with a dictionary syntax, so you don't need extra event handlers and state on your Ship class. If you push the left arrow key, then self[key.LEFT] will be set to True. The only tricky part to remember is that the ship instance is now a key handler, so you need to do a window.push_handlers(ship) so Pyglet knows to pass it events.

If you only let the player fire when the spacebar is pressed, they'll get a bullet per frame, or 60 shots per second! Even if your computer is fast enough to handle hundreds of bullets onscreen, it makes the game a bit easy: it means you can fill the screen with bullets until there's nowhere for the alien to hide. You'll limit the number of shots by setting a timer whenever the ship fires a bullet ❷. Every update, you'll subtract dt from the timer, until it's 0 and the player is ready to fire again.

Firing is straightforward—you create an instance of the Bullet class going in the right direction ❹. You give the bullets a speed of 500, with the ship's velocity added in (otherwise you get weird effects when you're travelling fast or shooting while travelling sideways). You store the bullet instance in ship.bullets, because if you don't have a reference to them somewhere, Python's garbage collector will remove them, and you'll wonder why your bullets aren't appearing on the screen.

❺ is the class you use whenever you fire a bullet. Bullet updates are easy, because they're not affected by gravity and move in a straight line.

Figure 9.13
Your ship firing—ready to
take on the alien armada

You don't want bullets hanging around forever, so they have their own timer. Once they've been around for 5 seconds, you delete them from `ship.bullets` and let Python handle the rest ❸. You also check for collisions with the planet, the same way you did for the ship.

Because there are potentially so many bullets, it makes sense to use Pyglet's `Batch` class, which makes sprite rendering much faster if you have lots of sprites to draw. To use the `bullets` batch, you pass it in when creating the bullet sprite and then call `bullets.draw()` to draw all the bullets at once ❻. You should see something like the next figure.

Now you can fly around the galaxy, doing good deeds and destroying alien scum. Hang on—you don't have any alien scum to shoot yet. Let's fix that next.

Evil aliens

What good are bullets without aliens to try them out on? In this section, you'll add an alien spaceship whose sole purpose in life is to destroy the evil Earthling intruder. To make life easier, you'll assume the alien has advanced technology that isn't influenced by gravity, and that they can enter and leave the planet's atmosphere at will. You're going to be a little lazy and not worry about all those vectors and collisions with the planet—only whether the alien has hit the player. The next listing gives you all the code you need to put an alien in your game.

Listing 9.10   A random alien

```
import random                          ◁──┐  ❶ Factor out vector
...                                        │     functions
alien_image = pyglet.resource.image('alien.png')   │ ❷ Alien class
center_anchor(alien_image)                          │
...
def make_vec((x1, y1), (x2, y2)):
    """distance and angle from (x1,y1) to (x2,y2)"""
    dx = x1 - x2
    dy = y1 - y2
    distance = math.sqrt(dx**2 + dy**2)
    if distance == 0:
        return (0,0)
    angle = math.acos(float(dx) / distance)
    if dy < 0:
        angle = 2*math.pi - angle
    return (distance, angle)                         ❸ Accelerate
                                                        in random
def vec_to_xy(distance, angle):                         direction
    x = distance * math.cos(angle)
    y = distance * math.sin(angle)
    return (x,y)


def dist_vec_to(source, target):
    return make_vec(
        (source.x, source.y),
        (target.x, target.y))
...
class Alien(pyglet.sprite.Sprite):
    def __init__(self, image, x=0, y=0,
                 dx=0, dy=0, batch=None):
        super(Alien, self).__init__(
                 image, x, y, batch=batch)
        self.x = x
        self.y = y
        self.dx = dx
        self.dy = dy                                  ❷ Alien class
        self.radius = self.image.width / 2
        self.life_timer = 2.0
        self.accel_spd = 200.0
        self.max_spd = 400.0
        self.alive = True
```

```
    def reset(self):
        self.alive = True
        self.life_timer = 2.0   # seconds until respawn
        self.x = random.random() * window.width
        self.y = random.random() * window.height
        self.dx = random.random() * (self.max_spd/2)
        self.dy = random.random() * (self.max_spd/2)

    def update(self, dt):
        if not self.alive:
            self.life_timer -= dt
            if self.life_timer > 0:
                return
            else:
                self.reset()

        if random.random() < 0.2:
            accel_dir = random.random() * math.pi*2
            accel_amt = random.random() * self.accel_spd
            accel_x, accel_y = vec_to_xy(accel_amt, accel_dir)
            self.dx += accel_x
            self.dy += accel_y

        self.dx = min(self.dx, self.max_spd)
        self.dx = max(self.dx, -self.max_spd)
        self.dy = min(self.dy, self.max_spd)
        self.dy = max(self.dy, -self.max_spd)

        self.x += self.dx * dt
        self.y += self.dy * dt
        self.x = wrap(self.x, window.width)
        self.y = wrap(self.y, window.height)
...
alien = Alien(alien_image)
alien.reset()

@window.event
def on_draw():
    ...
    if alien.alive:
        alien.draw()

def update(dt):
    ...
    alien.update(dt)
```

② Alien class

① Factor out vector functions

④ Don't go too fast

② Alien class

HOW DO YOU *DO* THAT, SID?

THRASHING PITR? OH, THAT JUST COMES NATURALLY.

NO ... THE GAME.

One thing I've done in this section of code is pull the vector functions out of the class and made them more standalone ❸. I've left them as is here, but, ultimately, you'll probably want to put them into their own module or find a vector library you can reuse.

The Alien class ends up being similar to the Ship class, except for its update method ❷, so there shouldn't be any major surprises in this part. You have all the same concepts—speed, acceleration, wrapping the x and y position, death, and respawning after a countdown.

Your alien has a simple AI—every so often, it accelerates in a random direction ❶. The frequency of the acceleration and the parameters set in __init__ give the alien enough changes in direction that shooting it can be a bit of a challenge.

Finally, I noticed while play-testing that it's possible for the alien to accelerate to ridiculous speeds ❹, which makes it hard to shoot. To stop it from doing that, you check that the x and y speeds are within the alien's maximum speeds and reduce them if they aren't.

NOTE   The alien is one thing in this game that you definitely want to experiment with. The rough rule of thumb is that an alien should be easy enough for the player to shoot some of the time, but hard enough to be a challenge. Without the right balance, your game won't be fun.

The last thing you need to do is make the alien interact with the other objects you have onscreen: it should be killed by bullets and should kill the player when it runs into the ship. You'd also like some sort of reward system for the player, so you'll add a score. Every time the player does something wrong, like crash into the planet or the alien, you'll subtract 100 points. If the player shoots the alien, then you'll add 100 points.

Listing 9.11   Making the alien interact

```
class Alien(pyglet.sprite.Sprite):
    def update(self, dt):
        ...
```

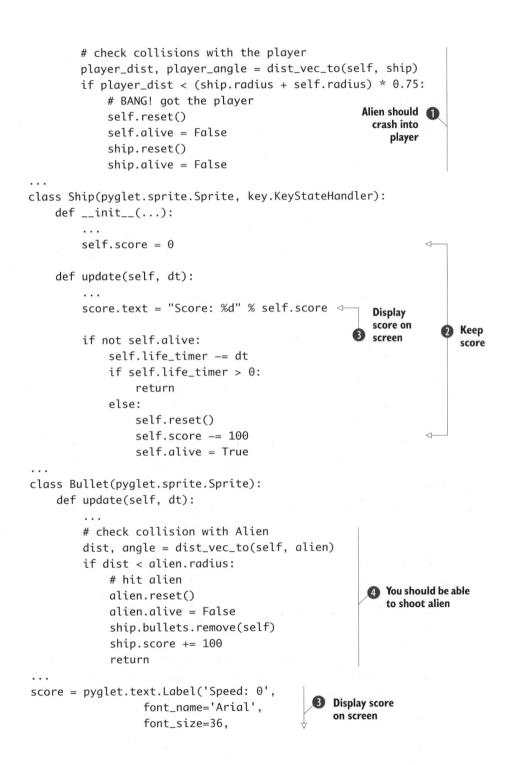

```
        # check collisions with the player
        player_dist, player_angle = dist_vec_to(self, ship)
        if player_dist < (ship.radius + self.radius) * 0.75:
            # BANG! got the player
            self.reset()
            self.alive = False
            ship.reset()
            ship.alive = False
...
class Ship(pyglet.sprite.Sprite, key.KeyStateHandler):
    def __init__(...):
        ...
        self.score = 0

    def update(self, dt):
        ...
        score.text = "Score: %d" % self.score

        if not self.alive:
            self.life_timer -= dt
            if self.life_timer > 0:
                return
            else:
                self.reset()
                self.score -= 100
                self.alive = True
...
class Bullet(pyglet.sprite.Sprite):
    def update(self, dt):
        ...
        # check collision with Alien
        dist, angle = dist_vec_to(self, alien)
        if dist < alien.radius:
            # hit alien
            alien.reset()
            alien.alive = False
            ship.bullets.remove(self)
            ship.score += 100
            return
...
score = pyglet.text.Label('Speed: 0',
                font_name='Arial',
                font_size=36,
```

1 Alien should crash into player

2 Keep score

3 Display score on screen

3 Display score on screen

4 You should be able to shoot alien

```
                  x=10, y=10,
                  anchor_x='left', anchor_y='bottom')
score.color = (255, 255, 255, 255)

@window.event
def on_draw():
    ...
    score.draw()
```

❸ Display score on screen

You'd like the alien to be an extra hazard for the player to avoid, so you check the distance between the ship and the alien ❶—the same way you do for the ship and the planet. It's up to you whether you want the alien to disappear when it collides with the player.

A score ❷ is how you let players know that they've done something right according to the rules of the game, so you give them 100 points for shooting the alien and subtract 100 points if they run into the alien or the planet.

The bullets should have an effect on the alien ❹. So, for each bullet, you check the range to the alien. If it's within the alien's radius, then you've shot the alien! Resetting the alien works in pretty much the same way it does for the player—only you draw the alien if it's alive and have a short delay between the alien dying and its reappearance.

Players need to be able to see their score on the screen ❸, so you add a Label class in the bottom of the screen, 10 pixels from the lower-left corner. Setting the color looks a little odd, because you might be expecting three numbers for red, green, and blue. The fourth is the alpha value—255 is opaque and 0 is completely transparent—which is useful for fading text in and out.

You should see something like the next figure, complete with alien scum!

Now you have a full-blown space-alien-shooting-get-as-many-points-as-you-can-but-don't-run-into-the-planet game (I'm sure you can think of a catchier title). You can send the game to your friends and even compete with each other.

Figure 9.14   Die, alien scum!

Where to from here?

You can make a number of improvements or changes to the game, either to refine what's already there, expand on the game play, or turn the game into something completely different. Here are some ideas.

Extending the game play

There are a number of other elements that would normally be in a game like this. A good idea might be to pick your favorite space-shooting game and see how many of its features you can add. You might want to make the alien shoot back, tweak its AI to make it nastier, or add more aliens. Adding extra, harder levels with each wave of aliens and limited lives for the player would be another feature. Sound effects are also good for setting an atmosphere.

Altering the game play

Another option is to extend the game in a completely different direction—after all, perhaps you're not a big fan of space-alien destruction. If you add a second player, and make your shots affected by gravity, you'll have something pretty close to Spacewar!, the original space shooting game, written for the PDP-1 back in 1962.

If shooting at stuff isn't really your thing, you could add extra planets and turn the game into a space-trading game or a 3D version of Lunar Lander. Limited fuel and lighter or heavier gravity on different planets would add to the challenge of the game, in addition to trading well.

Pyglet comes with several examples you can use to add text input and other features.

Refactoring

Now that you understand the program, there are some areas where the code could be improved. For example, there's quite a bit of duplication in terms of the objects and how their positions are updated—making them derive from a subclass could make your code clearer and easier to extend.

You could also use an external vector class within your objects, so you don't have to look at (or debug) all that geometry code. It helps to know what's behind the vector library before you start.

Unit tests would be a big help in ensuring that your program is functioning properly when you make these changes. It's difficult to test visual and game play aspects, but you can still check that collisions are detected properly by manually placing ship, bullet, and alien objects and checking whether they overlap. Other game data, such as forces and velocities, can be tested in the same way.

Get feedback

Another thing to bear in mind is that you're writing a game. You can write the most beautiful code, with all sorts of features, but all that will be for nothing if your game isn't fun to play. One good way to design and develop games is to create a minimal version that includes the elements you think will be fun and test it out on a few people, tweaking the various parts as necessary.

SURE. GAMES ARE ALL GEOMETRY BEHIND THE SCENES. ONCE YOU SEE THROUGH TO THE MATH UNDERNEATH, YOU CAN WIN AT ANYTHING.

OH YES, I WAS THE STATE NATIONAL GEOMETRY CHAMPION WHEN I WAS AT SCHOOL …

Summary

In this chapter, you learned how to write your own arcade game. You used Pyglet graphics classes to display images onscreen and move them around. To make your objects move realistically, you used some geometry and physics modeling to update their positions onscreen.

You added several types of objects and learned how to make them interact with each other—your ship could run into a planet and fire bullets; then, finally, you added an alien that could run into the ship and be shot by bullets.

Along the way, you learned about other game elements, such as collision detection and scheduling actions to take place over time.

Finally, we covered some aspects of game design: your game needs to be fun and include some familiar elements to attract people. It's important to get feedback from others: what's fun for you might not be fun for anybody else.

In the next chapter, you'll learn more about Django and how you can make the web applications you write available on the internet for other people to use.

## 10

Twisted networking

This chapter covers

- *Writing networked programs in Python*
- *Designing multiplayer games (including testing them on your friends)*
- *Issues you'll encounter when writing asynchronous programs*

In this chapter, we'll be revisiting the adventure game you wrote in chapter 6 and extending it so you can log in and play it with other people via the internet. Normally these games are referred to as MUDs, which stands for Multi-User Dungeon. Depending on the person creating them, MUDs can range from fantasy hack-and-slash to science fiction, and players can compete or cooperate to earn treasure, points, or fame.

To get you started quickly, we'll use a framework called Twisted, which contains libraries for working with many different networking protocols and servers.

Installing Twisted

The first step is to install Twisted and get a test application running. Twisted comes with installers for Windows and Macintosh, which are available from the Twisted homepage at http://twistedmatrix.com/. Some

Figure 10.1 Installing Twisted on Windows

versions of MacOS ship with Twisted already installed, in which case it's easier to use that version. If you're using Linux, there should be packages available through your package manager.

HEY SID—I'M TURNING MY ADVENTURE GAME INTO A MUD!

The installer will pop up a window as it compiles things, but once you see the window on the right in figure 10.1, Twisted is installed!

The only other thing you need is a Telnet application. Most operating systems come with one built-in, and there are many free ones you can download. I normally use an SSH terminal program called PuTTY, which is available for Windows.

Your first application

You'll start by writing a simple chat server. The idea is that people will be able to log into it via a program called Telnet and send each other messages. It's a little more complex than "Hello World!" but you can extend this program and use it in your game later on in this chapter. Open a new file, and save it as something like chat_server.py.

Let's start with the first part of your application: the protocol for the chat server. In Twisted terminology, a *protocol* refers to the part of your application that handles the low-level details: opening connections, receiving data, and closing connections when you're finished. You can do this in Twisted by subclassing its existing networking classes. The next listing shows a simple chat client, which you'll build on when you write your game in later sections.

Listing 10.1   A simple chat-server protocol

```
from twisted.conch.telnet import StatefulTelnetProtocol

class ChatProtocol(StatefulTelnetProtocol):
    def connectionMade(self):
        self.ip = self.transport.getPeer().host
        print "New connection from", self.ip
        self.msg_all(
            "New connection from %s" % self.ip,
            sender=None)
        self.factory.clients.append(self)

    def lineReceived(self, line):
        line = line.replace('\r', '')
        print ("Received line: %s from %s" %
                (line, self.ip))
        self.msg_all(line, sender=self)

    def connectionLost(self, reason):
        print "Lost connection to", self.ip
        self.factory.clients.remove(self)

    def msg_all(self, message, sender):
        self.factory.sendToAll(
            message, sender=sender)

    def msg_me(self, message):
        message = message.rstrip() + '\r'
        self.sendLine(message)
```

1 ChatProtocol is like Telnet

2 Override connectionMade

3 New connection

4 Handle data

5 Close tconnection

6 Convenience methods

For your chat server, you use Twisted's `StatefulTelnetProtocol` **1**. It takes care of the low-level line-parsing code, which means you can write your code at the level of individual lines and not have to worry about whether you have a complete line or not.

You're customizing the protocol by overriding the built-in connectionMade method ❷. This will called by for each connection the first time it's made.

You're taking care of a bit of housekeeping here—storing the client's IP address and informing everyone who's already connected of the new connection ❸. You also store the new connection so you can send it broadcast messages in the future.

The Telnet protocol class provides the lineReceived method ❹, which gets called whenever a complete line is ready for you to use (that is, whenever the person at the other end presses the return key). In your chat server, all you need to do is send whatever's been typed to every-one else who's connected to the server. The only tricky thing you need to do is to remove any line feeds; otherwise, your lines will overwrite each other when you print them.

If the connection is lost for some reason—either the client disconnects, or is disconnected by you—connectionLost will be called so you can tidy things up ❺. In this case, you don't really need to do much, just remove the client from the list of connections so you don't send them any more messages.

To make the code easier to follow, I've created the msg_all and msg_me methods, which will send out a message to everyone and just you, respectively ❻. msg_all takes a sender attribute, which you can use to let people know who the message is coming from.

NOTE   *Factory* is a programming term for something that creates a class for you to use. It's another way to hide some of the complexity of a library from the programmers who make use of it.

That takes care of how you want your program to behave. Now, how do you link it to Twisted? You use what Twisted refers to as a Factory, which is responsible for handling connections and creating new instances of ChatProtocol for each one. You can think of the Factory

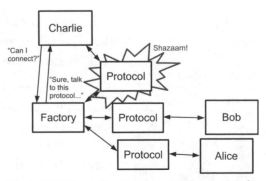

Figure 10.2 A Factory creating protocols

as a switchboard operator: as people connect to your server, the Factory creates new protocols and links them together, similar to figure 10.2.

So how do you do this in Twisted? Easy! Add a factory class, as shown in the next listing.

Listing 10.2 Connecting your protocol

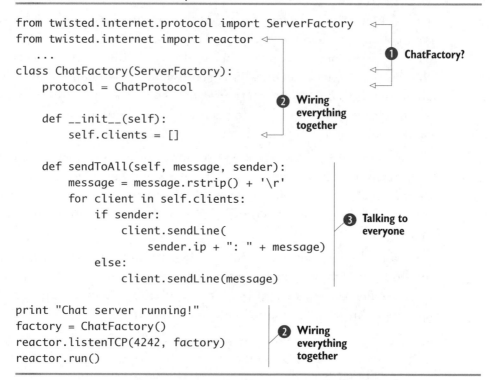

```
from twisted.internet.protocol import ServerFactory
from twisted.internet import reactor
    ...
class ChatFactory(ServerFactory):
    protocol = ChatProtocol

    def __init__(self):
        self.clients = []

    def sendToAll(self, message, sender):
        message = message.rstrip() + '\r'
        for client in self.clients:
            if sender:
                client.sendLine(
                    sender.ip + ": " + message)
            else:
                client.sendLine(message)

print "Chat server running!"
factory = ChatFactory()
reactor.listenTCP(4242, factory)
reactor.run()
```

❶ **ChatFactory?**

❷ **Wiring everything together**

❸ **Talking to everyone**

❷ **Wiring everything together**

SID?
IT'S LIKE AN ADVENTURE GAME, ONLY YOU CAN PLAY IT WITH OTHER PEOPLE OVER THE INTERNET.

A Factory is object-oriented terminology for something that creates instances of another class ❶. In this case, it will create instances of ChatProtocol.

The ChatFactory is the natural place to store data that is shared among all of the ChatProtocol instances. The send–ToAll method is responsible for sending a message to each of the clients specified in the clients list ❷. As you saw in listing 10.1, the client protocols are responsible for updating this list whenever they connect or disconnect.

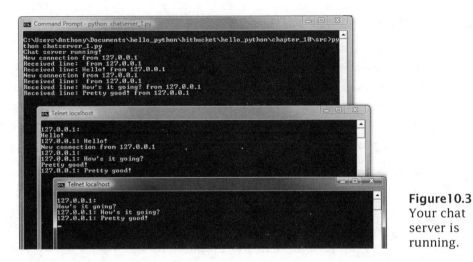

Figure 10.3
Your chat server is running.

The final step is to let Twisted know about your new protocol and Factory. You do this by creating an instance of ChatFactory, binding it to a particular port with the listenTCP method, and then starting Twisted with a call to its main loop, reactor.run() ❸. Here you use 4242 as the port to listen to—it doesn't matter too much which one you use, as long as it's above 1024 so it doesn't interfere with existing network applications.

If you save the program and run it, you should see the message "Chat server running!" If you connect to your computer via Telnet on port 4242 (usually by typing telnet localhost 4242), then you should see something like figure 10.3.

It may not seem like much, but you've already got the basic functionality of the MUD server going. If you'd like to explore the chat server further, there's a more fully featured version included with the source code, available from http://manning.com/HelloPython/. That version adds commands to change your name and see who else is connected, as well as limit some common sorts of misbehavior and allow you to remove anyone who's behaving badly.

UM, YEAH .... I USED TO PLAY THEM ... A WHILE AGO ...

First steps with your MUD

Now you're ready to start connecting your adventure game to the network. You'll base it on the chat server, but instead of only broadcasting what's typed to everyone who's connected, you'll feed it directly into the adventure game. This is a common way to get things done when programming—find two programs (or functions or libraries) that do separate parts of what you need, and then "glue" them together.

The basic gist is that you'll have multiple players logged in at once, all trying to execute commands (such as "get sword") at the same time. This could potentially cause problems for the server because you're mixing real-time Twisted code with the one-step-at-a-time of your adventure game. You'll head off most of the issues by queuing up player commands and updating your game's state once per second.

Let's get started. Copy your adventure code from chapter 6 into a new folder, along with the chat-server code you just created. You'll probably also want to rename chat_server.py to something like mud_server.py, to help keep things straight, and rename your classes and variables as in the next listing.

Listing 10.3 *Updating your chat protocol*

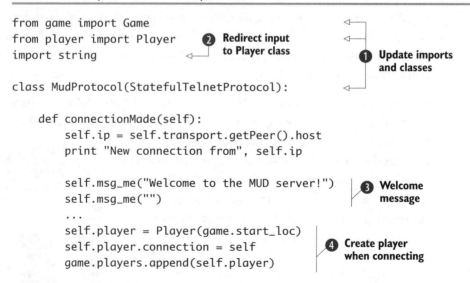

```
from game import Game
from player import Player        ❷  Redirect input          ◁──
import string                        to Player class         ◁──
                                                               ❶  Update imports
                                                                  and classes
class MudProtocol(StatefulTelnetProtocol):                   ◁──

    def connectionMade(self):
        self.ip = self.transport.getPeer().host
        print "New connection from", self.ip

        self.msg_me("Welcome to the MUD server!")            ❸  Welcome
        self.msg_me("")                                         message
        ...
        self.player = Player(game.start_loc)                 ❹  Create player
        self.player.connection = self                           when connecting
        game.players.append(self.player)
```

```
def connectionLost(self, reason):
    ...
    game.players.remove(self.player)      ❺  Remove players when
    del self.player                           disconnecting

def lineReceived(self, line):
    line = line.replace('\r', '')
    line = ''.join([ch for ch in line
                if ch in string.printable])   ❷  Redirect input
    self.player.input_list.insert(0, line)       to Player class
```

The first step is to import the `Game` and `Player` classes into your code ❶. I've also changed the name of the protocol so it's obvious what you're trying to write.

Next, you give a nice, friendly start when someone first connects to your MUD ❸.

Now you'll start to do the real work. But it turns out to not be that hard. I've assumed the game

GREAT! I'LL EMAIL YOU THE DETAILS, AND YOU CAN LOG IN AND PLAY!

will keep track of its players somehow, and added a new player object to the game's list of players ❹. To make it possible for you to talk to the player from within the game, I've also added the protocol to the player. You'll see how that works in a minute.

You'll still need to handle the case where a player disconnects from the server ❺. But, again, it's straightforward: remove them from the game's list of players, and delete them.

Once players are connected, they'll want to type commands, like "go north" and "attack orc" ❷. First, you sanitize the input you've received (in testing, I found that different Telnet programs can send different weird characters). When it's trimmed down to only printable characters, you assume the player has a list of commands waiting to be executed, and push this one to the end.

Your protocol is done, but what about the Factory and the rest of it? It turns out that you don't need to do too much to your Factory—just change a few lines.

Listing 10.4 Updating your chat Factory

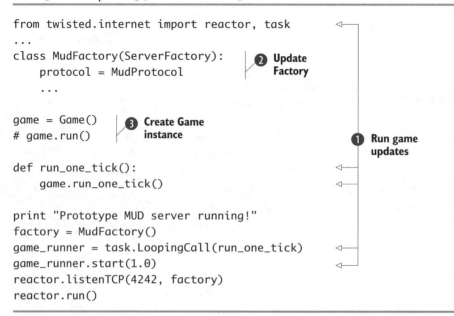

```
from twisted.internet import reactor, task
...
class MudFactory(ServerFactory):        ② Update
    protocol = MudProtocol               Factory
    ...


game = Game()        ③ Create Game
# game.run()            instance                    ① Run game
                                                       updates

def run_one_tick():
    game.run_one_tick()


print "Prototype MUD server running!"
factory = MudFactory()
game_runner = task.LoopingCall(run_one_tick)
game_runner.start(1.0)
reactor.listenTCP(4242, factory)
reactor.run()
```

NO, THAT'S OK. I'M ... BUSY.

You don't need to do too much to update your Factory ② —change its protocol and rename it.

You'll need a `Game` object, too, so you create it here ③. You don't want to use the old `run` method, though, because it still handles things the old way.

The design calls for you to run a game update once per second. Because you're using Twisted's event loop (that's the `reactor.run()` part), you'll need to use Twisted's `task.LoopingCall` to call the game's update method ①, `run_one_tick`, which you'll also create shortly.

That should be all you need to do to the network code for now. You've made a few assumptions about how the game code will work, but often this is easier than jumping back and forth between the `Game` and `Mud-Protocol` classes and trying to fit it all together. Now that your protocol is written, you have to make `Game` and `Player` play along, too.

Listing 10.5   Changing your game code to work with the new interface

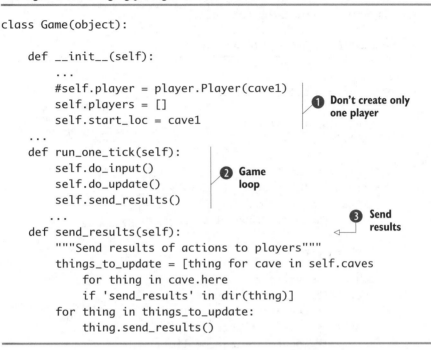

```
class Game(object):

    def __init__(self):
        ...
        #self.player = player.Player(cave1)
        self.players = []                        ❶ Don't create only
        self.start_loc = cave1                      one player
    ...
    def run_one_tick(self):
        self.do_input()
        self.do_update()         ❷ Game
        self.send_results()         loop
    ...
    def send_results(self):
        """Send results of actions to players"""
        things_to_update = [thing for cave in self.caves
            for thing in cave.here
            if 'send_results' in dir(thing)]
        for thing in things_to_update:
            thing.send_results()
```

❸ Send results

The single-player version of the adventure game had one player, but you'll potentially have many, so you'll make it a list instead ❶. You're also giving the starting cave a sensible name.

❷ is the main loop you called from the networking part of your code. You should be able to follow what it's doing from the names—get input for each Player object (including monsters), run the update, and then send the results back.

You already have methods for getting input and processing orders, but you'll need something to send back the results of each player's actions ❸. To do that, you'll make another assumption: that each Player object knows how to send results back to the player.

Now you have only two assumptions left to fill in, and they're both in the Player class. The first is that Player will have a list of pending commands, and the second is that it will have a way to send the results of any commands or events back to the player. The other thing you need to do is make sure the `Player` class reads from the list of pending commands, rather than using `raw_input`.

Listing 10.6   Changing the Player code

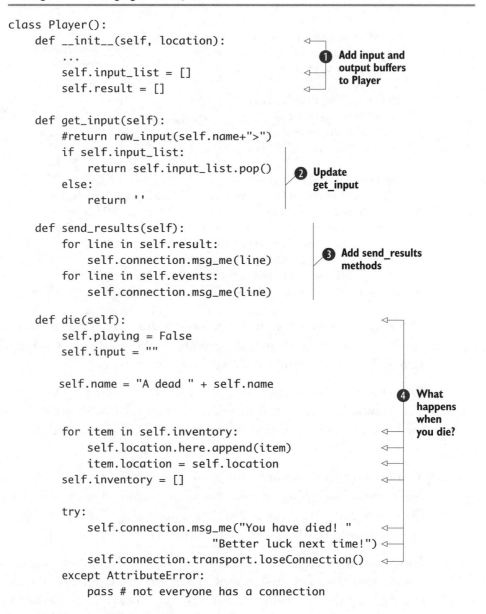

```
class Player():
    def __init__(self, location):
        ...
        self.input_list = []
        self.result = []

    def get_input(self):
        #return raw_input(self.name+">")
        if self.input_list:
            return self.input_list.pop()
        else:
            return ''

    def send_results(self):
        for line in self.result:
            self.connection.msg_me(line)
        for line in self.events:
            self.connection.msg_me(line)

    def die(self):
        self.playing = False
        self.input = ""

        self.name = "A dead " + self.name


        for item in self.inventory:
            self.location.here.append(item)
            item.location = self.location
        self.inventory = []

        try:
            self.connection.msg_me("You have died! "
                            "Better luck next time!")
            self.connection.transport.loseConnection()
        except AttributeError:
            pass # not everyone has a connection

class Monster(player.Player):
```

① Add input and output buffers to Player

② Update get_input

③ Add send_results methods

④ What happens when you die?

```
...
def send_results(self):
    pass

def get_input(self):
    if not self.playing:
        return ""
    player_present = [x for x in self.location.here
        if x.__class__ == player.Player
            and x.playing]
```

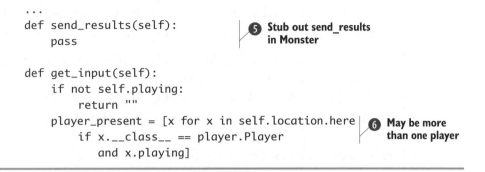

5 Stub out send_results in Monster

6 May be more than one player

You start by creating your list of pending commands and the result that needs to be sent back to the player **1**. They're just lists, and when they're in use they'll have a list of strings.

You can't use raw_input any more, so you need to read your next command from self.input _list **2**. pop removes the command for you so you don't have to worry about removing it from the list later. pop called on an empty list raises an exception, so you check for that case and assume the command is blank if there's nothing there.

HEY AJ! WANT TO SIGN UP FOR MY MUD?

A MUD? COOL! KINDA 80S, BUT STILL COOL ...

To send the results of a player's actions **3**, you use the self.connection object that you set up in mudserver.py. Note that even if the player isn't doing anything, other players and monsters are, so you have two separate sections: one for the results of your actions and another for events.

In the old version of the game, when the player died, the game ended. That's no longer the case, so you'll need to gracefully handle the situation where a player dies **4**. To do that, you make the player drop whatever they're carrying, send them a message, and drop the connection. If you extend your game, you might want to make the player keep their items. Alternatively, you can allow other players to "get sword from Anthony" if you're feeling mean.

Monsters don't connect over the network and don't have the self.connection object, so the default send_results from the Player class won't work. They don't need to know the results of their actions, so you'll stub out their version of send_results and return immediately ❺.

The previous adventure game looked at the player's name to figure out whether to attack them. Now that you have multiple players, who probably all have different names, you'll need to be a bit more discerning ❻. A better way is to examine the class of the object the monster is looking at, using the __class__ method. That will return the class, which you can compare to player.Player.

> **NOTE**   This works so well because your game has only one point of communication with the player: the commands the player types and the responses the game returns.

That should be all you need to do. Now, when you run your server and connect via Telnet, you'll see your familiar adventure-game prompt, and you can run around the server collecting loot and slaying monsters. Go ahead and bask in the adventure and glory.

Well, sort of. Although the game works, and you can explore and do everything you need to, there are a few more things to take care of before your game is playable.

Making the game more fun

I made the previous code available to some of my friends online and got feedback from them. They raised two major issues: the monster was too hard to beat, and there wasn't enough interaction between the players. Normally, in an adventure game like this, you'll be able to change your name and description, talk to other players, look at their description, and so on.

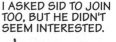

I ASKED SID TO JOIN TOO, BUT HE DIDN'T SEEM INTERESTED.

DIDN'T YOU KNOW? SID USED TO BE A MUD JUNKIE.

Bad monster!

The problem with combat is pretty obvious once you run into the orc for the first time. You're limited to the actions you type in—but the monsters react at computer speed. The next figure shows what I mean.

```
Telnet localhost
Welcome to the MUD server!

look
Wumpus lair

Items here:
sword
coin
Exits:
west: Winding steps
east: Dripping cave
north: Underground lake
south: Black pit
The orc misses you!
The orc misses you!
The orc hits you!
The orc misses you!
The orc misses you!
The orc hits you!
The orc misses you!
The orc misses you!
The orc has killed you!
```

Figure 10.4   Bad monster! No beating on the player!

The solution that most MUDs use is what's known as an *angry list*. Rather than attacking things directly, the game maintains a list of monsters and other players you're angry at. If you're not explicitly doing anything else, and there's something present that's on your angry list, then you'll attack it. If something attacks you, then it will go on your angry list, too, so you'll at least put up a token defense. Let's look at how you can implement the angry list in your game.

Listing 10.7   Angry lists

```python
class Player(object):
    def __init__(self, game, location):
        ...
        self.angry_list = []              ❶ Add angry
                                             list

    def update(self):
        self.result = self.process_input(self.input)

        if (self.playing and
            self.input == "" and
            self.angry_list):
            bad_guys = [x for x in self.location.here    ❷ Attack
                        if 'attack' in dir(x) and           bad guys
                            x.name in self.angry_list]
```

```
        if bad_guys:
            bad_guy = random.choice(bad_guys)
            self.events += bad_guy.do_attack(self)
```

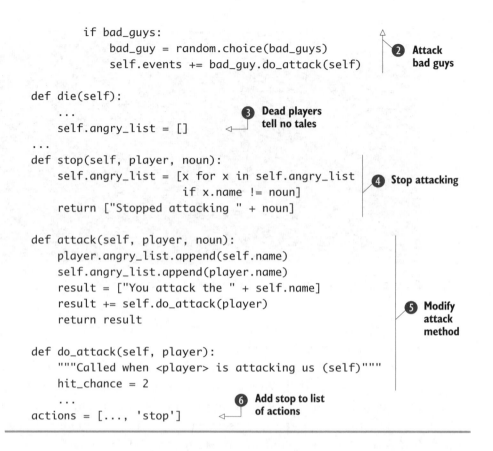

2 Attack bad guys

```
def die(self):
    ...
    self.angry_list = []
```

3 Dead players tell no tales

```
...
def stop(self, player, noun):
    self.angry_list = [x for x in self.angry_list
                       if x.name != noun]
    return ["Stopped attacking " + noun]
```

4 Stop attacking

```
def attack(self, player, noun):
    player.angry_list.append(self.name)
    self.angry_list.append(player.name)
    result = ["You attack the " + self.name]
    result += self.do_attack(player)
    return result
```

5 Modify attack method

```
def do_attack(self, player):
    """Called when <player> is attacking us (self)"""
    hit_chance = 2
    ...
actions = [..., 'stop']
```

6 Add stop to list of actions

A MUD JUNKIE? COME ON. THERE'S NO SUCH THING …

NO, REALLY. HE HAD TO BE HOSPITALIZED FOR A WHILE …

Both players and monsters will need a way to remember who they're angry at. You'll make it a list **1**, because you're not expecting it to grow too large.

Next, you'll modify your update method. If your input attribute is blank, you know that the player (or monster) hasn't entered any commands, and you can go ahead and attack if necessary. You build a list of all the things you're angry at that are present, and then attack one of them **2**.

If a player or monster is dead, they shouldn't keep attacking, so you clear their angry list **3**.

The players will also need a way to stop attacking things (maybe they're friends again). The stop command will remove an attacker from the list of things that the player is angry at ❹.

The final major thing you'll do is make the attack command modify the angry lists of both the attacker and attacked ❺. Now, when something gets attacked, it will automatically fight back. Note how you build your result before you do the attack. That way, if the target dies, you won't see "You attack the dead orc." do_attack is the mechanism from your old attack attribute with a different name.

The final, final thing is to add stop to your list of commands ❻—otherwise you won't be able to use it!

Now the player should have half a chance against the orc. If the orc beats the player now, the player will at least feel that they haven't been completely robbed by the game. If you pick up the sword, you'll find it helps a lot, which is what you want. There are plenty of other opportunities for improving the combat system, but you need to deal with a more pressing problem, instead.

Back to the chat server

The second problem is that players can't interact with each other. This is often a big draw when it comes to a multiplayer game—players will come for the game but stay for the company. Fortunately, making your game more social is easy to do. You'll add a few extra commands to the Player class.

Listing 10.8   Social gaming

```
help_text = """
Welcome to the MUD

                                                                    ❶ Help!
This text is intended to help you play the game.
Most of the usual MUD-type commands should work, including:
...
"""


class Player(object):
    ...
```

```
def help(self, player, noun):
    return [help_text]
```
❶ Help!

```
def name_(self, player, noun):
    self.name = noun
    return ["You changed your name to '%s'" % self.name]

def describe(self, player, noun):
    self.description = noun
    return ["You changed your description to '%s'" %
            self.description]
```
Change name ❷
and description

```
def look(self, player, noun):
    return ["You see %s." % self.name, self.description]
```
❸ **Look**

```
def say(self, player, noun):
    for object in self.location.here:
        if ('events' in dir(object) and
            object != self):
            object.events.append(
                self.name + " says: " + noun)
    return ["You say: " + noun]
```
❹ **Talk to**
people

If a player is completely new to the game, you need to give them at least half an idea of what they can do. You'll make "help" output some helpful instructions ❶. The full help text I added is in the source code.

Another easy win is to let players customize their appearance by changing their name and description ❷. Rather than being "player #4," the player can now be "Grognir, Slayer of Orcs."

Of course, the description's not much good if other players can't see it ❸.

HE'S ON SOME SORT
OF COURT-SPONSORED
NETHACK PROGRAM
NOW. I THINK ...

You'll also need to add to most important case of all: a say command, so your players can talk to each other ❹. All this command needs to do is send what you've typed to every other object in the current room. This simple change will allow players to interact on a human level, which will in turn help keep them coming back.

One of the issues you'll run into is that with the new commands, the old `find_handler` method will sometimes call the wrong thing. For example, both the `player` and the `location` have a `look` method, and which one is correct will depend on the context. Additionally, some of the commands you've just added only apply to the players themselves, and you shouldn't look for an object to apply them to. The following listing has an updated version that is a lot more explicit about which objects it should look at.

Listing 10.9   Updating `find_handler`

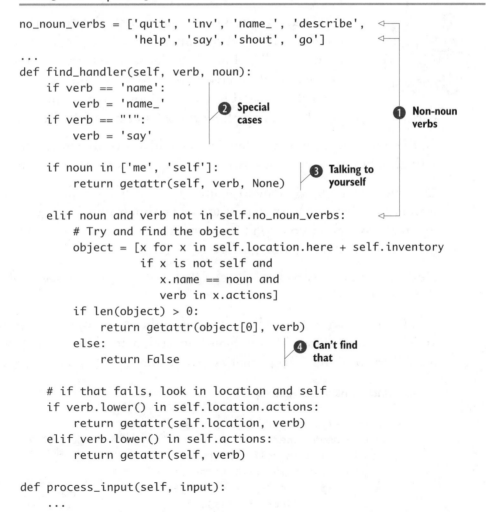

```
no_noun_verbs = ['quit', 'inv', 'name_', 'describe',
                 'help', 'say', 'shout', 'go']
...
def find_handler(self, verb, noun):
    if verb == 'name':
        verb = 'name_'
    if verb == "'":
        verb = 'say'

    if noun in ['me', 'self']:
        return getattr(self, verb, None)

    elif noun and verb not in self.no_noun_verbs:
        # Try and find the object
        object = [x for x in self.location.here + self.inventory
                    if x is not self and
                        x.name == noun and
                        verb in x.actions]
        if len(object) > 0:
            return getattr(object[0], verb)
        else:
            return False

    # if that fails, look in location and self
    if verb.lower() in self.location.actions:
        return getattr(self.location, verb)
    elif verb.lower() in self.actions:
        return getattr(self, verb)

def process_input(self, input):
    ...
```

1 Non-noun verbs

2 Special cases

3 Talking to yourself

4 Can't find that

```
    handler = self.find_handler(verb, noun)
    if handler is None:
        return [input+"? I don't know how to do that!"]
    elif handler is False:
        return ["I can't see the "+noun+"!"]
actions = [..., 'name_', 'describe', 'look', 'help', 'say',...]
```

④ Can't find
that

THAT WAS A CRAZY
BUG, GREG. HOW DID
PITR MANAGE TO
ATTACK HIMSELF?

Let's pay close attention to word choice. Some verbs don't apply to nouns, or else they implicitly apply to the player ❶.

There are a few special-case commands ❷ that you can't handle with your current system. You could rewrite the entire handler, but it's easier to catch those commands and explicitly convert them to something you *can* handle. Of course, if it becomes more than a handful of conversions, then you'll have to rethink things; but it will do for now.

So that you can see how you look, you'll add a `self` object, too ❸. "Look self" should return your description as it appears to other people.

❹ is another improvement to make things easier for the new player. Rather than have one error message when things go wrong, you'll have one for a command you don't understand, and another when you can't find what the player's looking for.

Now your players can chat to each other and compliment each other on their fine threads.

Finally, what would social gaming be without the opportunity to be antisocial, too? Most MUDs have the option to shout, which works much like speaking, except that everyone connected can hear you.

Listing 10.10 Antisocial gaming

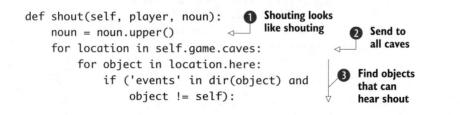

```
def shout(self, player, noun):
    noun = noun.upper()
    for location in self.game.caves:
        for object in location.here:
            if ('events' in dir(object) and
                object != self):
```

❶ Shouting looks
like shouting

❷ Send to
all caves

❸ Find objects
that can
hear shout

```
              object.events.append(
                    self.name + " shouts: " + noun)
        return ["You shout: " + noun]
```
❸ Find objects that can hear shout

```
class Player(object):
    def __init__(self, game, location):
        self.game = game
        ...
```
❹ Update Player class

```
class Monster(player.Player):
    def __init__(self, game, location, name, description):
        player.Player.__init__(self, game, location)
        ...

class Game(object):
    def __init__(self):
        ...
        orc = monster.Monster(self, self.caves[1],
                'orc', 'A generic dungeon monster')

class MudProtocol(StatefulTelnetProtocol):
    def connectionMade(self):
        ...
        self.player = Player(game, game.start_loc)
```
❺ Update all Player and Monster instances

First, you'll convert the text to uppercase ❶, SO THAT IT LOOKS A LOT MORE LIKE SHOUTING!

Now you need to visit each cave in turn—but there doesn't seem to be any way to find out what the caves are. For now, you'll assume you have access to the game's list of caves ❷.

This is pretty much the same as when players talk to each other ❸. Merging the two together—for example, by pushing the code into the location class—is left as an exercise for the reader.

OH, I MESSED UP THE INDEX IN THE ROOM'S LIST OF THINGS.

IS NOT FUNNY!

Now you need to give your Player class access to the caves list from the game ❹ by making it a variable you pass in from the game when you create a player or monster. Then, update each place where you create an instance of a player or monster ❺, so it now knows about the *game* object and can tell where all the caves are.

There! That's a few more rough edges smoothed off your game. There's plenty left to do, but you won't be writing any new features for the game now. Instead, you'll focus on making the infrastructure around the game a bit more robust, so players won't be put off by having all their hard work disappear.

Making your life easier

If you only want to write the game for your friends, you can probably stop here; they can connect and play your game, after all. Currently, though, there are still a few issues that will make your life harder than it needs to be. Anyone can log on as anyone else, so the game isn't particularly secure; and the game doesn't save any progress, so every time you restart the game server, the player will have to start over from scratch.

Let's fix that. You'll add usernames and passwords to the game, as well as a mechanism to allow new players to register. Once you know who's logged on, you can save the players' progress every so often, and also when they quit the game. You'll need to learn a bit more about Twisted, though, because you'll be digging into the guts of one of its Telnet classes. But don't worry; it's straightforward once you get the hang of it.

Exploring unfamiliar code

Twisted is a large codebase and has a huge number of modules to help you network your application. That's great, because it means you don't have to write your own code to handle the networking in your application, but it raises a related problem: you must have at least a basic understanding of how everything fits together before you can make use of all that great code.

Ideally, the documentation for libraries like Twisted would be 100% up-to-date and cover everything you need to do with a nice, gentle introduction—but this isn't always the case. Often, you'll be able to find something close, but then you'll need to piece together how the code works with some guessing, experimentation, and detective work.

It sounds hard, but in practice it's usually pretty easy. The trick is not to get too overwhelmed, and to use *all* the resources at your disposal. Here are some ideas on how you can get a grip on a large codebase and make it work in your application.

NEVER MIND, PITR. I'M SURE YOU'LL GET THAT VORPAL WABBIT SOMEDAY ...

FIND AN EXAMPLE

Searching for "twisted tutorial" online gives you a number of starting points, and you can also add "telnet" or "telnet protocol" into the mix. As you learn more about Twisted, you'll find other keywords or method names that will help you narrow down what you're looking for. You can also start with a working example that sort of does what you need, and then tweak it until it covers exactly what you need it to do.

THE TWISTED DOCUMENTATION

There's reasonably comprehensive documentation available in the Conch section of the main Twisted site, http://twistedmatrix.com/documents/, but it doesn't cover all of what you need to do. There are some simple examples of SSH and Telnet servers, which you can skim through to get an idea of how everything fits together.

THE TWISTED API DOCS

Detailed, automatically generated documentation is available for the entire Twisted codebase, which you can see at http://twistedmatrix.com/documents/current/api/. Don't let the sheer number of packages put you off—we'll focus on the Telnet one: http://twistedmatrix.com/documents/current/api/twisted.conch.telnet.html.

THE TWISTED CODE

You can also read most of the Twisted code directly. The Windows version of Python stores its libraries at C:\Python26\Lib\site-packages\twisted; under Linux, it will be somewhere like /usr/lib/python2.6/dist-packages/twisted; and under Mac, it's usually at /Developer/SDKs/

MacOSX10.6.sdk/System/Library/Frameworks/Python.framework/ Versions/2.5/Extras/lib/python/twisted. All the Twisted code is stored there, and you can open the files and read the code to find out exactly what a method does.

INTROSPECTION

If a library doesn't have API documentation, all is not lost. You can still create instances of classes and use dir(), help(), and method.__doc__ to find out what they do. If you have a one-off method you need to know about, this can often be easier than reading the code or documentation.

In practice, none of these sources will cover all the details you need to know when writing your program, so you'll end up using a combination of them going back and forth as you learn new parts or run into problems.

Putting it all together

Let's get started putting together your login system. From a quick scan of Twisted's Telnet module, it looks like the best starting point is the AuthenticatingTelnetProtocol class. You'll get that working with your code, then make it register new players, and finally make the game able to save player data.

To start with, I looked at the Twisted documentation and the API reference for AuthenticatingTelnetProtocol. It sort of made sense, but from the methods and classes it's hard to see how to tie everything together. The protocol needs a Portal, which in turn depends on a Realm, an Avatar, and a PasswordChecker. Hmm, confusing. It looks like it's time to try to find an example of how the classes fit together.

AFTER ALL, "IS ONLY CUTE LITTLE BUNNY. HOW TOUGH CAN IT BE?"

There are a few different searches you could try: "twisted telnet," "twisted telnet example," and so on, but I didn't find much until I put in some terms from the code. The search "twisted telnet TelnetProtocol example" led me to www.mail-archive.com/twisted-python@ twistedmatrix.com/msg01490.html, which, if you follow it through to the end, gives you some example code that is enough to see how the classes work together.

The basic gist is something like this: set up a `Realm` class, along with a `Portal` to get into it. The docs don't say whether it's a *magic* portal, but it should do. A `Portal` controls access to your `Realm`, using one or more password `Checkers`, via a `TelnetTransport`. Of course, the `Authenticating-TelnetProtocol` only handles authentication, so you'll need to hand off to another protocol like your `MudProtocol` once you're logged in.

Got all that? No, me neither. I had to draw a picture to see how it all worked, and without the example I probably would've been lost. Figure 10.5 shows what I came up with.

Using the diagram and the example code, you can get a simple login going. The following listing shows how I changed the mudserver.py file.

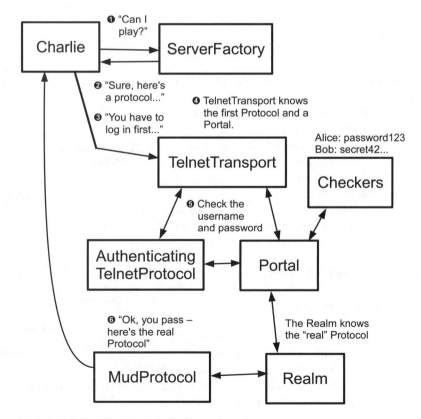

Figure 10.5 The Twisted class structure

Listing 10.11 Mudserver.py

```python
import sys

from zope.interface import implements
from twisted.internet import protocol, reactor, task
from twisted.python import log

from twisted.cred import portal
from twisted.cred import checkers
from twisted.cred import credentials

from twisted.conch.telnet import AuthenticatingTelnetProtocol
from twisted.conch.telnet import StatefulTelnetProtocol
from twisted.conch.telnet import ITelnetProtocol
from twisted.conch.telnet import TelnetTransport

...
class Realm:
    implements(portal.IRealm)

    def requestAvatar(self, avatarId, mind, *interfaces):
        print "Requesting avatar..."
        if ITelnetProtocol in interfaces:
            av = MudProtocol()
            print "**", avatarId, dir(avatarId)
            print "**", mind, dir(mind)
            av.name = avatarId
            av.state = "Command"
            return ITelnetProtocol, av, lambda:None
        raise NotImplementedError("Not supported by this realm")

...
class MudProtocol(StatefulTelnetProtocol):

    def connectionMade(self):
        ...
        # self.factory.clients.append(self)
        self.player.name = self.name
        checker = portal_.checkers.values()[0]
        self.player.password = checker.users[self.player.name]
        game.players.append(self.player)

    def connectionLost(self, reason):
        print "Lost connection to", self.ip
```

Annotations:
- ❶ Lots of imports!
- ❷ Create Realm
- ❸ Use debugging strings
- ❷ Create Realm
- ❻ Set up ServerFactory
- ❹ Find player's username and password

```
        if 'player' in dir(self):
            if self.player in game.players:        ④ Find player's
                game.players.remove(self.player)       username and
            del self.player                            password

if __name__ == '__main__':
    print "Prototype MUD server running!"

    realm = Realm()                                    Set up Realm and ⑤
    portal_ = portal.Portal(realm)                     PasswordCheckers
    checker = checkers.InMemoryUsernamePasswordDatabaseDontUse()
    checker.addUser("AA", "aa")
    portal_.registerChecker(checker)

    game = Game()
    ...
    factory = protocol.ServerFactory()
    factory.protocol = lambda: TelnetTransport(        ⑥ Set up
        AuthenticatingTelnetProtocol, portal_)            ServerFactory

    log.startLogging(sys.stdout)                ⟵┐   Send logging
    reactor.listenTCP(4242, factory)             ⑦  to screen
    reactor.run()
```

To start, you'll import all the bits of Twisted you need ❶. There are a lot, but think of it as code you don't have to write.

The `Realm` is the core class that represents your game's login ❷. You only need to override one method: the one to get an `Avatar`. `Avatar`s are instances of the `MudProtocol` and represent the player's login. Notice that you set the player's name so you have access to it in `MudProtocol`, and set `state` to `"Command"`; otherwise, you'll get logged out right away.

NOTE   The "code that you don't have to write" part is important. It's easy to overestimate how hard it is to learn how existing code works, and underestimate how hard it is to write new code that's as well tested.

While you're figuring out how everything works, it's perfectly fine to print out things to the screen to try and work out what each object does ❸. You can use what you learn to search online, or through the code to find out what else uses these classes.

WHAT'S ALL THIS FUN AND FRIVOLITY I CAN HEAR?

Most of `MudProtocol` is unchanged, but you'll need to know your player's username and password for later ❹, when you start saving to a file. The `Realm` has already given you the username, so you can use that to get the password from the checker. The other thing you change is the `connectionLost` method—if you lose the connection to the player, you want to clean up properly.

Now we're into the section where you set the code in motion. The first thing to do is create a `Realm` and then attach a `Portal` and `Checkers` to it. Once you've done that, you can insert usernames and passwords into your checker ❺. `InMemory..DontUse` is fine for your purposes, even though, in theory, it's insecure and you're not supposed to use it. There's also a file-based checker available, but it doesn't support saving new users back to the file.

Now that you're using `TelnetTransport` and your `Realm` to control things, you don't need a custom Factory, and you won't need to manually track the clients in the factory any more ❻. The `TelnetTransport` will use `AuthenticatingTelnetProtocol` to handle usernames and passwords, but once that's done it will hand off to the `Realm` to get the final protocol.

One last thing is that Twisted uses Python's log facility. To see what it's up to, you can add this line ❼, which will redirect the logging to `sys.stdout`—that is, print it on the screen.

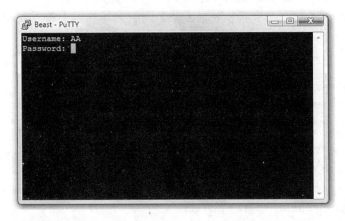

Figure 10.6 Logging in to your game

What does all this give you? Well, if you run your server now and try to connect to it, you should be presented with a login request instead of a password, similar to what's shown in figure 10.6. If you enter the username and password that are in the script, you should connect to the game.

That's not all you need to do, though. Remember that you want to allow players to register their own username and password. For that you'll have to learn a bit more about Twisted.

AHEM! ER ... SO, HOW'S THE GRAPHIC DESIGN COMING ALONG, AJ?

ER ... FINE, GREG! JUST FINE!

Write your own state machine

What you're going to do in this section is create a subclass of the class you've been using so far, which is `AuthenticatingTelnetProtocol`. It's what generates the `User-name:` and `Password:` prompts in the login. What you'd like instead is a prompt that asks the player whether they want to log in or register a new account. If it's a registration, then it still asks you for a username and password, but creates the account instead of checking whether it exists.

Let's first take a look at `AuthenticatingTelnetProtocol`, to see how it's done. You can find the Telnet module on your computer at C:\Python26\Lib\site-packages\twisted\conch\telnet.py, or somewhere like /usr/lib/python2.6/ site-packages/twisted/conch/telnet.py if you're using Linux or MacOS X. If you open that file and scroll to the bottom, you'll find the class you're looking for; it's also shown in listing 10.12.

Listing 10.12 Twisted's `AuthenticatingTelnetProtocol` class

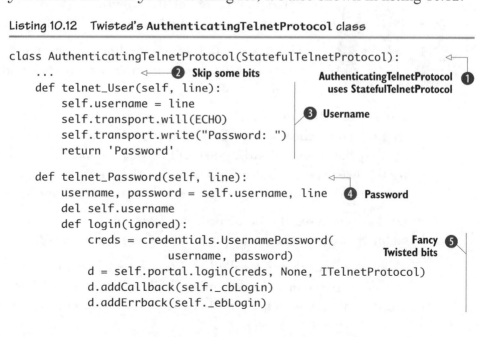

```
class AuthenticatingTelnetProtocol(StatefulTelnetProtocol):
    ...                                  Skip some bits
    def telnet_User(self, line):
        self.username = line
        self.transport.will(ECHO)                    Username
        self.transport.write("Password: ")
        return 'Password'

    def telnet_Password(self, line):
        username, password = self.username, line          Password
        del self.username
        def login(ignored):
            creds = credentials.UsernamePassword(            Fancy
                        username, password)             Twisted bits
            d = self.portal.login(creds, None, ITelnetProtocol)
            d.addCallback(self._cbLogin)
            d.addErrback(self._ebLogin)
```

① AuthenticatingTelnetProtocol uses StatefulTelnetProtocol

② Skip some bits

③ Username

④ Password

⑤ Fancy Twisted bits

```
        self.transport.wont(ECHO).addCallback(login)
        return 'Discard'
```
6 If everything goes great: callback

```
    def _cbLogin(self, ial):
        interface, protocol, logout = ial
        assert interface is ITelnetProtocol
        self.protocol = protocol
        self.logout = logout
        self.state = 'Command'

        protocol.makeConnection(self.transport)
        self.transport.protocol = protocol
```
7 If everything goes bad: errorback

```
    def _ebLogin(self, failure):
        self.transport.write("\nAuthentication failed\n")
        self.transport.write("Username: ")
        self.state = "User"
```

GREG? I NEED TO BORROW YOUR PC FOR A MINUTE …

NO, GREG! DON'T LISTEN TO HIM!

All the `Telnet` classes we've looked at so far are state machines—there are multiple steps involved in logging in, and the next one depends on the input you get. You're initially in the "User" state, which means input is fed to the `telnet_User` method **1**. Each method returns a string, which determines the next state.

There are a few other methods: `connectionMade` and `connectionLost`, but you don't need to deal with them in this case **2**.

The first line (after the initial greeting) goes to `telnet_User` and sets the username within the instance **3**. The `transport.will()` call tells the local client that the server (that is, you) will be responsible for echoing anything the user types—but in this case, it's the password, so you don't. Then "Password" is returned, so the next line goes to `telnet_Password`.

Now that you have the password, you can compare it with what you have for that username in the portal's password checker **4**.

Twisted has a mechanism called a *Deferred*, that helps to speed up the server **5**. A password checker might look at a file on disk, or connect to a different server to see whether the password is correct. If it waits

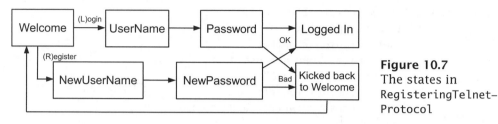

Figure 10.7
The states in
`RegisteringTelnet-`
`Protocol`

for the result (normally known a *blocking*), nobody else will be able to do anything until the disk or remote server responds. Deferred objects are a way to say "When we get a response, handle it with this function" and then continue with other tasks. There are two possibilities: a callback and an error back.

If the checker responds that the password is right ❻, you can go ahead and do the rest of the login, which means storing some values, setting your state to `"Command"`, and switching out your protocol for the final one.

If the checker tells you the password or the username is wrong ❼, then you can tell the user off and switch back to the `"User"` state. The user will need to type in the username and password again—and you the user will get it right this time.

How can you subclass `AuthenticatingTelnetProtocol`? The answer is to add some new states so there's a registration branch as well as the normal login one, similar to the flowchart in figure 10.7.

The next listing adds a new protocol with three extra states— `"Welcome"`, `"NewUserName"`, and `"New Password"` —along with methods to handle each of them.

Listing 10.13   RegisteringTelnetProtocol

```
from twisted.conch.telnet import ECHO
class RegisteringTelnetProtocol(
        AuthenticatingTelnetProtocol):
    state = "Welcome"

    def connectionMade(self):
        self.transport.write("Welcome to the server!")
        self.transport.write("(L)ogin or (R)egister "
                        "a new account? ")
```
❶ Welcome
  to server

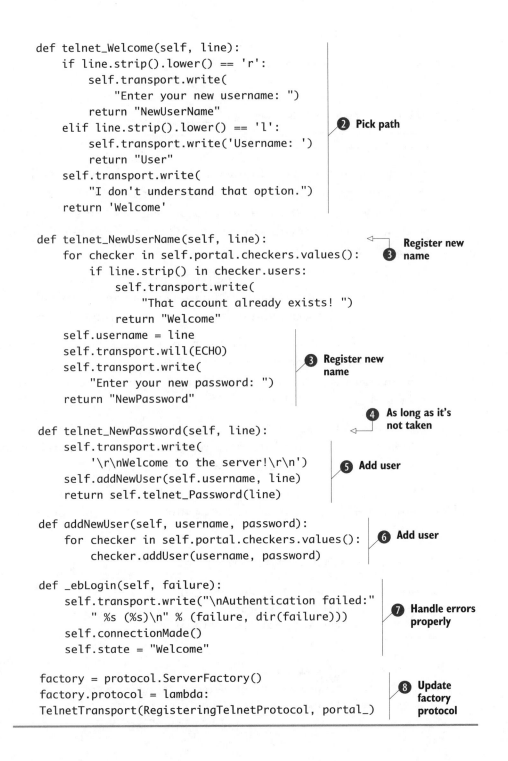

```
def telnet_Welcome(self, line):
    if line.strip().lower() == 'r':
        self.transport.write(
            "Enter your new username: ")
        return "NewUserName"
    elif line.strip().lower() == 'l':
        self.transport.write('Username: ')
        return "User"
    self.transport.write(
        "I don't understand that option.")
    return 'Welcome'
```

2 Pick path

```
def telnet_NewUserName(self, line):
    for checker in self.portal.checkers.values():
        if line.strip() in checker.users:
            self.transport.write(
                "That account already exists! ")
            return "Welcome"
    self.username = line
    self.transport.will(ECHO)
    self.transport.write(
        "Enter your new password: ")
    return "NewPassword"
```

3 Register new name

3 Register new name

4 As long as it's not taken

```
def telnet_NewPassword(self, line):
    self.transport.write(
        '\r\nWelcome to the server!\r\n')
    self.addNewUser(self.username, line)
    return self.telnet_Password(line)
```

5 Add user

```
def addNewUser(self, username, password):
    for checker in self.portal.checkers.values():
        checker.addUser(username, password)
```

6 Add user

```
def _ebLogin(self, failure):
    self.transport.write("\nAuthentication failed:"
        " %s (%s)\n" % (failure, dir(failure)))
    self.connectionMade()
    self.state = "Welcome"
```

7 Handle errors properly

```
factory = protocol.ServerFactory()
factory.protocol = lambda:
TelnetTransport(RegisteringTelnetProtocol, portal_)
```

8 Update factory protocol

Welcoming the user to the server ❶ is pretty much the same as the previous example, only with different values. You're prompting the user to enter R to register or L to login.

Because your previous state was "Welcome", the first method is telnet_Welcome. The code is straightforward: R sets the state to "NewUser-Name", L to "User", and anything else will kick them back to "Welcome" ❷.

telnet_NewUserName is the same as telnet_User, too ❸. It prompts slightly differently and passes to a different state: "NewPassword" instead of "Password".

Of course, you can't have two Gandalfs or Conans running around your server, so you need to check that the username doesn't already exist on the server ❹. If it does, you kick the user back to "Welcome". Pick something more original!

Now that the player has passed all the hurdles you've set, you should probably add the player to the server ❺. To make life easier for the player, you also automatically log the player in.

JUST ONE LITTLE ORC? IT CAN'T HURT! JUST ONE!

NO, SID! I CAN'T LET YOU DO IT TO YOURSELF!

The last bit didn't add the user, it only pretended to. ❻ will do the trick. You're calling each of your checkers in turn and calling their addUser method. Note that this won't work if you use the file-based checker, twisted.cred.FilePasswordDB — or at least not permanently, because it won't write the players back to the file.

If the login raises an error, you should return to the initial "Welcome" state ❼, rather than to "User", so the user can register instead if the user can't remember their username (or if you've deleted it for some reason).

Finally, you need to update your factory's protocol so it uses Registering-TelnetProtocol instead of the old AuthenticatingTelnetProtocol ❽.

Awesome! Now you won't have to enter usernames and passwords for everyone who wants to check out your cool new game. In practice, this will mean you'll get more players, because it sets the bar to entry much lower, and the players won't have to wait around for you to check your email. The next step, if you're interested, is to include a password-reset or -retrieval mechanism, so the players (if they've set their email address in-game) can be sent their password if they forget it.

Making your world permanent

You have a few more pressing concerns now: players can register and log in, but if you restart the server for some reason (say, to add a new feature), then they lose all their progress and have to reregister! You don't have to save *everything*, though—what you'll do is save only the players and their items and restart all the monsters from scratch. This is common practice in most MUDs, so the monsters, puzzles, and stories reset each night.

NOTE   One of the other reasons to implement saving is that it breaks the player's suspension of disbelief if everything suddenly vanishes. You want the player to believe on some level that the world you're creating is real, and real worlds don't disappear in a puff of virtual smoke.

Listing 10.14   Loading players

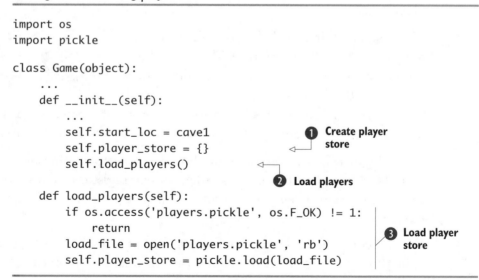

```
import os
import pickle

class Game(object):
    ...
    def __init__(self):
        ...
        self.start_loc = cave1          ❶ Create player
        self.player_store = {}             store
        self.load_players()             ❷ Load players

    def load_players(self):
        if os.access('players.pickle', os.F_OK) != 1:
            return                          ❸ Load player
        load_file = open('players.pickle', 'rb')     store
        self.player_store = pickle.load(load_file)
```

You don't need to store every player, because you're only interested in players' data—what they've called themselves, how they look and which items they're carrying. You'll put that information into the store ❶ so you can call it out at will.

The next thing you'll do is figure out how you're going to call the code you'll use to load the player store ❷. I think you'll be alright if you create a method.

The method to load the player store ❸ turns out to be pretty simple. Check to see if the file exists—if it does, then open it and load the player_store from it using Pickle.

Easy! Of course, you're not done yet—that only loads the player store. Now you need to work out what goes in the store, and save it to a file.

Listing 10.15   Saving players

```
class Game(object):
    ...
    def save(self):
        for player in self.players:
            self.player_store[player.name] = \
                                player.save()          ❶ Save each
                                                          player
        print "Saving:", self.player_store
        save_file = open('players.pickle', 'wb')       ❷ Save file
        pickle.dump(self.player_store, save_file)

class Player(object):
    def __init__(self, game, location):
        ...                                            Add password
        self.password = ""                          ◁─┘ to player

    def save(self):
        return {
            'name': self.name,
            'description': self.description,           ❸ Create
            'password': self.password,                    player
            'items': [(item.name, item.description)       store
                        for item in self.inventory], }
```

You add each player to the player store in typical object-oriented fashion—by calling player.save to find out what should be stored for each player ❶.

Once you've refreshed the store, you can go ahead and save it to disk
❷, ready for the next time you start the game.

All the player.save method needs to do is make a dictionary of all of the
player's data and return it ❸.

Now your game.save method should be working, and you can load from
it. The last step is to trigger game.save at appropriate points and make
sure the players are loaded with all their data when they log in.

Listing 10.16   Updating the server

```python
from item import Item

class Player(object):
    ...
    def load(self, config):
        self.name = config['name']
        self.password = config['password']
        self.description = config['description']
        for item in config['items']:
            self.inventory.append(
                Item(item[0], item[1],
                    self.location))
    ...
    def quit(self, player, noun):
        self.playing = False
        self.game.player_store[self.name] = self.save()

        # drop all our stuff(?)
        for item in self.inventory:
            self.location.here.append(item)
            item.location = self.location
        self.inventory = []

        return ["Thanks for playing!"]
...
class Game(object):
    def connectionMade(self):
        ...
        self.player.password = \
            checker.users[self.player.name]
```

❶ Load player

❷ Update quit method

```
            if self.player.name in game.player_store:
                self.player.load(
                    game.player_store[self.player.name])
            game.players.append(self.player)
if __name__ == '__main__':
    ...
    def do_save():
        print "Saving game..."
        game.save()
        print "Updating portal passwords..."
        for player in game.player_store.values():
            for checker in portal_.checkers.values():
                checker.users[player['name']] = \
                              player['password']

    do_save()
    game_saver = task.LoopingCall(do_save)
    game_saver.start(60.0)
```

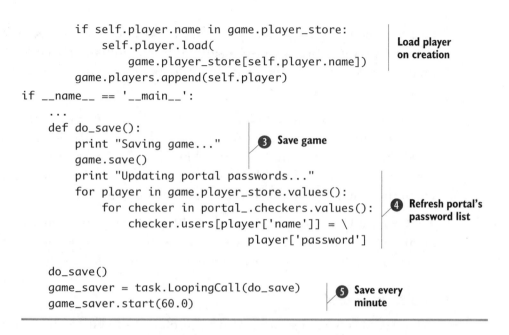

Load player on creation

❸ **Save game**

❹ **Refresh portal's password list**

❺ **Save every minute**

Loading the player is much the same as saving it ❶, only the other way around. Rather than dump your state into a dictionary, you update the state from one.

Rather than have the players die whenever they quit, they'll now save themselves and exit nicely ❷. For this game you only have one sword and one coin to share among all the players, so you'll drop all your items; but that's not normal practice for an adventure game.

To save everything ❸, you'll set up another periodic function using Twisted.

The players can change their passwords in game, so it makes sense to refresh the server's password list along with saving the game ❹. You do this right after the call to game.save(), so you know game.player_store is as fresh as possible.

Note that there's a bug in this code: when a player changes their name, the old name isn't removed. You'll want to either update the

NYAHHH! LET ME!
MY PRECIOUS!

NOW, SID—TIME
FOR SLEEPIES ...

OW!
NOOOOo ...

STAB!

name-changing code in Player to delete the old name from both the portals and player_store, or else disable the name-changing code. Disallowing name changes is probably the best option, because it also discourages bad behavior.

Once your function is complete, you only call it when you start up, and every minute or so after that ❺. I've picked 60 seconds as a reasonable timeframe, but you might find that a longer or shorter span works better for you. In practice, it will be a tradeoff between the load on the server when the game is saved, and the risk of losing your players' stuff.

That should be it. Now you have a stable base for your future development, and you don't have to worry about players not being able to log in, or having to respond to everyone who wants to log in.

Where to from here?

Your MUD is working and feature complete, but you've only scratched the surface of what you could do. One way to find out what needs to be done is to invite some of your friends to play—make sure they know it's a work in progress—and ask them for suggestions and bug fixes. If you don't have any friends who are into MUDs, the following is a list of some ideas you could try:

⊙ Make the orc respawn once you've killed it (in a different location), or add different monsters. They might have different attacks, take more or fewer hits to kill, and drop different sorts of treasure.

⊙ Saving the cave layout as well as the players' info will help players identify it more strongly as an actual place. Also, most MUDs will let you log in as a "wizard" and extend the game while you're playing it, adding rooms or monsters.

POOR SID—NEVER MIND. THE HOME FOR DERANGED GAMERS WILL HAVE YOU BACK ON YOUR FEET AGAIN IN NO TIME …

⊙ Different items, armor, and weapons can add an extra level of interest, as players explore or save up their gold for new ones.

⊙ Let the players gain experience and levels, with higher-level characters being tougher and more powerful. Different character classes and statistics (strength, intelligence, dexterity, and so on) can help players identify with the game and make it more enjoyable.

- A number of open source MUDs are available, in several languages; download them and see how they work. Most of the core components will be similar, so you'll know what to look for when you're trying to make sense of them.

Summary

In this chapter, you learned how to add networking to a game and about the issues you need to deal with in networked environments. You started with a simple chat server and learned about Twisted's Protocol and Server classes, before creating a similar setup so you could play your game over Telnet. Because Twisted is asynchronous (does lots of things simultaneously), you also needed to learn how to use Twisted's task.LoopingCall for your game loop.

Once you'd done that, you opened your game for testing and discovered a few issues with the game play in the new environment. To fix these, you added some new features, such as angry lists, talking to other players, and commands to change player names and descriptions.

Finally, you set up a system so new players could log into your system without you having to add them to a list of users. You learned a bit more about the details of Twisted, particularly its Telnet implementation, but also about how it interfaces with Protocols, Servers, and also Deferreds—one of Twisted's lower-level features.

11

Django revisited!

This chapter covers

- *Adding authentication*
- *Unit-testing and functional-testing applications*
- *Updating the database when models change*
- *Serving static images and CSS style sheets*

In Chapter 8, you built a simple todo list with Django, which allowed you to keep track of tasks you needed to do. Although useful for you, it's not helpful to other people. In this chapter, we'll look at some of the polishing steps you need to take to make your Django application useful to others. Let's get started!

Authentication

Your application was pretty much finished from a functionality point of view—you can delete and change any of your todos, and add as many as you like. Here's the problem: so can anyone else, if that person has access to your web interface. If that person is malicious, then all your todos might be deleted, or your important ones could be tampered with.

In order for your application to be safe, you'll need to restrict who can access your application, and you shouldn't be able to tamper with anyone else's todos. In practice, this means you'll introduce the following checks:

- You should need to log in to the application.
- Once logged in, you should only see your own todo items.
- Whenever you try to add, change, or delete a todo, it should only work if it's your todo.

Once these three constraints are in place, you should be safe against anyone trying to fiddle with anyone else's todo list.

SALES ARE STILL DOWN FOR WEB2.0TODO ...

Logging in

Let's start with logging in to your application. Django provides a built-in application called auth, along with middleware to handle sessions and store user data. It makes user-based applications such as yours much more straightforward, and it's a lot more robust and secure than creating your own from scratch.

Listing 11.1   Django authentication and login views

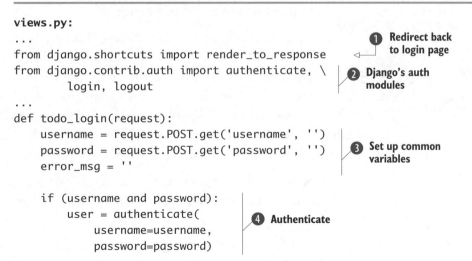

```
views.py:
...
from django.shortcuts import render_to_response
from django.contrib.auth import authenticate, \
        login, logout
...
def todo_login(request):
    username = request.POST.get('username', '')
    password = request.POST.get('password', '')
    error_msg = ''

    if (username and password):
        user = authenticate(
            username=username,
            password=password)
```

1 Redirect back to login page

2 Django's auth modules

3 Set up common variables

4 Authenticate

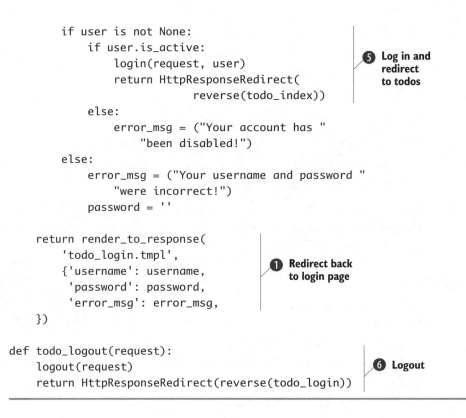

```
        if user is not None:
            if user.is_active:
                login(request, user)
                return HttpResponseRedirect(
                            reverse(todo_index))
            else:
                error_msg = ("Your account has "
                    "been disabled!")
        else:
            error_msg = ("Your username and password "
                "were incorrect!")
            password = ''

    return render_to_response(
        'todo_login.tmpl',
        {'username': username,
         'password': password,
         'error_msg': error_msg,
    })


def todo_logout(request):
    logout(request)
    return HttpResponseRedirect(reverse(todo_login))
```

⑤ Log in and redirect to todos

❶ Redirect back to login page

⑥ Logout

You start with the three functions you need to import to use Django's authentication ❷.

This view is used in a few different ways: as the initial display of the login form and for checking a username and password. So that you don't run into Key-Error exceptions, you're setting up the username and password variables ❸ from the request.post dictionary's get method; this way, if those values aren't set in the request, they'll default to being blank. You also set error_msg to a blank string.

If you have a username and password, then someone is trying to log in, and you use Django's authenticate function ❹ to check them against your list of users.

If the username and password check out OK, then authenticate will return a User object. If not, it will return None. That's easy to test for, but the other thing you need to look for is where a user has been deactivated. If both of those tests pass, then you can log in the user with login and redirect to the todo index ❺.

If you haven't been redirected to the index page, you'll pass through to this section, where you redisplay the login page ❶. So that you can repopulate the form if there's an error, you pass back the username and password, along with any error messages you've generated. You're also using one of Django's convenience functions, render_to_response, which will find and render a template directly when given the template name and a dictionary of variables.

Logging out is even easier—call the logout function with the request, and it will remove any session data and cookies the user's been using ❻. Once you've done that, you redirect back to the login page.

Great—now you only need a template to display the login form. That's not too hard to do. The following listing shows my version, which I put in todos/templates/todo_login.tmpl.

Listing 11.2   Login template

```
<html>
<head>
<title>Todo Login</title>
<style type="text/css">
    body { font-family: Arial, Helvetica, sans-serif;
           color: black;
           background: #ffffff; }
    .error { color: red; }
</style>
</head>
<body>

{% if error_msg %}
    <p class="error">{{ error_msg }}</p>
{% endif %}

<form action="" method="POST">
    <table>
    <tr><td valign="top">Username:
        <td><input type="text" name="username"
                   value="{{username}}">
```

❶ Show any errors

❷ Login form

```
<tr><td valign="top">Password:
    <td><input type="password" name="password"
                value="{{password}}">
<tr><td colspan="2">
    <input type="submit" value="login">
</table>
</form>

</body>
</html>
```

❷ **Login form**

CAN WE HAVE ONE OF THOSE ON OUR SITE?

If you get an error back from the view, you'd like to display it, so ❶ is a section of template code that does just that. You've also added an error class, which displays the error in red.

Other than including the username and password as values, the form is a standard username and password login ❷. You're including the username and password that are fed in, so if there's an error, the user doesn't have to retype everything. Little touches like this go a long way toward making your application look professional.

Last but not least, you'll tell Django about the views so it can display them. Here's the plumbing from urls.py to link everything up—login and logout go straight to the relevant views:

```
(r'^login$', views.todo_login),
(r'^logout$', views.todo_logout),
```

Now, if you go to http://localhost:8000/todos/login in your browser, you should be able to type in your username and password and have it redirect you to the index page. It should also give you a nice red error message if you mistype your password or username.

NOTE   If you'd rather not enter users by hand, there's a Django application called django-registration that will let people add their own accounts via email.

Adding users

The other thing you're probably wondering at this point is how to add new users. It's easy—use Django's admin screen (http://localhost:8000/admin/) to create some. I'm not sure what your friends' names are; I'll call my friend "Bruce," to save confusion.

Click Users in the admin screen, and you should see something like the first screen in figure 11.1. Fill in the username and password, and your user will be created. Then, edit the relevant fields. If you look carefully at the permissions list, you'll see that there are permissions for adding, editing, and deleting todos. You won't use them in this application, because they apply to every todo, but they're available if you need them.

What's next? Now that you have to log in to your application, let's make the todos a bit more secure.

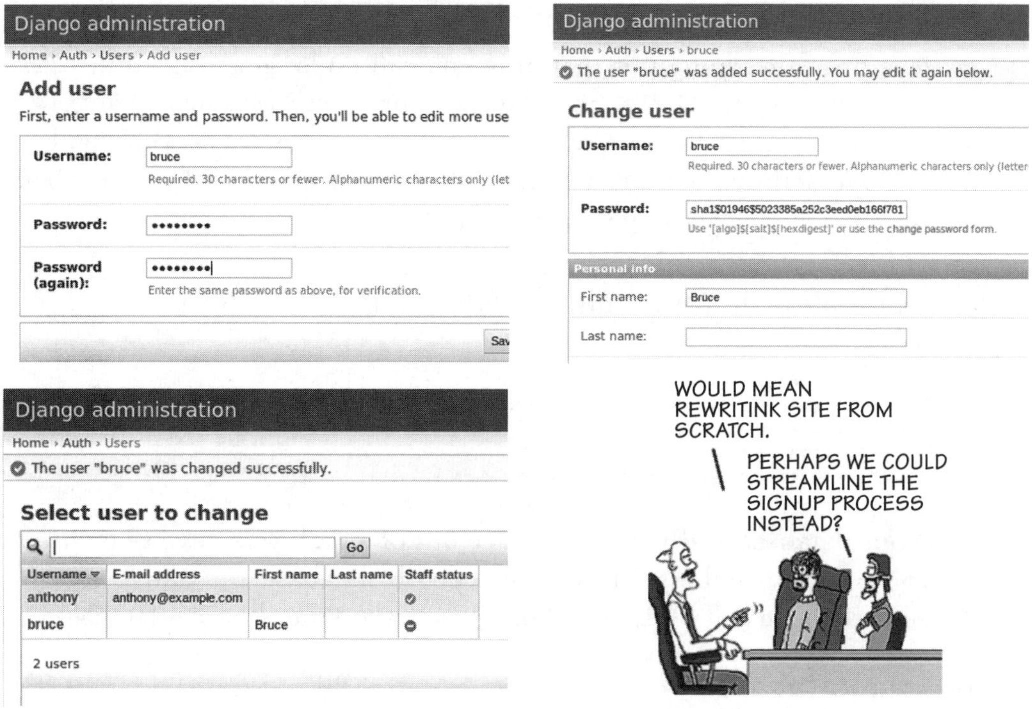

Figure 11.1 Adding a user through Django's admin screen

Listing only your own todos

Now that your users can log in, you can start making changes to how your application displays. Currently, your index page still lists every todo in the database, but you'd like it to only show the todos that have been created by the current user. Come to think of it, you don't have any way to tell which todos belong to which user. You'd better fix that part before you do anything fancy.

To add a link to the owner of a todo, you add a foreign key to the Todo class in models.py, something like this:

```
class Todo(models.Model):
    ...
    owner = models.ForeignKey(User)
```

Don't forget to import the User model from Django as well:

```
from django.contrib.auth.models import User
```

The problem, though, is that now you can no longer use python manage .py syncdb to update your database. For safety reasons, Django will only add new tables, not tamper with your existing ones. But you have to do something, because Django will give you an error if you try to use the todo model, as shown in figure 11.2.

OperationalError at /admin/todo/todo/

no such column: todo_todo.owner_id

Request Method:	GET
Request URL:	http://localhost:8000/admin/todo/todo/
Exception Type:	OperationalError
Exception Value:	no such column: todo_todo.owner_id
Exception Location:	/var/lib/python-support/python2.6/django/db/backen

Figure 11.2
Your database is broken!

Your database and your model are out of sync! You have two choices at this point: either remove the todo.db database file and start from scratch, or install SQLite and use it to update the existing database.

Fixing your database

You'll take the second option—although it's somewhat harder, you'll need to be able to update the database like this once you start working on applications where you have existing data. Don't worry, it's not too difficult to do once you know a few simple commands. If you don't already have the sqlite3 program installed, SQLite is available from www.sqlite.org, and all you need to do is put the executable somewhere where your operating system can find it. The following listing shows how I updated my database.

NO—DEFINITELY NOT! WE NEED ALL THAT VALUABLE MARKETING INFORMATION!

Listing 11.3   Adding a field to the database backend

```
anthony:~/todos$ python manage.py sql todo          ◁     What
BEGIN;                                                 ❶  to add?
CREATE TABLE "todo_todo" (
  "id" integer NOT NULL PRIMARY KEY,
  "title" varchar(200) NOT NULL,
  "description" text NOT NULL,
  "importance" varchar(1) NOT NULL,
  "owner_id" integer NOT NULL REFERENCES \
                              "auth_user" ("id")
);
COMMIT;
anthony:~/todos$ sqlite3 todo.db
SQLite version 3.6.10
Enter ".help" for instructions
Enter SQL statements terminated with a ";"
sqlite> .tables                                       ◁
auth_group               auth_user_user_permissions
auth_group_permissions   django_admin_log
auth_message             django_content_type          ❷  Common
auth_permission          django_session                  SQLite
auth_user                django_site                     commands
auth_user_groups         todo_todo
sqlite> .schema todo_todo                             ◁
CREATE TABLE "todo_todo" (
    "id" integer NOT NULL PRIMARY KEY,
    "title" varchar(200) NOT NULL,
    "description" text NOT NULL,
    "importance" varchar(1) NOT NULL
);
```

```
sqlite> alter table todo_todo
   ...> add column "owner_id" integer NOT NULL
   ...> REFERENCES "auth_user" ("id");
SQL error: Cannot add a NOT NULL column with \
    default value
sqlite> select * from auth_user;
1|anthony|||anthony@example.com|sha1$7405c$ ...
2|bruce|Bruce|||sha1$01946$ ...
sqlite> alter table todo_todo
   ...> add column "owner_id" integer NOT NULL
   ...> DEFAULT 1 REFERENCES "auth_user" ("id");
sqlite>
```

❸ Alter table, take one

❹ Alter table, take two

First, you need to figure out what to add ❶. manage.py won't make any changes for you, but it still knows what should be there. python manage.py sql todo will tell you the exact SQL needed for the database you're using, which beats having to rack your brain trying to create the right SQL command.

It pays to know common SQLite commands ❷. If you need to find your way around the database, .help, .tables, and .schema are three useful commands to know.

Next, you issue an alter table command, with the SQL syntax cribbed from manage.py ❸. Unfortunately, SQLite won't accept it—you've told it that the field shouldn't be NULL, but you haven't given it a default either, so SQLite won't know what to do with that field for all your existing todos. To fix the alter command, you can either drop the NOT NULL clause or add a reasonable default.

In this case, you make the default be that the existing todos are owned by the admin user (with id=1) ❹.

TIP   A Django application called South can automatically alter your database for you based on your models.py file. It doesn't get everything (such as field renames), but it can be a lifesaver if you have a complex application.

Now that you've added your owner column and Django knows about it, your application is a lot more useful, and you can use the owner field to do all sorts of cool stuff. For example, the Django admin system will

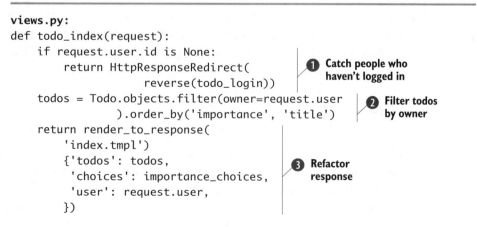

Figure 11.3
Changing the owner of a todo

now let you change the owner of a todo with a convenient drop-down menu, as shown in figure 11.3.

The Django admin application is good at reading your models and making appropriate choices about how to display your data. All it needs is for the right relationships to be defined.

Back on track...

Your original plan was to only show todos owned by the person who's logged in. That's now easy to do—the following listing shows updated todo_index and add_todo views that will filter the todo list you're shown when you log in.

Listing 11.4   Showing only your todos

```
views.py:
def todo_index(request):
    if request.user.id is None:
        return HttpResponseRedirect(
                    reverse(todo_login))          ❶ Catch people who
                                                     haven't logged in
    todos = Todo.objects.filter(owner=request.user
                ).order_by('importance', 'title')  ❷ Filter todos
                                                     by owner
    return render_to_response(
        'index.tmpl')
        {'todos': todos,                           ❸ Refactor
         'choices': importance_choices,              response
         'user': request.user,
        })
```

```
def add_todo(request):
    t = Todo(title = request.POST['title'],
             description = request.POST['description'],
             importance = request.POST['importance'],
             owner=request.user)
    t.save()
    return HttpResponseRedirect(reverse(todo_index))
```

④ Set owner in add_todo

... AND THEY'VE CONCLUDED THAT THE SITE NEEDS MORE "BLING."

If someone hasn't logged in, they could still manually type in the index URL, or bookmark the index page and forget to log in. That will mess up your application, so if they're anonymous, you redirect them to the login page ❶.

Instead of returning all the todos, this database query ❷ will return those where the user is the same as the one currently logged in.

In general, once you've found a clever new way to do things, it's a good idea to go back and clean up the code you've already written. Here's your old template-calling code from chapter 8, but now it uses the new render_to_response function ❸.

The only thing left is to add the owner to all your new todos ❹. Easy peasy!

Now you can view only your todos, and nobody else can see what you're up to. When you create a new todo, it's linked to your user ID. All you need to do is perform the same checking when editing or deleting your todos. They won't appear in the list of todos, but that won't stop evil people from noticing that your todos are referenced by IDs and seeing what happens when they put in a different ID. Oops! Just deleted someone else's todo!

Covering all your bases

Here's where Django's simplicity comes into play. Your views are just functions that are fed certain things depending on the request that comes in, and you can use that simplicity to your advantage. Rather than rewrite the entire view—and throw away all your work—you can wrap the view with some of your own code to check the request, and then pass your values to the generic view if the request is OK. The following listing shows you how.

Listing 11.5 Wrapping the update and delete views

```python
from django.views.generic.create_update \          ❶ Import generic
    import update_object, delete_object                views
from django.shortcuts import render_to_response, \
    get_object_or_404
                                                     ❷ Another handy
...                                                      shortcut
def update_todo(request, todo_id):    ◁——❸ Old view
    todo = get_object_or_404(Todo, id=todo_id)
    if todo.owner.id != request.user.id:
        return HttpResponseRedirect(
            reverse(todo_index) +                    ❹ Check that it's
            "?error_msg=That's not your todo!")         your todo
    return update_object(
        request,
        object_id=todo_id,
        model=Todo,                                  ❺ Call generic
        template_name='todo_form.html',                update
        post_save_redirect='/todos/%(id)s'             function
    )


def delete_todo(request, todo_id):
    todo = get_object_or_404(Todo, id=todo_id)
    if todo.owner.id != request.user.id:             ❻ Delete todos
        return HttpResponseRedirect(
            reverse(todo_index) +
            "?error_msg=That's not your todo!")
    return delete_object(
        request,
        object_id=todo_id,
        model=Todo,

    template_name=('todo_confirm_delete.html'),
        post_delete_redirect='..'
    )
```

❶ are the generic views, but you're importing them in views.py rather than urls.py.

You may notice the stub view we looked at earlier in the chapter ❸, but you're expanding it. You only need the request and the ID of the todo you're editing.

get_object_or_404 is another Django shortcut ❷. It tries to access the model with that ID, and, if it can't, it triggers a 404 error.

Before you get to the generic view, you want to check that the todo is owned by the person trying to edit it ❹. If the ID of todo.owner doesn't match the one in the request, then you redirect to the index page with an error.

If you get here, then the user owns the todo, and you can pass control through to the generic view ❺. All the same arguments that were in urls.py previously are here, but they're specified as function arguments rather than keys and values in a dictionary.

Deleting a todo follows exactly the same steps as updating a todo ❻, except that the variables passed to the generic view are slightly different.

Now you need new URLs to point to your new views. The following listing shows a much cleaner version of the previous urls.py.

Listing 11.6   New urls.py

```
from django.conf.urls.defaults import *

import views

urlpatterns = patterns('',
    (r'^login$', views.todo_login),
    (r'^logout$', views.todo_logout),

    (r'^$', views.todo_index),
    (r'^add$', views.add_todo),
    (r'^(?P<todo_id>\d+)/{0,1}$', views.update_todo),    ❶ Updated
    (r'^(?P<todo_id>\d+)/delete$', views.delete_todo),        URLs
)
```

You should be able to follow these updated URLs easily by now ❶. (?P<todo_id>\d+) matches an ID and feeds it to the view as an argument.

You also add an optional forward slash to the editing URL, in case someone adds one by hand.

Updating your interface

The last thing you need to do is update your index page so it can take an optional error argument. That's easy to do, and you've already done this for the login form, so you can cut and paste it into the relevant sections here.

Listing 11.7   Error messages on the index page

```
views.py:
def todo_index(request):
    ...
     'user': request.user,
     'error_msg': request.GET.get('error_msg', ''),     ❶ Pass in error
    })                                                      messages


index.tmpl:
    .error { color: red; }
...
{% if error_msg %}                                        ❷ Show error
    <p class="error">{{ error_msg }}</p>                     messages on
{% endif %}                                                  index page
```

The first step is to pass in any error messages from the request into the template ❶. You're using a one-liner here that is similar to the way you handle usernames and passwords in the login script.

THAT SHOULD BE OK, BUT I'D BETTER CHECK IT ...

Now you can update the template to show a nice red error message if one is set in the URL ❷.

With that, your application is done! You can look at, add, edit, and delete todos from your todo list. Your interface is also limited to only those people whom you choose to give a username and password. Additionally, if you go back and look through the code you've written, you'll notice it's nicely broken up—everything to do with display is in your templates, your models contain all the data and data-formatting functions, and your views handle logins, data extraction, and redirecting when something happens.

Testing!

In your original todo application, you developed it with unit testing, but so far you haven't seen any testing code. You can get away without having any testing code while your project is small, but as it grows, it will need some sort of testing to keep it in check. Also, Django's testing infrastructure is cool. Let's take a quick look at how you can test your Django applications.

Unit testing

The first thing you need to know how to do is how to create unit tests to test your model. You can also use unit tests for other functions and classes that are independent and don't depend on any other infrastructure. The following listing shows how to create unit tests for your application. You should put it in a file called tests.py in your application folder.

Listing 11.8   Unit testing (tests.py)

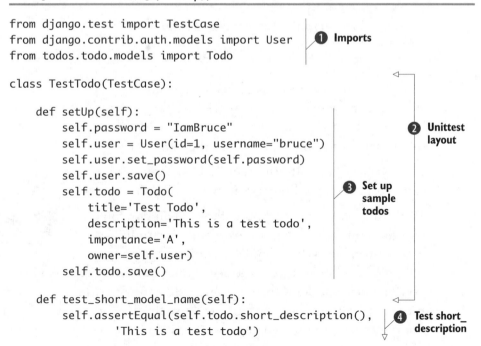

```python
from django.test import TestCase
from django.contrib.auth.models import User          ❶ Imports
from todos.todo.models import Todo

class TestTodo(TestCase):

    def setUp(self):
        self.password = "IamBruce"
        self.user = User(id=1, username="bruce")
        self.user.set_password(self.password)
        self.user.save()
        self.todo = Todo(
            title='Test Todo',
            description='This is a test todo',
            importance='A',
            owner=self.user)
        self.todo.save()

    def test_short_model_name(self):
        self.assertEqual(self.todo.short_description(),
                'This is a test todo')
```

❷ Unittest layout

❸ Set up sample todos

❹ Test short_ description

```
self.todo.description = "Test\nMultiple\nLines"
self.assertEqual(self.todo.short_description(),
        'Test')

self.todo.description = ("A"*50) + ("B"*50)
self.assertEqual(self.todo.short_description(),
        ("A"*50) + ("B"*30))
```

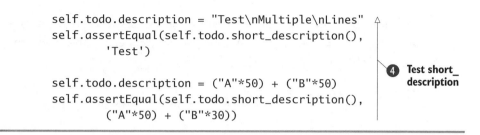

4 Test short_description

You're using Django's TestCase class to organize your testing code. It's mainly modeled on the xUnit style of testing, although it's possible to use doctests with Django, too. Your Todo class needs to link to a user, so you're importing that as well as the Todo class **1**.

AUUGH!

BLING!

xUnit tests are structured with a parent class and multiple test_ methods within it **2**. The parent class gives you lots of convenience methods to test for equality, truth, exceptions being raised, and so on.

xUnit also has the concept of a setUp method, which is called before each test method and is used to do things like set up common data structures. Here you're setting up a user and a todo you need for your tests **3**. There's also a corresponding tearDown, which is called after each test.

4 is one example of what a unit test might look like. You're testing the short_description method of the Todo class, so you're setting up your test todo with different descriptions and making sure the method returns the right value using TestCase's assertEqual method.

You'll typically have a number of unit tests for each of your models, to test all of their functionality, but what about the views? They're even more important to test, because they typically define most of your application and link everything together.

Functional testing

For views.py and urls.py, you'll need to use functional tests to make sure everything's working. For functional testing, Django lets you submit "pretend" forms with the Client class, which mimics a browser and the entire web request/response process. The following listing shows a few simple functional tests.

Listing 11.9   Functional testing

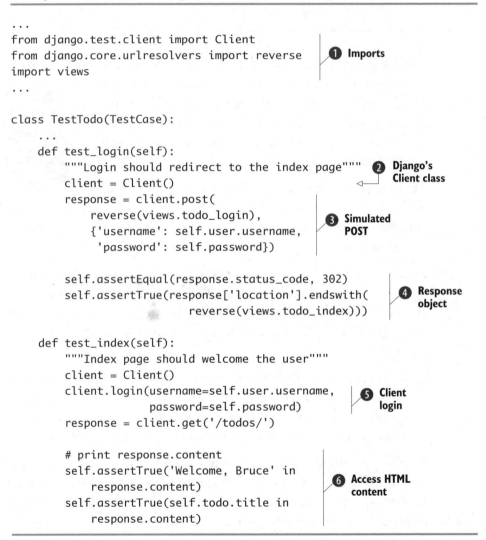

```
...
from django.test.client import Client
from django.core.urlresolvers import reverse          ❶ Imports
import views
...

class TestTodo(TestCase):
    ...
    def test_login(self):
        """Login should redirect to the index page"""   ❷ Django's
        client = Client()                                  Client class
        response = client.post(
            reverse(views.todo_login),                   ❸ Simulated
            {'username': self.user.username,                POST
             'password': self.password})

        self.assertEqual(response.status_code, 302)
        self.assertTrue(response['location'].endswith(   ❹ Response
                    reverse(views.todo_index)))             object

    def test_index(self):
        """Index page should welcome the user"""
        client = Client()
        client.login(username=self.user.username,        ❺ Client
                password=self.password)                     login
        response = client.get('/todos/')

        # print response.content
        self.assertTrue('Welcome, Bruce' in             ❻ Access HTML
            response.content)                               content
        self.assertTrue(self.todo.title in
            response.content)
```

Because you're testing views, the imports ❶ will be the same as the ones you set up in your views.

Creating an instance of the Client class is easy ❷—it doesn't require any arguments.

Once you have a Client class, you can use its .post method to send data to your application ❸. .post takes a URL and a dictionary of POST arguments and returns a response object. Notice that you're using reverse here—as with views, it's important to keep your unit tests independent of where you happen to store your code. There's also a corresponding .get method, which doesn't need the argument dictionary.

The response object ❹ contains everything that's returned from the POST request you've just run, such as status code, content, headers, cookies, and so on. Here you're interested in two things: that the response is a redirect, and that the redirect is to the index page (because you've logged in successfully).

You don't want to have to send in a login request every time you test something in your application, so Django provides the login method for the client ❺. It creates all the cookies and session variables needed to simulate an actual login.

If you're testing a more normal request and you need to test what it returns, you can access it through response.content—it's a string containing the HTML, as if you were viewing the source of a page in your browser ❻.

Now you have your tests, but that's not much good—you need to be able to run them and make sure your code tests OK. The beauty is that finding your test code and running your tests is done automatically.

Running your tests

Django's manage.py contains a test command that will collect your test code and run it, as well as set up all the associated database infrastructure, and so on. The following listing shows a sample test run against the todo application.

Listing 11.10 Test run

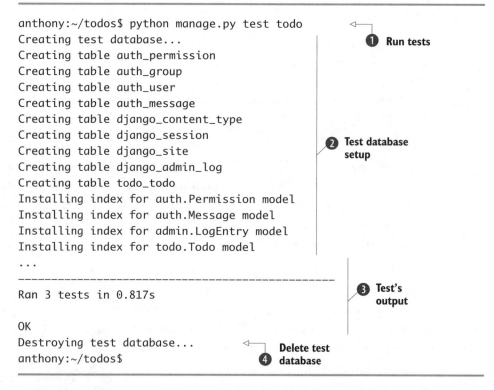

```
anthony:~/todos$ python manage.py test todo                    ❶ Run tests
Creating test database...
Creating table auth_permission
Creating table auth_group
Creating table auth_user
Creating table auth_message
Creating table django_content_type
Creating table django_session                                  ❷ Test database
Creating table django_site                                        setup
Creating table django_admin_log
Creating table todo_todo
Installing index for auth.Permission model
Installing index for auth.Message model
Installing index for admin.LogEntry model
Installing index for todo.Todo model
...
--------------------------------------------------------
Ran 3 tests in 0.817s                                          ❸ Test's
                                                                  output
OK
Destroying test database...                         Delete test
anthony:~/todos$                                  ❹ database
```

If you only want to run your tests against one application, then include
the application's name after the test command ❶. Otherwise, Django
will test all of your installed applications, including applications like the
admin interface, which might not be what you want.

For each test run, Django will create a test database and connect to
that instead of your live database ❷. This makes your testing independent of the data you have stored in your application—you can even run
tests against a live server if you need to.

Output from the tests is much like what you would have for a standard
unit-test style test run ❸. Each test will get a dot (pass), an E (error), or
an F (failure). Once the tests have run, you'll get a report on how many
failed, and tracebacks for any errors or failures.

When the testing is complete, Django will delete the test database ❹.

Now you know how to make sure your applications run according to plan, even if you need to pull them apart and refactor them completely. You can make sure your releases don't have any known bugs and that your code doesn't regress when you're developing—all you need for a robust, healthy, stress-free project.

Images and styles

One of the last things you need to do is to configure serving images and style sheets. Up to this point, you've been hard-coding style sheets into the HTML; but if you want to make a change later, you'll need to edit every template. Django refers to images, style sheets, JavaScript, and other bits and pieces like that as *media*.

First, let's look at a simple way to serve media directly from Django, and then a more robust method where your media is delivered with a server such as Apache or Nginx.

Serving media from Django

First, a warning: this method is only really suitable for a development server. Django is written in Python and is slow at serving flat files such as images when compared to a server written in C. If you get any significant traffic on your server, it won't be able to handle the load.

TIP　　Do one thing, and do it well. Django's built more for returning HTML populated with results from a database, so it's best to use it for that, and use something else to serve images.

That said, let's look at how to configure Django to serve static media files using one of Django's built-in views, `django.views.static.serve`. You'll need to make changes to both settings.py and urls.py.

Listing 11.11　Serving static files with Django

```
settings.py:
MEDIA_ROOT = '/home/anthony/todos/'
MEDIA_ROOT = 'C:/Documents and Settings/
              Anthony/Desktop/todos/media/'
```

❶ Pick directory to store files

```
...
MEDIA_URL = '/site_media/'
```

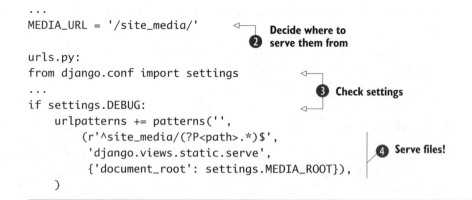 **Decide where to serve them from** ❷

```
urls.py:
from django.conf import settings
...
if settings.DEBUG:
    urlpatterns += patterns('',
        (r'^site_media/(?P<path>.*)$',
         'django.views.static.serve',
         {'document_root': settings.MEDIA_ROOT}),
    )
```

❸ **Check settings**

❹ **Serve files!**

IF YOU WOULD BE PROOFREADING? IS HARD TO CHECK WHEN WORDS ARE BURNT ONTO RETINAS.

AH. I'LL GET MY WELDING GOGGLES.

BLING!

First, pick a directory to store your media ❶. To make it easy, I normally call it "media" and put it in the root of my project. I've included versions for both Windows and Linux—note that the second and third lines are one line, and that Django uses forward slashes, even under Windows.

You'll also want to pick a URL from which to serve your files ❷. You're free to pick any URL you like, but be aware that if you choose /media/ you'll interfere with the admin application's media setting. /site_media/ is the convention for most Django applications.

To be absolutely certain you're not going to use Django to serve up images when your site goes live, you check the value of DEBUG from settings.py ❸. If it's set to True, then you're in development and should be safe.

Finally, you set up the django.views.static.serve view ❹. The two variables it needs are the path and the document root; other than that, it can take care of itself. To save duplicating your setup, you're also including the MEDIA_ROOT from settings.py.

Once you've made those changes, you can restart the server and begin adding images and style sheets. Figure 11.4 shows the Django logo displayed on my development server.

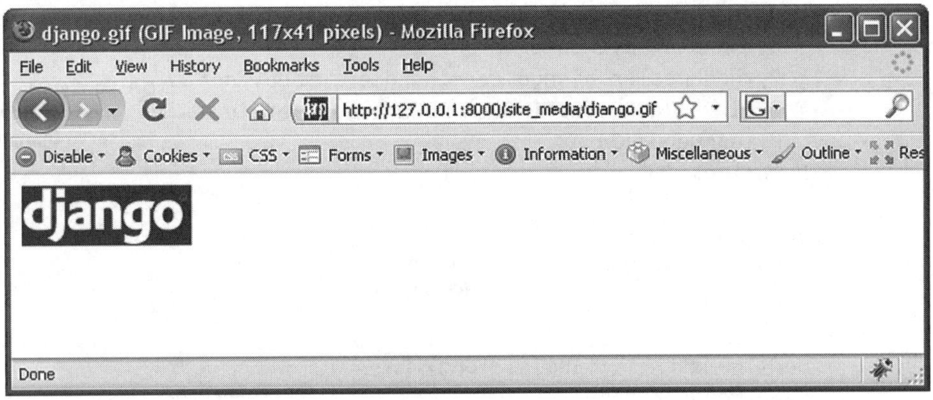

Figure 11.4   Serving up images with Django

Now you can include images, CSS files, and JavaScript in your application templates by referencing /site_media/ like this:

```
<link rel="stylesheet" type="text/css"
     href="/site_media/style.css">
<img src="/site_media/images/todo_logo.gif">
```

Actually creating a logo for your todo list is left as an exercise for the reader!

Serving media from another server

A better way to serve media, though, is to use a program expressly designed to serve static content, such as images and style sheets, and save Django for dynamic pages. This is relatively easy to do with most web servers, and there are a number of ways to achieve the same end. The following listing gives an example of how you might configure Apache with mod_python to serve requests for media and images, but pass other page requests on to Django.

Listing 11.12   A sample Apache **mod_python** configuration

```
<VirtualHost *>
ServerName www.example.com
DocumentRoot /var/www/www.example.com
```

```
<Location "/">
    SetHandler python-program
    PythonHandler django.core.handlers.modpython
    SetEnv DJANGO_SETTINGS_MODULE todos.settings
    PythonDebug On
</Location>
```

❶ Configure mod_python to serve Django

```
<Location "/media">
    SetHandler None
</Location>
```

❷ But not for /media

```
<LocationMatch "\.(jpg|gif|png)$">
    SetHandler None
</LocationMatch>
```

❸ Or anything involving images

```
</VirtualHost>
```

BLING!

WARNING: USE OF THIS SITE MAY CAUSE FITS OR SEIZURES IN PEOPLE PREDISPOSED TO EPILEPSY, AND THOSE WHO HAVE TASTE AND/OR GRAPHIC DESIGN SKILLS. SIDE EFFECTS OF USING THIS SITE MAY INCLUDE DIZZINESS, NAUSEA, LOSS OF BODILY FUNCTIONS, DISMAY ...

BLING!

❶ is pretty much a stock Django-with-mod_python configuration section. You use Django's mod_python handler, use your todos.settings as the settings module, and switch on debugging—at least, while you're setting up and testing everything.

For /media, though, you'd like Apache to serve files normally, which means it will fall back to the normal document root for the server and display the media you've stored in /var/www/www.example .com/media ❷.

You can do much the same thing with a Location-Match directive, so URLs like http://www .example.com/not_a_media_folder/logo.gif will fall back to the image stored at /var/www/www.example.com/not_a_media_folder/logo.gif ❸.

Note also that you're not limited to using subfolders like this—you can use completely separate domains. For example, if you had www.example.com serving Django pages, then it's possible to serve media from media.example.com or images.example.com. If your application model supports it, arranging your URLs like this can save a lot of configuration.

Last but not least

The final thing you need to do is to edit your settings.py file and find the DEBUG setting. With this set to True, Django will give you detailed information whenever something goes wrong. It's useful while developing, but this information can be dangerous in the wrong hands. Once you've switched it to False, Django will return a standard 500 error if your site breaks and will keep your application's innards safe.

Where to from here?

Your application is now fully functioning, plus you can install it on a server on an intranet or the internet and give out accounts to all your friends. It's still somewhat bare-bones, though, so here are some ideas for extending it to make it more useful:

- Now that you can use separate style sheets, you can pretty up your application, add logos and icons to your main page, and put your forms in tables. A little beautification can make a big difference to how seriously people take your application.

- Your todos are fairly basic. What about adding some extra data to them, such as deadlines? If you recorded email addresses, the system could also email people when their deadlines are a week or a day away.

- Once you have a few users, you could consider making the application more collaborative. Perhaps you could add a field to mark todo items as public. Other people's public todo items would be included in your list, and you'd be able to view but not edit them. A list of users in the system and what people are working on might also be useful.

- Or, the ability to add notes to your todos might be useful; you might even allow other people to add comments.

A wealth of information is available on advanced aspects of Django. The Django documentation, for example, is excellent and freely available from the Django website.

You can also download some of the many Django-based applications and read through them. It's a good way to learn how to structure your project and about new libraries to make development even easier. A good place to start is the Pinax website (http://pinaxproject.com/), which provides a number of reusable modules such as user registration and pagination (breaking a big list into smaller pages of 10 or 20). There are also modules for integrating external services like PayPal or Facebook, and entire applications such as content-management systems.

Summary

In this chapter, you learned about some of the issues associated with hosting and maintaining Django. You started with adding users and logins to your system and saw how to update the database when you made changes to your model. Then, you took a look through your system so far and secured all your pages and forms so different users (or even external attackers) couldn't access todo lists that were supposed to be private. In the process, you got a lot more hands-on with your views and saw how to wrap some of Django's built-in views so you could add extra features without having to reimplement the views from scratch.

You then saw how to add tests to your Django application, and how Django allows you to easily add functional tests by providing a `Client` class that acts like a web browser.

Finally, we looked at how you can serve your static content, such as images and style sheets—both with a built-in view in Django and through a more efficient mechanism like Apache.

That's all the Python programming you'll learn in this book. In the next chapter, you'll find out what your next steps should be to improve your Python skills even further, and you'll learn about several sources of assistance if you get stuck on your journey.

12

Where to from here?

This chapter covers

- *Further improving your Python skills*
- *Making contact with other Python programmers*
- *Other Python libraries you may find useful*

If you've gotten to this point in the book, you've learned several different Python programs in a number of different styles. We started out with a straightforward program in chapter 2, when you wrote Hunt the Wumpus. Since then, we've covered libraries, classes, event-based programs, and interacting with the web. You could think of *Hello! Python* as a tasting plate, letting you try different styles of Python programming before you delve too deeply into one particular topic.

Although we've covered a lot of ground in this book, we've only scratched the surface of what you can do with Python. This chapter is intended as a springboard for the next stage of your development as a programmer.

Read some more code

One of the best ways to learn how to write better programs is to look at how other people have written their programs and figure out what they've done and why. There's something of an art to reading other people's code—experience definitely helps.

I find that the best way to understand new code is to skim its structure first for an idea of the design of the program (so you won't get *completely* lost) and then dig into the details of how it's written. To get a good grasp of the design, ask yourself questions as you go. Why have they split up the program this way? Why a dictionary instead of a list here? Is there a better way to do this? How could I extend it if I needed to do something differently? Is there a library that will help?

Bear in mind that not all the program code you find on the internet is of production quality—some might be throwaway prototyping or proof of concept, and some might be for older versions of Python. Asking questions will also help you avoid these sorts of pitfalls.

Here are some places where you can find code to read.

Python Standard Library

A fair chunk of the Python library itself is written in Python. By digging into it, you can find out how common Python features and libraries are implemented—by the people who wrote them. Bear in mind, though, that some of the libraries might be somewhat older and use techniques that have been deprecated.

Python recipes

Sites like http://code.activestate.com/recipes/langs/python and http://djangosnippets.org provide Python functions and modules that illustrate a particular technique or solve a specific (small) problem. They're useful when you know exactly what you need to do—for example, check a book's ISBN code or find out how to solve an anagram—but they're also easier to follow when you're first starting out.

Open source projects

Once you've read a few small code samples, you might want to look into larger programs. A number of open source projects are available on sites like SourceForge (http://sf.net) and Project Hosting on Google Code (http://code.google.com/hosting), both of which will let you search specifically for Python-based projects. Sites like http://ohloh.net will also give you statistics on the age of the project, number of developers, and lines of code, so you can pick established code or smaller projects, depending on your comfort level.

Join the Python community

Another good way to find out how to improve your programming is to make contact with other people who know Python. Asking questions about what they're up to is a good way to learn more about what's possible.

Sign up for some mailing lists

A good place to ask questions (if you've searched online and haven't found a solution, or if you're stuck) is the Python Tutor list. (You can subscribe at http://mail .python.org/mailman/listinfo/tutor.) Don't forget to search the list archives before you ask your question, or you might be asking a question that has been asked a hundred times before.

Also, don't forget to "pay it forward"—once you find you've outgrown the tutor list, stick around and help some other people learn how to use Python. Don't worry if there's a question that you don't know how to answer; but if you can help out, jump in. The site is run by volunteers who will be more than happy to have the help.

There are also mailing lists dedicated to other areas that you might be interested in learning about, such as Django and Pyglet. Through the mailing lists, you'll not only pick up a number of techniques and learn about useful libraries, but also be able to read the discussions and find out why things are written a certain way or discover limitations before you run into them.

Find a local user group

WHACK!

Python meetups and user groups are an excellent way to find Python programmers who are active near you. They'll often have regular meetings or get-togethers and are a good source of advice and new ideas. It's one thing to read websites about what Python can do; it's another thing entirely to talk to people about their projects in person.

Help out an open source project

If there's an open source Python project that you use on a regular basis, you might want to consider signing up for the developer mailing list, becoming familiar with its code, and contributing patches. Most open source projects have some sort of tracker you can use to find bugs you think you can fix. Even verifying that a bug exists and investigating possible causes is a good start—you don't necessarily have to fix it all in one go. Alternatively, add a minor feature, write documentation or a tutorial, or add a unit test.

Scratch your own itch

The next time you have a problem or a cool idea, you can start your own project: a website, game, todo list, or data-processing application (don't laugh—I know a few people who've used Python to manage their fantasy football or sports betting pool, both of which are heavily data-intensive).

Once you're on your feet with Python, the best way to continue to learn is by doing. Pick a project—something you're interested in, something that annoys you and needs improvement, or something that could be useful—and start trying to develop it. Don't forget to begin with one small chunk; otherwise, you'll risk becoming overwhelmed.

Another option is to build on the code in this book. I've covered a lot of ground, so there will be something close to what you're trying to write, or something you can use as a scaffold. Writing a program is a lot easier once you have a basic idea of your project and which direction to take it.

When you're ready to share your project with the world, there are plenty of sites you can use to publish your code, provide documentation, and track bugs and feature requests. These include SourceForge and Google Code, mentioned earlier, as well as GitHub (http://github.com) and Bitbucket (http://bitbucket.org).

Look at more Python libraries

As your programs grow in scope, you'll find that you need to be able to do more and more things. Perhaps you'll need to talk to other programs over the internet, load specific data formats, or run programs more quickly. In this book, we've covered several libraries that can help extend what you can do. Here are a few others you might otherwise miss. Some of them are included with Python; others you'll need to download and install separately.

Profiling code

If you're writing code that needs to run quickly, or if it's running a lot slower than you thought it would, Python comes with a profiler called cProfile, which can tell you how long the individual parts of your program are taking to run. You can use this information to rewrite only the parts that are slow (or cache or pre-generate them) instead of having to guess why your program's running slowly.

Logging

Python also has built in support for logging—writing status reports to a file so you can tell what your program's up to. You can log at different levels, produce only some lines if you've configured your program for debugging output, and log to several different destinations, such as a file, printing to the screen, or syslog if you're using Linux.

Subprocess and multiprocessing

Sometimes you might need to run several processes at the same time—usually, if you're running as a system program in the background, or if you're doing something processor-intensive and need to make use of all of your system's CPUs. The subprocess module is the standard way of running separate processes, and you can use multiprocessing if you need to run processes in parallel for extra speed.

Better parsing

You already used shlex (along with some cus-tom code) when writing your adventure game, but there are other solutions if you need a more featured parser. Pyparsing is easy to get started with and allows you to define more complex types of grammar, rather than splitting on just quotes and spaces; but many other types of parsers are available, depend-ing on your experience and needs.

WHAT'D YOU HIT ME FOR?

WITHIN BAMBOO POLE LIE ALL THE SECRETS OF PYTHON!

SIGH. YES, MASTER.

PIL and image processing

If you're doing any sort of image processing work in Python, the Python Image Library (PIL) is essential. With it, you can crop and resize images, merge them, accept binary image data over the web, check it, and save it to disk—even generate images from scratch.

XML, ElementTree, and JSON

For XML and XHTML parsing, it's hard to beat ElementTree. It was added to the Python standard library in version 2.5 and has several dif-ferent models for parsing and inspecting XML data. Python also has xmlrpclib: handy if you need to communicate with other programs that use XML-RPC.

If XML seems a bit heavyweight for you, there are a number of other formats you can try. JSON is ideal if you're working with data on a

JavaScript-enabled site, but it's broadly useful even when storing data or transmitting it between programs.

Summary

Now you know not only how to program in Python, but also where to find help or further inspiration if you need it. To take your next steps on the path to mastery, you'll want to read code, talk to other programmers, look for new libraries and techniques, and, most important, experiment and create programs of your own. You won't even need to be hit with a bamboo pole!

Index